ETIQUETTE FOR ALL

A Comprehensive Guide
For Social Skills & Proper Manners

Library of Congress Control Number: 2024949616

ISBN: 9781961420342

KHAYAT®
Publishing House

WASHINGTON, DC
UNITED STATES

www.khayatpublishing.com
www.khayatbooks.com

DR. RIAD NOFAL

ETIQUETTE
FOR
ALL

A Comprehensive Guide
For Social Skills & Proper Manners

Contents |

- Preface

- **Section One**
  - Communication & Behavior ... 3
  - Protocol ... 5
  - Etiquette (Manners) ... 7
  - Relationship Between Etiquette & Politeness ... 11
  - Relationship Between Protocol & Etiquette ... 15

- **Section Two**
  - Titles ... 23
  - Order of Precedence ... 25
  - Introduction and Presentation ... 27
  - Visit Cards ... 31
  - Greetings ... 33
  - Hugging and Kissing ... 41

- **Section Three**
  - Clothing Etiquette ... 47
  - Orders, Decorations & Medals ... 69

- **Section Four**
  - Telephone Etiquette ... 77
  - Conversation and dialogue etiquette ... 81
  - The Virtue of Silence ... 89
  - The Virtues of Apologizing and Forgiveness ... 91
  - Correspondence Etiquette ... 93

- **Section Five**
  - Theater Etiquette ... 107
  - Museum and Art Gallery Etiquett ... 111
  - Dance Etiquette ... 113
  - Borrowing Books Etiquette ... 117
  - Playing Cards Etiquette ... 119

- **Section Six**
  - Religious Places Etiquette ... 125
  - Funeral Etiquette ... 129

- **Section Seven**
  - Gift etiquette ... 135

- **Section Eight**
  - Women's Etiquette ... 143
  - The Elderly Etiquette ... 149
  - People with Special Needs Etiquette ... 151
  - Patient's Etiquette ... 163
  - Etiquette Toward Misconduct ... 167
  - Etiquette Toward Enmity ... 171
  - Foreigner and Visitor Etiquette ... 173

- **Section Nine**
  - Police Etiquette ... 179
  - Secretarial Etiquette ... 181
  - Workplace Etiquette ... 185
  - Elevator Etiquette ... 191

- **Section Ten**
  - Travel and Transportation Etiquette ... 199

- **Section Eleven**
  - Banquet Etiquette ... 211
  - Children's Eating Etiquette ... 239
  - Coffee Etiquette ... 241
  - Wine Etiquette ... 245
  - Smoking Etiquette ... 257
  - Etiquette Toward Obesity and Dieters ... 261

- **Section Twelve**
  - Pet Etiquette ... 267
  - References ... 271
  - The Author ... 275

Acknowledgment

In the course of my work as a lecturer, trainer and diplomat, I encountered a multitude of questions and issues that were often controversial and put me in front of challenges and responsibilities that prompted me to write on the topics of this work and condense them into a comprehensive book. In fact, the completion of this book required more than five years of effort, including the verification of information from a multitude of references, as well as the application of my academic and practical experience accumulated over many years.

I would be remiss if I did not acknowledge the warm welcome and supportive environment that Brazil has provided me and my family, a beautiful country whose grandeur and splendor is sometimes unknown even to many Brazilians themselves. In this vein, I would like to extend my gratitude to my wife and children for their support and assistance. I am also indebted to my esteemed friends Sheri Smith and the renowned artist Nasr Warour, who did their best in bringing this work to fruition.

Preface

The question of writing—What is it? Why do it? For whom?—has been a matter of argument for a long time. Despite the implicit skepticism in this question, writing continues, and writers, "the poor intellectuals," continue in their amusing misery. Such a question may have multiple answers that differ according to each person's vision of writing. Some think of it as self-expression and others may consider it the lungs through which they can breathe.

While I am still not certain about the specific reasons behind my writing, I am sure about my heartfelt desire to do so. I find myself following what the great writer and philosopher Gibran Khalil Gibran said: "Half-hearted desire is half of life, but indifference is half of the death." Moreover, I consider that writing, like many other art forms, is a reflection on experience coupled with a responsibility to reveal an intense part of one's thinking.

Perhaps I would feel guilty if I did not present to readers a summary of what I have in mind based on my life journey. I have had the opportunity to combine two rich experiences. The first is my professional career. I worked for about three-and-a-half decades in public relations and protocol departments in the Syrian Parliament, the Prime Ministry, and the Ministry of Foreign Affairs. The second is my academic career, which I maintained through that period, working as a lecturer in several universities, diplomatic institutes, and training centers in Syria as well as a visiting lecturer in several other countries.

I consider myself lucky to have both taught and learned as well. I had the chance to visit more than a third of the world's countries (approximately 60), where I witnessed and experienced many cultures, customs, behaviors, and traditions.

Being obsessed with etiquette, I have sought detailed research in the field, especially because we rarely find relevant and reliable references to provide satisfying answers for those who've been puzzled in some situations about etiquette and manners, or even attire.

Although I don't claim to be a pioneer in this subject, I have tried to simplify the concepts and principles, unlike those who intentionally associated etiquette with only elites, putting much emphasis on class distinctions and giving them false esteem.

In this work, I hope I have been able to reshape this subject of etiquette to lower it from an ivory tower and make it more popular and indiscriminately accessible. Etiquette should be used in the daily life of all people as opposed to only palace dwellers, diplomats, and senior "white collar" officials, who have often become used to the privilege of elegance, albeit along with complexity and strictness.

Life is rich and beautiful if it is simple. Burdensome if complicated. This is my wish and hope. And, as Fyodor Dostoyevsky once said, "When hope is lost life stops."

Riad Nofal

Section One

Communication
& Behavior

"Human behavior flows from three main resources: desire, emotion, and knowledge."[1]

Communication is a practice important to humans and non-humans, as we witness it among animal groups. Without communication, humans would be abnormal, diseased beings or withdrawn people living in a limited world. Through communication and intermingling, the various societies mold their customs, traditions, and concepts, regulating the way they behave and deal with each other as individuals and in groups. Hence, the relationship between communication and behavior.

According to specialists in education, sociology, and psychology, human behavior is not static. It varies according to the customs and traditions of the people's environment.

When we talk about any environment, we refer to the conditions in which the individual lives, interacts, and develops his ethics and values. This includes loyalty, honesty, humility, justice, courage, and respect. It also includes a person's behavior in various situations.

" *An individual's values on one side and behaviors on the other side can be considered the code of protocol and etiquette.* "

---

1 Plato (427-347 B.C.), Greek philosopher, who was the student of Socrates and teacher of Aristotle. He founded the Academy in Athens, which was the first institution of higher learning in the Western world.

Protocol

- **Etymology and significance:**

Originally, the source of "protocol" is the Byzantine Greek word "prōtókollon," which was the first sheet glued onto a manuscript. It is formed from πρῶτος (prôtos, "first") + κόλλα (kólla, "glue"). In French, it gradually evolved to mean "official account" then "official record of a transaction," then "diplomatic document," and finally, "formula of diplomatic etiquette."

In English, "protocol" was borrowed from French in 1896 to mean "diplomatic rules of etiquette." Later, it began to convey the general sense of "conventional proper conduct." Robert Anson Heinlein[3] said:

" *Anyone who considers protocol unimportant has never dealt with a cat.* "

- **Implications of the word:**

Over time, this word has several implications:

- **Protocol as a document:**

A protocol could be a kind of accord, such as a convention, agreement, or treaty. It is less important than other accords, even though it is subject to the same procedures of signature, ratification, and conclusion.

---

2 Juan Evo Morales Ayma (born, 1959), president of Bolivia from 2006 to 2019. He is the country's first president from the Indigenous population.

3 Robert Anson Heinlein (1907-1988): An American science fiction author.

- **Protocol as the protocol administration/department:**

It is one of the departments of royal or presidential palaces, prime ministries, ministries of foreign affairs, parliaments, etc. It is responsible for:

- Ensuring the proper implementation of the rules of courtesy.
- The organization of meetings and visits.
- Taking care of diplomatic privileges and immunities.
- Preparing the procedures for signing agreements as well as the arrangements for giving medals, decorations, and official gifts. In fact, without the application of the protocol, chaos, and confusion may prevail in any official activity.

Protocol as a diplomatic concept:

In the relationships between the states and their representatives, the protocol has a great role in safeguarding the norms of dignity and sovereignty of the states.

Any intentional or unintentional omission (even due to ignorance) of any protocol rule might be considered a deliberate insult or violation of the principles of courtesy and good conduct.

In the diplomatic field, protocol may refer to:

- The set of procedures, rules of precedence, customs, and traditions that should be observed in international and diplomatic relations.
- The set of procedures that should be applied in formal events, such as meetings, visits, formal banquets, and receptions.
- The set of procedures applied in granting and wearing orders, decorations, and medals.
- The official correspondences.
- The minutes that include the summaries of discussions.
- The procedures for convening regional and international meetings and conferences.

Etiquette
(Manners)

*"Etiquette and good manners are to react discreetly
to the other's misbehavior and bad manners."* [4]

• Etymology and significance:

"Etiquette" is a French word (originally Latin). In Old French, it was "estiquette," meaning "label or ticket," and later small cards written with instructions for how to behave properly; but since 1750, it has become "etiquette," to mean "prescribed behavior."

Then "etiquette" was later used to refer also to the cards circulated in royal palaces and distributed to people who had meetings with the king, princes, and ministers, including instructions about how to appear and how to behave in their presence. Since then, the word etiquette has become associated with behavior, or with what some people tend to say: good or sophisticated behavior.

To avoid endless and controversial discussions about abstract concepts such as "good" or "sophisticated," about which everyone has their own opinion and vision, I would rather say etiquette is simply how to behave.

Historically, there is no real documentation displaying who first spoke about etiquette, when, and where; but some consider the oldest written etiquette notice was in 2560 B.C., in which an Egyptian had given some guiding instructions to his son about how to behave properly with others.

---

4   The author.

- ## Beginnings of standards-based etiquette:

  - ### Spanish Etiquette:

    The fundamental evolution of etiquette standards and norms began in Europe. Although some principles of French and English etiquette prevailed, the real etiquette originated in Spain, particularly during the reign of King Charles V (1500-1558), who initiated many procedures that suggested power and authority, including, for example, those who were entitled to wear certain kinds of clothes, colors, and jewelry.

    Furthermore, during his reign, the arrangements of hunting trips and royal visits were subject to special and binding procedures.[5]

  - ### French Etiquette:

    The basic French etiquette dates back to the Bourbon dynasty rather than to the older Spanish Etiquette. It was strict etiquette[6] but had already started to fade and lose its momentum. During the reign of King Louis XIV[7] of France (1643-1715), the real French etiquette appeared and was strictly applied until the French Revolution in 1789. After that revolution, many of the previous etiquette norms, values, and principles were changed. Some practices have vanished, and other new practices have arisen. The most prominent event, in this connection, was what happened during Napoleon Bonaparte's crowning in 1804.[8]

---

5 The following is an example of both a tragic and funny situation, which shows the extent to which etiquette was strict and obligatory. The instructions stipulated that the queen should never be touched except by the close princes of the royal family. Once, the queen had fallen off her horse, but her foot was stuck in the spindle. While the horse was running, no one dared to approach and touch the queen in order to save her, due to fear of committing a crime that requires punishment. For her good luck, two princes were there and hurried to save her.

6 When Cardinal Richelieu (Prime Minister of France between 1624 and 1642) fell ill and King Louis XIII came to visit him in his bed, another bed was brought for the king to lie on, as it was not common for the king to be standing while others were sitting.

7 During the reign of the French King Louis XIV, the chief administrator of Versailles Palace gardens had placed written cards in some of the gardens' spots, forbidding people to pass over the newly planted grass, but the nobles ignored that. He referred to the king himself who issued a royal decision banning and warning those who pass over grass. The cards became binding. The gardeners used to say to those who ignore the cards: "Please, keep to etiquettes." Since then, the word "Etiquette" has become synonymous to action and behavior according to specific conduct and manners.

8 Starting from the coronation of King Charles the Great "Charlemagne" (768-814) by Pope Leo III, on Christmas Day AD 800, at Roman's Old St. Peter's Basilica, there was a special coronation procedure in the Vatican for the kings of Europe. But during the coronation of Napoleon Bonaparte in the great cathedral of Notre Dame de Paris (1804), when Pope Pius VII was about to put the crown on Napoleon's head, Napoleon grabbed the crown and placed it on his own head by himself. That was a violation of the customary etiquette and protocol procedure of about one thousand years, stipulating the Pope puts the crowns on the heads of kings.

- **English Etiquette:**

Making use of Spanish and French etiquette, English etiquette played a pivotal role in the development of etiquette in general. It can be considered the most stringent one that began to impose itself on Europe and has become the main reliable source for diplomatic and business practices in most regions of the world, especially in Anglo-Saxon countries.

- **Russian Etiquette:**

Russian etiquette had its own character, which was derived from the Orthodox Church and influenced by both the Slavic culture and the legacy of the Byzantine Empire. It continued to exist in the Cesarean palaces until the reign of Peter the Great[9] (1672-1725) when Russian etiquette began to be influenced more and more by the French.

- **American Etiquette:**

Unlike etiquette in Europe, which was derived, largely, from royal, ecclesiastical, and cultural heritage, etiquette in the United States of America was a mixture of European etiquette principles. It is still linked, in general, to business and people of financial influence.

---

9 Peter the Great (1672-1725), who ruled the Russian Empire from 1682 until his death in 1725. Through several successful wars, he expanded Russia into a much larger empire. He led a cultural revolution that replaced some of the traditionalist and medieval social and political systems with ones that were modern, scientific, and based on the Enlightenment. Peter's reforms had a lasting impact on Russia, and many institutions of the Russian government trace their origins to his reign. He is also known for founding and developing the city of Saint Petersburg, which remained the capital of Russia until 1917.

Relationship Between Etiquette & Politeness

"Learn good manners from those who don't have them."[10]

Some may describe politeness as a kind of acquired behavior, while I say that good behavior is an innate politeness that leads us to act properly for the satisfaction of others and avoid disturbing them as much as possible. Polite gestures and behaviors count and never fail to impress.

As etiquette corresponds to customs and traditions, it is also largely interlinked with politeness. Etiquette and politeness cannot be separated without falling into a mistake. Moreover, both constitute a tributary to law and complement it.

Politeness and etiquette can address some ethical and moral issues and matters that are not covered by the law. For example, the law may not punish someone who looks or gazes at another with disdain or disrespect, while etiquette and politeness convey that this behavior is wrong and deserves to be described by society as vulgar behavior. That is why it is possible to say etiquette is complementary to law and intervenes in the so-called "gray area" where law has no clear role.

There is no doubt philosophers, intellectuals, the various educational systems, and the different cultural heritages glorify and encourage people to behave well. Jean Jacques Rousseau said,[11] "What wisdom can you find greater than kindness." Yet, there are great differences in this regard. People

---

10 Persian proverb

11 Jean-Jacques Rousseau (1712-1778), a Swiss francophone philosopher and writer whose thoughts and political philosophy largely influenced the French Revolution and contributed to the development of modern politics and education.

in some societies may behave in a given situation oddly compared to other societies, depending on their social background, customs and traditions, and cultural heritage. It is not surprising, therefore, that to find normal behavior in a certain region may seem disapproved, impolite, or even outrageous in another one. For example, burping is an improper and embarrassing behavior for most people in many countries of the world and requires an apology, while it is common and natural in China, several Southeast Asian regions, and some African countries. Therefore, any behavior cannot be considered appropriate or inappropriate if it is taken out of its context and own environment.

Coming to etiquette and politeness, we find ourselves faced with the question of what is the optimal behavior if inconsistency occurs between the requirements of etiquette and politeness. To which side do we stand? An answer to this question might be found in the following fable:

"When his vacation was over, he got the plane back to his country. Next to him on board was an old woman who had the appearance of a simple peasant. The passengers were served meals with several items including a piece of white dessert. The woman took that piece and began to eat it with a piece of bread, thinking, due to its white color, that it was a piece of cheese. Discovering her mistake, she felt very embarrassed. The man next to her pretended not to notice her mistake and after a few seconds, he took his piece of dessert and ate it with a piece of bread as well. The old woman laughed...He said to her 'Why did you not tell me it was dessert?' She said, 'I also thought that it was a piece of cheese."

Certainly, he knew that what was served within the meal was a piece of dessert, not a piece of cheese, but his taste led him to be polite and not abide by etiquette so as not to embarrass the woman.

For more clarification, let's look at another fable:

> **" A leader was offered a cup of tea on a tray provided to him. He took it, but with a saucer of a cup of coffee (not the saucer of a cup of tea) after noticing that the two women near him, out of ignorance, did so before him. To be courteous with them, he violated the etiquette intentionally. "**

He acted according to the requirements of politeness rather than the requirements of etiquette. He did not act as a leader, but as a polite man, considering the feelings of the others. He ignored some of the simple mistakes that could be overcome.

Proper behavior sometimes requires breaking strict etiquette rules. One should adapt behavior, as much as possible, to go along with the prevailing behaviors of the environment. It is not fair to impose some rules of etiquette suddenly. Some of these rules need more time to change and become accepted. Etiquette rules cannot be put into force by laws and decrees. They are unwritten laws that creep slowly into our consciousness before becoming mainstream and recognized by most people in society.

This is why we say politeness precedes etiquette and should be taken into consideration first until the opportunity comes to accept both. Hence, if one's misfortune leads him once to be accompanied by naïve and roistering people, he should show pleasure rather than disgust with some of their actions. Then, after, he will quietly withdraw without hurting their feelings. Bismarck[12] said, "Even in a declaration of war one observes the rules of politeness."

In the following, I will remind you of some of the values that may help to make one consistent with etiquette and politeness.

› Etiquette tips:

· With family, one should pay attention to their dispositions, and temper, and be a good example for the children.

· In the community, what one utters and expresses, and how they behave are among the most important norms according to which they would be evaluated and considered.

· As much as one can control their emotions, they will gain respect. On the contrary, being abruptly angry, reckless, and nervous is the fastest way to lose people's respect and confidence.

· No one can be respectful just according to their style or appearance, but also according to their behavior, character, and way of thinking. All of which, require them to be honest, polite, and positively interact with others.

· Without good sense, one could be civilized one time and the opposite another time. A young man who attends a rock concert can dance and shout perhaps,

while he should not talk or laugh at opera houses, reading rooms, places of worship, and so on. Only good sense leads him to this or that behavior.

· Each one has their own privacy and secrets and does not like others to interfere in that.

· In return, one is required not to interfere in the private life and affairs of others, and not to release arbitrary judgments, in this regard.

· Being punctual, keeping appointments, and observing deadlines all reflect on a key aspect of one's personality and respect for others.

· As much as one is modest, educated, and knowledgeable, they avoid superiority or pretending to be elite and distinguished over others who might be inferior in one area.

· When accompanied by others, it is not fair to look at one's watch from time to time. This would make them feel their presence is not desirable; furthermore, if guests are at one's house, this gesture indicates the host wants them to leave.

· When accompanied by others, yawning, snapping fingers, or tapping the table are not proper behaviors. They may make others feel one is indifferent or not interested.

· When walking, one is expected to move normally, and not to boast or sway as a peacock.

· Giving orders and instructions in an imperative way does not reflect one's strength and authority; on the contrary, it proves one's lack of self-confidence and leads to others' resentment.

---

12 Otto von Bismarck: (1815-1898) a Prussian statesman who was the first Chancellor of the German Empire between 1871 and 1890.

· One is supposed to be moderate in eating and drinking. Extravagance displays greediness and has nothing to do with etiquette.

· Certainly, rubbing hair, picking teeth, and putting a finger in the nose, in the presence of others, are disgusting habits.

· Providing help to a woman by not letting her drag a chair to sit on, or bend to pick up a glove and the like is compatible with etiquette.

· It is inappropriate to disturb and embarrass others by disrespecting their privacy, as in entering a room without knocking on the door or reading a message on a cellphone in the hands of someone nearby.

Relationship Between Protocol & Etiquette

"Applying etiquette and protocol costs nothing."[13]

It can be said that protocol is generally related to procedures and arrangements, while etiquette is related to behavior, the implementation of the procedures' details, and how to comply with them. If the protocol requires, for example, that a formal dress should be worn for a formal event, the color, style, and quality of that dress are the details that belong to etiquette requirements.

Therefore, the relationship between protocol and etiquette is very close and interactive.

- **Are protocol and etiquette rules final, fixed, and non-changeable?**

As long as protocol and etiquette are part of customs and traditions, and as long as customs and traditions evolve and change according to time, place, and circumstances, protocol and etiquette consequently change according to the same process.

Furthermore, it is certain that protocol and etiquette change from one period to another in the same region. Men in Eastern countries, for example, used to walk in front of women (a behavior still common in many

———————— 13 The author.

rural areas), but this has changed in cities where women have the privilege of entering doors and being served first.

> **" In any case, the only non-changeable rule in this context, which contradictorily stresses the concept of change and diversity, is well expressed by the proverb "When in Rome, do as the Romans do. "** [14]

It means one should act and behave in Rome as its people do. Rome is metaphorically any place in the world. Hence, good behavior in Damascus may not be proper in Beijing and vice versa.

Therefore, internationally speaking, anyone is generally supposed to follow the same protocol and etiquette rules that prevail in that region, regardless of their opinion about those rules.

▪ Where to apply etiquette and protocol rules?

As I mentioned before, for a long time, etiquette and protocol were thought of as being exclusive to royal and presidential palaces, and high and rich classes. That was a wrong assumption adopted by some social classes and elites.

It is easy to prove that simple groups such as Bedouins in tents, for example, have a kind of protocol and etiquette rules that govern their behaviors, as well as the way they deal with others. Protocol requires that Arab Bedouins, for example, welcome known or unknown guests and host them for three days, before even asking about the purpose of their visit. Their etiquette stipulates that the Bedouin host offers Arabic coffee to his guests upon arrival.

The way coffee is offered includes some interesting rituals and etiquette details concerning who drinks coffee first, which hand is used in handling and getting the cup of coffee, refraining from drinking, etc. [15]

---

14 "When in Rome, do as the Romans do," is a proverb or saying often shortened to "When in Rome..." It is said that Saint Monica and her son Saint Augustine (from Milan) planned to visit Rome one Saturday in 1777, to discover that, unlike the case in Milan, it was observed as a fast day in Rome. So, they consulted Saint Ambrose who told them: "When you are in Rome, do as the Pope does." In fact, when I am in Milan, I do not fast on Saturdays, while in Rome I do fast on Saturdays. That reply is said to have brought about the proverb or saying "When in Rome, do as the Romans do," meaning it is best to follow the traditions or customs of the place being visited.

15 Arabic coffee etiquette: The host and guest use only their right hands to offer and get the cup of coffee. After sipping the first or second cup of coffee (as the guest desires), the guest shakes the cup, with a half-circular motion, left and right before giving it back to the host, as a sign of satisfaction (otherwise the host will continue to add coffee to the guest). It is a kind of non-verbal language. If the guest takes the cup and puts it in front of him without sipping the coffee, it is a gesture indicating the guest has a certain request, and the host must take it into consideration. If the guest is distinguished and of high rank, after sipping the coffee offered to him, the host might break the cup directly. It is an honorific gesture indicating no one else deserves to drink again from the same cup.

• Some "odd" etiquette applications:

· An Eskimo guest shows and moves his tongue over his lips, in front of their host, after eating to indicate satisfaction.

· For the Inuit tribes, a good meal is praised by leaving one small piece of food on the plate after finishing eating.

· In the Middle East, people used to eat almost silently, applying the etiquette rule of "No talking while eating." Now, the situation has drastically changed.

· In Tibet, people stick out their tongues, as a traditional method of greeting and bidding farewell.

· In many Asian countries, including Sri Lanka, white is the color of mourning.

· In Japan and the Philippines, the yellow color (not white) is the color of joy and happiness.

· Foot washing is a widespread tradition across different cultures in India. While some have the tradition where the bride's parents wash the groom's feet, others make the bride herself wash his feet.

· In Afghanistan, when bread is dropped on the floor, it is lifted and kissed.

· In China, a host can tell their guest enjoyed the meal if a mess is left around his table.

· In China, leaving just a bit of food on one's plate shows they are full.

· In China, it is rude to leave any rice left over in a bowl.

· In China, belching is another way of complimenting the host on the food and is not considered rude.

· In Ghana, a man may slightly slip his dress from his shoulder to greet others.

· In Egypt, one is supposed to refill their neighbor's glass when needed, but it is never acceptable to refill their own glass.

· It is inappropriate in many Muslim and Arab countries to sit down cross-legged in the presence of elder people, some dignitaries, and clergymen.

· In England, a port is continuously passed to the left side of the table until it is finished.

· In Ethiopia, a tradition called "Gursha" is practiced, in which people give food into the mouths of other people sitting at the same table as a symbol of love, friendship, and loyalty.

· In France, bread could be used as a utensil to scoop food off the plate and into the mouth.

· In Georgia, toasting lasts very long. Everyone at the table goes around in a circle making toasts before emptying their glasses in one big sip. Georgians only toast with wine or vodka, or with beer if they wish someone bad luck.

· In Austria, people do not clink beer glasses.

· In Italy, if the pizza served does not have Parmesan[16] on it, it is not a good idea to ask for it.

· In Japan, slurping, usually when eating noodles or soup, is a sign of appreciation for the chef. The louder the slurp, the greater the thanks.

· In Korea, to be sociable, one should always say yes to the first drink, but without being the first to pour.

· In Korea, one must first serve everyone before serving anyone again.

---

16 Parmesan is an Italian hard, granular cheese produced from cow's milk and aged at least 12 months.

· In Mexico, using a fork and knife to eat a "taco"[17] is considered silly and snobby. It's polite to eat it with your hands.

· In some Middle Eastern areas, India, and parts of Africa, eating with the right hand is commonplace, but never the left one.

· In countries such as Portugal and Egypt, it is inappropriate to add salt or pepper to a served dish. Reasonably, the food is perfect and does not need more seasoning.

· In Russia, vodka is always drunk neat. Adding any mixer, even ice, is seen as polluting vodka's purity.

· In Russia, offering someone a drink is a sign of friendship, and turning it down is very offensive.

· In Russia, even if you are invited only to a cup of tea, it is better not to eat before. The Russians are generous and have the habit of offering abundant food to the guests.

· In parts of Peru, Argentina, Chile, and Bolivia, diners might pay respect to "Pachamama" (the Andean goddess of fertility and harvest), by spilling a few drops of their drink on the ground.

· In Thailand, forks should only be used to put food that is not rice-based into the mouth.

· In Thailand, forks are mainly used to push food into a spoon.

· In Tanzania, eating on a carpet or mat is customary. However, showing the soles of the feet is seen as impolite.

· In Venezuela, one should make sure to arrive for dinner about 15 minutes late. Being early, or even on time, is seen as rude.

· In Brazil, for an informal invitation, such as dinner at seven o'clock, guests are expected to attend at eight. An hour delay is a common rule.

· In Germany, men and women enter the same sauna while they are naked, assuming that everybody adheres to the rule of not looking at others.

---

17 A taco is a traditional Mexican dish consisting of a corn or wheat tortilla folded or rolled around a filling.

Section Two

Titles

"It is not titles that honor men,
but men that honor titles."[1]

" The title, as a privilege granted to its holder, is an official or honorific name that displays the prestige and respect of its owner. "

Some countries still have the old and traditional titles. The United Kingdom (U.K.), for example, has royal and hereditary titles such as queen/king, prince/princess, duke/duchess, marquise/marchioness, earl/countess, viscount/viscountess, lord/lady, and baron/baroness, as well as honorary and order titles such as knight, commander, etc. Nevertheless, most countries have already diminished or abolished all titles and adopted instead "**Mr.** /**Mrs.** /**Miss**" for all persons, ranks, and positions.

While it is difficult to identify titles in all countries, some of the titles are internationally used and could be outlined as follows:

- ## Common titles:

· A king is addressed as "**His Majesty**" and "Your Majesty."

· A queen, "Her Majesty' and "Your Majesty."

· A prince and princess of a king's close family, "His/Her Royal Highness," and "Your Highness."

· Prince and princess of the royal dynasty, "His/Her Highness," and "Your Highness."

---

1 Niccolò Machiavelli (1469-1527), an Italian diplomat, politician, historian, philosopher, and writer. He has often been called the father of modern political science. He wrote his most renowned work The Prince (Il Principe) in 1513.

In most countries, the titles "His/Her Excellency" and "Your Excellency" are used for heads of state, prime ministers, and heads of legislative bodies (first and second chambers).

Some countries like India, Pakistan, Sri Lanka, Bangladesh, Malaysia, and others use the title "The Honorable" for heads of state, prime ministers, and heads of legislative bodies.

Most countries use the title "Mr./Mrs." for ministers while some use the title "His or Her Excellency" and "Your Excellency."

For the rest of the political and administrative positions, most countries use the titles "Mr./ Mrs./Miss."[2]

For ambassadors, the titles used are "His /Her Excellency and Your Excellency."

For the wives or husbands of ambassadors and other members of the diplomatic corps, the titles of "His/Her Excellency" are not used.

Titles for military officers and other military ranks are numerous and vary from one country to another, and there is no room to mention all of them here.

Titles used for clergy are numerous and differ from one religion to another. Furthermore, they sometimes differ among sects of the same religion.

• Some abbreviations:

·   In English, "His Excellency', is abbreviated as "H.E."

·   In French, "Son Excellence', is abbreviated as "S.E."

·   In Spanish, "Su Excelance', is abbreviated as "S.E."

·   In Português, "Sua Excelência', is abbreviated as "S. Ex."

---

2   One should use "Miss" (without abbreviation) when addressing girls and young unmarried women. "Ms." should be used when unsure of a woman's marital status or if she is unmarried and prefers to be addressed with a marital-status neutral title.

Order of Precedence

*"A post gives an interim precedence; modesty
and honesty make it permanent."*[3]

Since the Vienna Conference (1815) and the Vienna Convention (held under the auspices of the United Nations in 1961), the issue of precedence is still a very complicated and delicate subject.

No formal or semi-formal event can be organized without applying the principle of precedence.

Applying the principle of precedence requires too much effort and experience to ensure the exact rights and privileges of all people, without causing any kind of prejudice to anyone. In fact, without precedence, chaos would prevail.

In this regard, it is necessary to mention the following:

There is no single international precedence order (or system), except for the diplomatic corps and countries (and consequently countries' flags).

Each country has its order of precedence, which may be a written one, or a custom applied.

- **The order of precedence is usually considered according to:**

1. Positions or posts (as classified into general categories): Such as the categories of ministers, governors, ambassadors, directors, etc.

2. The ranking (or hierarchy) within each post (category). Within the post of ministers, for example, there is a precedence order, usually stipulated in the decree/s of their appointment/s (That is, the precedence of each minister is according to his name sequence in the decree related

───────── 3 The author.

to the formation of the government and its amendments, if any).

The order of precedence among ambassadors is considered according to the submission dates of their credentials.

› Etiquette tips:

– Precedence cannot be interchanged or passed to another person. When a minister, for example, assigns a deputy to replace them at a meeting or an event, the deputy does not take the minister's seat, but rather the deputy's own seat according to precedence. Otherwise, the deputy might go ahead of some other ministers.

– A wife takes precedence order of her husband. It is an international custom practiced all over the world. The wife of a king is a queen, the wife of a head of state is a first lady, and the wife of a governor is to be treated as a governor and so on, at all events.

– Husbands do not take precedence order of their wives. Husbands of the queens of the U.K., the Netherlands, and Denmark, for example, are not kings. Similarly, husbands of women ministers are not treated as ministers. They all take their precedence within the categories or posts to which they belong.

– It is worth mentioning that, regardless of the previous protocol rule, event organizers can seat the husbands and wives next to each other if the event is social or cultural, such as concerts, operas, theater shows, and the like. In these cases, the husband is to be seated next to his wife, not far or in another row.

– Married women have precedence over single women unless they have certain official status.

– Children do not benefit from the precedence of any of their parents.

– Widows retain their previous precedence, i.e., the same precedence they used to have before the death of their husbands.

– In case of equal precedence between man and woman, the woman is given priority.

– An ex-dignitary retains their previous precedence but comes after the last one in the category to which they used to belong.

– When seating people, the system of precedence begins first with the one that has the highest preference or the guest of honor.

– A person of the highest rank (or the guest of honor) is usually seated in the middle, and then the others are seated on his right and left alternatively.

– For certain events, it is possible to give precedence to the high dignitary responsible for the event, regardless of their precedence. When a prime minister, for example, is present at a university's event, the minister of higher education is usually seated on their right, the rector of that university is seated on their left, and then the other ministers and dignitaries, according to the system of precedence.

– Clergy persons, regardless to which religion they belong, are usually given precedence in some form.

Introduction
and Presentation

*"The pure force of life
is in communication with each other."[4]*

It is natural that people look for acquaintance with others and try to make friends and build relationships with them. Hence, it is fundamental for people to introduce themselves, to be introduced, and to present to others.

The way people introduce themselves to others as well as the way they accomplish the introduction of others, is one of the aspects of determining first impressions. Moreover, the first impressions that come from the first acquaintance, whether positive or negative, usually last long and are not easy to change. Therefore, people's introductions to each other requires careful knowledge of the rules of etiquette that govern this sensitive matter.

- **Here are some considerations and etiquette rules:**

▷ **Visual communication:**

In all cases of presentation and introduction, eye contact with the person we are introduced to must be maintained. Otherwise, the matter could be interpreted as a lack of interest.

▷ **Titles and occupations:**

Civil, religious, military, or honorific titles precede names. For example, "The two businessmen and brothers Bassam and Hanna"; "Professor Marcos"; and "Captain Edward."

---

4 Paulo Coelho de Souza (Born, 1947), a Brazilian lyricist and novelist and the recipient of numerous international awards. He is the writer with the highest number of social media followers.

Declaring titles and occupations of people during introduction, helps them find topics for conversations.

▷ **Introduction depending on age:**

The younger person is to be presented to the older one.

▷ **Introduction depending on status or rank:**

A person of a lower rank is to be introduced to a person of a higher one. It is not easy to know the status and ranks of all people, which requires experience. However, without applying this rule, confusion may happen and lead to a problem.

The following is an example of the introduction of two people with two different professional statuses to one another (one is a minister and the other a professor). The minister's title is used to first draw his attention:

"Mr. Minister, I would like to present to you Ms. Camila Oliveira Macêdo, she is a professor of Portuguese." Then after, I would say to Ms. Camila: "This is H.E. Mr. George Touma, minister of education."

▷ **Introduction of foreigners:**

The name of a foreigner's country should be mentioned, for example, "Mrs. Maria das Graça Dalvi from Brazil, an economist and executive advisor of a company," "Mr. Ziad Amer, a businessman and the honorary consul of Indonesia in Syria."

▷ **Introduction depending on gender:**

Men are introduced to women and not vice versa. For example:

"Mr. Pedro, let me introduce you to Mrs. Jaqueline and Mrs. Mery."

However, if men have high status or ranks, whether political, administrative, religious, social, cultural, and so on, or if they are elderly, women can be introduced to them.

▷ **Introduction of family members:**

The person's position in the family must be mentioned before mentioning his or her name, surname, and occupation. For example:
· "My husband Harold Luis, he is a lawyer."
· "My wife Nof Nofal, she is a doctor."
· "My relative Ousseima Imad writes the scripts of her plays. She directs her plays in which she acts as well."

▷ **Quick introduction:**

While introducing two people, they may be of similar age or status, and the name of one or both has been forgotten. To avoid embarrassment, one may resort to a quick way of introduction, so that neither of them would feel any slight. One may say: "I think you know each other" or "I do not think I need to introduce you to each other."

▷ **Mistakes during introduction:**

Any mistake in identifying name, surname, and occupation, could be corrected gently and politely without embarrassing the person who made the introduction. Furthermore, such mistakes could even be ignored or corrected later.

▷ **Compliments during introduction:**

An introduction should be accompanied by expressions of appreciation that highlight the person's achievements or services, whether scientific, administrative, social, or others (clearly, briefly, and without exaggeration).

▷ **Introducing oneself:**

A person may introduce themselves to others who are parallel or higher in status or rank.

▷ **Introduction of young people:**

For young boys and girls, it is enough to introduce them simply by mentioning their first or full names.

▷ **Introduction at dinners and banquets:**

While sitting at tables, each person should introduce themselves to the others sitting next to them, at their right and left, and try to chat with them equally.

▷ **Coming across someone:**

If you come across someone you know, but you have not met them for a long time and feel they have not remembered you, there is no need to say, "Guess who I am." This kind of introduction (and improper humor) is not acceptable. On the contrary, remind them of your name and the place where you had met before.

▷ **Introduction at cocktail parties and receptions:**

If a guest arrives late for a cocktail party or reception, and the host and hostess have already mingled, the guest introduces himself or herself to those whom they meet and then tries to find the host and hostess to greet them.

The guest should not impose themselves on two people engaged in an important or private conversation, just to introduce themselves.

One might be introduced to a famous person, whom they have never heard of before. The guest should never show ignorance of the person's fame; this will hurt the person and cause distress.

One who introduces people to each other must be sure they have the desire for that. Otherwise, it might cause embarrassment for someone who is not on good terms with another.

Visit Cards

*"Your visit card reflects part of
the first impression about you."*[5]

It is well known that visit cards have become an important part of the communication devices that many of us use, very often, in daily life.

▷ **Visit cards use:**

Visit cards are used in the following cases:

- To present oneself to others.
- To reciprocate a visit card offered by someone else.
- With a bouquet of flowers sent as a gift for a certain event.
- With a gift presented at a formal or personal event.
- To thank.
- To congratulate.
- To express condolences.
- To recommend someone else.

▪ **Formal visit cards:**

Formally speaking, a visit card is mostly white or beige, simple, and without any trimming or ornament.

A state's flag or emblem should not be printed on one's visit cards unless they are of a very high rank, such as minister, deputy minister, or the like.

A diplomat should not print on their visit cards a flag or emblem unless they are the head of a diplomatic mission.

▪ **Phrases that can be recorded on visit cards:**

It was customary in diplomatic (and even social) traditions that a diplomat may record some phrases or abbreviations on their cards sent to other people or diplomats in the Ministry of Foreign Affairs of the state to which

───────────── 5 The author.

they are accredited. These abbreviations are in French, but are used internationally as follows:

– For thanks, (Pour remercier), abbreviated as "p.r."

– For presentation, (Pour Presenter), abbreviated as "p.p."

– For congratulations on anniversaries, (Pour fêter), abbreviated as "p.f."

– For acquaintance, (Pour faire Connnaissance), abbreviated as ''p.f.c.''

– To congratulate on the New Year, (Pour fêter nouvelle année), abbreviated as "p.f.n.a."

– For condolences, (Pour Condoléances), abbreviated as "p.c."

– For vacations, (Pour prendre nouvelles), abbreviated as "p.p.n.''

And other phrases.

Note:

It is advisable to write all phrases mentioned above in pencil.

When sending a visit card with a gift, a diplomat is supposed to delete their occupation (Deleting should be done with a pencil, not a pen).

For the gift to be acceptable, it must be presented as a personal initiative of the sender, not because the diplomat represents the country or embassy.

- **Married women visit cards:**

Usually, regardless of her position (diplomatic, scientific, business, cultural, or any other position), she writes her name on a visit card coupled with her surname and her husband's surname.

- **Widows visit cards:**

It is customary to mention in a widow's visit cards her social status, with the name and surname of her husband, without mentioning the address or phone number.

- **Divorced women visit cards:**

A divorced woman writes her name on visit cards, along with the name of her own family, without mentioning the address or phone number.

- **Single women visit cards:**

A single woman writes her name on visit cards with her father's surname, without mentioning the word "Miss" or the address and phone number.

In Latin American countries, on their visit cards, men and women or unmarried/single mothers, write (as in official documents) the name accompanied by the mother's surname and then the father's surname.

Note:

It is unfair for a married or a single woman to send her visit card to an employee or someone else unless she is herself an employee and the necessities of work so require.

It is unfair for a man to ask for a woman's visit card. The woman herself decides to provide that or not.

In countries such as China, Japan, Korea, Malaysia, and other East Asian countries, people give and receive visit cards with both hands.

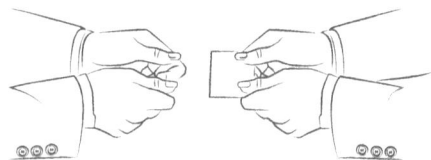

Greetings

*"You cannot shake hands
with a clenched fist"*[6]

> **" According to various
cultures, there are many
types of greeting used in
various parts of the world,
such as handshaking,
giving a bow, "Namaste,"
taking off the hat, etc. "**

- **Handshaking:**[7]

Handshaking, as a mutual movement between two people, is the most common type of greeting used between those who are already familiar with each other and is key for new contact between those who have just been acquainted with each other, for the first time.

The first documented instance of the practice of a handshake greeting is represented by a wall sculpture from 851 B.C.,

---

6 Indira Gandhi (1917–1984) was India's first and, to date, only female Prime Minister. She was the daughter of Jawaharlal Nehru, the nation's first Prime Minister.

7 The custom of shaking hands is believed to date back to the Stone Age, when a man had to be armed with a thick stick that he carried in his right hand, often to fight wild beasts or hunt animals for food. Man was the enemy of his fellow man, and when he began to learn or experience how to befriend neighbors, he had to devise a way to show those he befriended he was peaceful. The best way was to throw his stick on the ground and extend his right hand, free from the weapons of combat.

which portrays Babylonian King Marduk-Zakir-Shomei shaking hands with Assyrian King Shalmaneser III in a gesture of alliance between the two kingdoms.[8]

A wall sculpture on display at the Iraq Museum in Baghdad, Iraq.

Depending on the way it is applied, handshaking can be a positive or negative factor in the process of communication. Therefore, it is not just a mere manual movement, but also an important gesture of body language to convey feelings of safety and consent.

While handshaking is frequent and a daily habit among employees, colleagues, friends, and relatives in some communities, especially in the Middle East, it is not so often frequent in Western societies. This does not mean a lack of interest, but it is a result of cultural differences.[9]

> ### Etiquette tips:

– It is unfair to ignore someone else's hand extended for handshaking.
– The younger person begins greeting the older person unless the younger person is higher in rank or status (political, administrative, social, or religious).
– It is important to note that customs and traditions in some areas, particularly rural ones, still observe the practice of the elderly being greeted by younger people, regardless of rank or status.
– When a person with a lower status greets someone with a higher one, the person of lower status does not initiate extending for handshaking. The higher-status person decides this.
– If it happens and a person of lower status extends their hand first, by mistake, the higher-status person does not have the right to refuse that extended hand. This behavior, in no way, corresponds to etiquette.
– The person who comes to a place, wherein there are many persons, greets and advances to shake hands with them (unless they have a very high status).
– If someone shakes hands with one or more, they should continue shaking hands with all the people present, whether they know them or not.
– Unlike women, men cannot do handshaking while putting on gloves, even if he is outdoors and the temperature is very low.
– Men shake hands with men and women, young and old, always while standing.
– Men proceed to shake hands with women and not vice versa.
– A woman can shake hands with a man while sitting unless he is of a high status; in this case, she has to shake hands standing.

---

8 Introduction to the History of Ancient Civilizations, by Taha Baqer.

9 In times of some pandemics like COVID-19 and its variants, it has been important and obligatory to avoid handshaking as well as hugs and kisses, in addition to observing distance and using masks.

- A woman standing to shake hands with a man should not be considered a breach of rules, but rather a kind of additional respect.
- To greet clergy, women always stand.
- A woman stands while shaking hands with another woman.
- A woman does not need to stand to shake hands with a young woman.
- It is tactful for young women to stand and greet others (men and women).
- A female host should stand up to greet her guests, women, and men (whether the event is in or outdoors).
- During parties, a woman does not usually greet others, except those who are introduced to her, and does that by a slight nodding of her head.
- If a man meets a woman of his acquaintance on the street, he does not greet her unless they meet face to face.
- When witnessing a woman of his acquaintance on the street, a man should not try to draw her attention by any signal or voice. Otherwise, he may embarrass her.

- **Correct handshaking:**

When greeting by shaking hands, the two should have direct eye contact. Communicating with the eyes is so important in this case.

- Sunglasses should be taken off during a handshake to be able to make eye contact, which is very important in communication.
- One cannot do handshaking with someone while looking at and talking to someone else. This behavior will be interpreted negatively.
- When shaking hands, the right hand should be free from anything.
- Large or many rings in the right hand are not recommended.
- A handshake is naturally performed by extending one's hand with the palm and fingers open, and the thumb up.
- Handshaking should be avoided if one's hand is wet or sweaty.
- While handshaking, a distance of approximately 50 to 60 centimeters should be maintained between one person and another. This distance or personal space varies according to different cultures.
- One should not extend his hand while two are already performing handshaking.
- If someone is about to pass between two persons, they are supposed to wait for a moment before shaking hands. Otherwise, he will be hindered to pass.
- Finger signals or an unusual movement of any finger during a handshake (especially with the opposite sex) should be avoided.

• Types of handshaking:

▼ Normal/equal handshake.

▼ Dominating and submissive handshake.

▼ Crushing handshake.

▼ Flabby handshake (the dead fish).

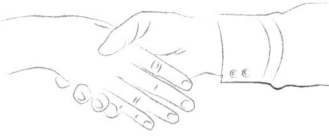

▼ Finger handshake.

▼ Sandwich handshake.

▼ Shaking hands with additional pats on the other person's arm or shoulder.[10]

• Greeting by kissing hand:

It is familiar in many parts of the world, especially in some Arab and Islamic countries to see a person kissing the hand of his father or mother. It demonstrates respect and gratitude.

In some Western societies, the hands of married women are sometimes kissed (instead of a handshake) as a symbolic gesture of further respect.
It is impermissible to kiss the hand of a woman wearing gloves.
The hands of a girl or a single woman are not supposed to be kissed for greeting.

• Namaste greeting:

Although a handshake is common in most countries, there are still other ways to greet.
In India, Sri Lanka, Nepal, and sometimes in Bangladesh, for example, "Namaste" is the common greeting style. Each individual brings their hands together and bows simply, without any hand contact between people, and says, "Namaste."

• Taking the hat off for greeting:

The practice of taking off the hat goes back to an ancient dueling tradition when both contestants used to lift their helmets before a fight. It was a kind of greeting, but moreover, a gesture to stir the horror and fear of the opponent.

---

10 Shaking hands with additional pats on the other person's shoulder is inappropriate unless the relationship is that friendly and allows for such behavior.

- A man can greet just by lifting his hat.
- In compliance with etiquette, taking the hat off, in specific situations, is not only a kind of greeting but also to show more respect for other people.
- When a man meets a woman of his acquaintance while outdoors, he removes his hat and keeps it in his left hand to shake hands with her. He does not put it on again as long as he is speaking with her.
- When a man enters indoor places like rooms, offices, houses, etc., he takes off his hat.
- When a woman enters an elevator, a man takes off his hat and keeps it in his hand until he leaves the elevator.
- In elevators of public places and commercial centers, men may not take off their hats. Men can show respect for women just by giving them comfortable space, no more.
- Outdoors, a woman might stop a man wearing a hat to ask about a certain place or other information. He takes off his hat, or lifts it over his head, for a short while, or at least touches it with his hand, as if he intends to remove it.
- A man removes his hat when introduced to another.
- A man removes his hat when he talks to an elderly man.
- A man removes his hat when he gives thanks or apologies to someone.
- A man removes his hat when a national anthem is played.
- A man removes his hat when a funeral is passing.

- **Giving a bow:**

Chinese bow >
< Japanese bow

Giving a bow is an elegant way of greeting as well as showing respect.

Giving a bow is a movement performed by people towards each other, often accompanied by a little flexing of knees, trunk, or shoulders or bending one's neck.

A bow is the only kind of greeting in China, Japan, and some other neighboring countries. The Chinese give a bow by bending their shoulders and neck, so the bow looks simple. The Japanese perform a bow at the waist; therefore, it appears more obvious.

- **Cases of bow greeting:**

During dance classes, schoolchildren are taught to bow to each other, at both the beginning and end of a dance.

Giving a bow is performed as an expression of greeting on one hand, and to show pleasure and satisfaction towards the performance of the dance partner, on the other hand.

- When entering a room or hall, wherein there is one woman or more, it is preferable to give a slight bow as a kind of apology, as well as greeting.
- When meeting several people, it is elegant for young girls to greet by giving a slight bow, often accompanied by a little flexing of knees and touching the edge of the dress or skirt.
- While having lunch or dinner in a restaurant, a man is supposed to rise and give a slight bow to a passing woman of his acquaintance.
- A man is supposed to give a slight bow, on the street, to greet a passing woman he knows before continuing his way.
- Formally, a woman is supposed to greet a man by giving a bow first, before he does.
- It is proper if a woman and a man give bows to each other reciprocally, at the same time.
- To only smile for a person giving a bow is incompatible with etiquette. The right response should be a bow in return.

• Greeting by rubbing noses:

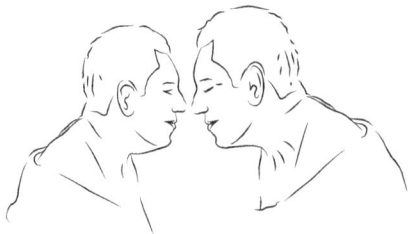

The Eskimos as well as the Maori (Indigenous people of New Zealand) greet each other by rubbing noses together.

In the Arab Gulf states, while shaking hands, people may also rub their noses.

• Greeting by kissing shoulders:

In some Arab regions, while shaking hands, people may kiss their shoulders.

• Greeting with hugs and kisses:

Due to many details, the next chapter is dedicated to this topic.

• Greeting by patting on the shoulders:

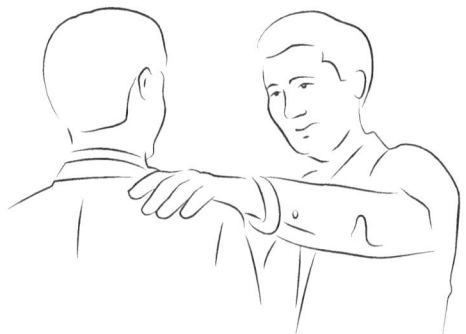

In some countries, Sudan, for example, greetings between two people can be performed just by patting each other's right shoulder.

- **Greeting by kissing head:**

In some Arab and Islamic countries, as a show of respect, a person may kiss the head of one of his parents. This can also be done toward older relatives.

- **Sticking out tongue:**

It is diplomatic in Tibet for a host to stick out his tongue when he says goodbye to his guests if he feels happy about their visit.

- **Greeting by a hand on the chest:**

In Arab and Islamic countries, a person can greet another person or group of people by placing his right hand on the left side of his chest.

Hugging and Kissing

"A hug is a great gift; one size fits all, and it's easy to exchange."[11]

It is important to know that hugging and kissing as a social behavior are subject to cultural aspects as well as customs and traditions.

Therefore, this behavior varies from one region to another. According to some sources, the origin of the tradition of cheek-kissing can be traced back to Saint Paul's Epistle to the Romans where he instructed followers to "greet one another with a holy kiss."[12] This "holy kiss" developed into a social kiss and common greeting among early Christians as an essential part of Catholic rituals.

> **Etiquette tips:**

· In South and North American countries, as well as Europe, people of the same sex can shake hands or exchange hugs, but generally do not give kisses. More likely, kisses could be exchanged if people are of different sexes.

· It is worth mentioning that Latin Americans are the biggest huggers and social kissers. In most Latin American countries, it is natural for men to greet girls or women they meet, even for the first time, by kissing and not just by handshaking.

· In Arab countries, it is common to have frequent hugging and kissing among people

---

11 Anonymous

12 The Bible: Romans 16:16.

of the same sex, even if they were together one or two days before.

· In Islamic and Asian societies, it is not common for men to kiss or hug women or girls, unless they are very close relatives or of the same family.

The number of greeting kisses varies from one place to another. It is worth knowing where one might turn a cheek and how many kisses to expect. In France for example, the count varies dramatically by region: Parisians consider two kisses the norm, while three is standard in Provence, and four throughout the Loire Valley.

- **Here's the common count for a sampling of some countries:**

One Kiss: Colombia, Argentina, Chile, Peru, Philippines, and other countries.

Two Kisses: Spain, Italy, Greece, Germany, Hungary, Romania, Croatia, Bosnia, Brazil (though, like France, the number may differ by region), some Middle Eastern countries (though not between opposite sexes, as mentioned before), and other countries.

Three Kisses: Belgium, Slovenia, Macedonia, Montenegro, Serbia, Netherlands, Switzerland, Egypt, Lebanon, Russia (where it's accompanied by a hug, locally called "bear hug"[13]), and other countries.

While it seems familiar to kiss babies and kids in many societies, including Arab and Islamic ones, this practice is inappropriate in Western societies and Latin American countries with people who are not friends or family, particularly in rural areas.

Furthermore, in part due to health concerns, in some countries, like the U.S., it is not appropriate even to touch children who are not close to you.

---

13 Bear Hug: A tight hug, with the huggers swaying left and right, resembling a fight with a bear.

Section Three

Clothing Etiquette

"Appearances are deceiving."[1]

Clothes are among the important elements of a nation's culture. They are essential components of traditions and customs and play an influential role in forming perceptions about any group of people.

Although some people may consider clothes secondary, they are considerably important in the appearance of any individual, and to some extent play a substantial role as a preliminary introduction of their personality.

Regardless of an individual's reality, a well-dressed person calls for respect unconsciously; William Shakespeare,[2] in his play, The Merchant of Venice says, "The world is still deceived by ornament."

" *Anyhow, a person's elegance should be as natural as possible, not extravagantly remarkable.* "

A person's style is supposed to reflect a positive and good impression, although it should not be the only focal point.

Fortunately, elegance is not as expensive as some might think, and the most expensive clothes are not necessarily the most elegant ones. A woman wearing the best of China's silk and ornamented with jewels

---

1 Portuguese proverb.

2 William Shakespeare (1564-1616), an English poet, playwright, and actor, widely regarded as the greatest writer in the English language and the world's preeminent dramatist.

like an Eastern princess might appear very vain and absurd.

Whatever a woman wears should be simple, harmonized in colors and sizes, and compatible with the event and location. Confucius said, "Life is really simple, but we insist on making it complicated." [3]

The British say a man can be elegant if he has just one suit and a dozen neckties. This indicates that a man is not required to diversify his clothes so much. It is almost enough to wear the same suit for a few days and just change necktie every day, to give the impression he is different.

If just one piece of the worn clothes or the jewels used is extravagantly noticeable more than the other components of the attire or ornaments, a big defect would happen, and elegance would be a failure.

Women should know men notice their defects more than their overall clothing.

It is to keep in mind that the choice of appropriate clothing is also age-related, so what young people wear might be unusual at an advanced age. A 70-year-old man wearing a young man's clothes would inevitably look like a philanderer.

The situation is even worse if, for example, an old woman tries to wear the same as her daughter. She would look playful, as if trying hard to turn back the wheels of time.

For men and women to look elegant, it is important to remember that the body shape is important in choosing the appropriate clothing.

If a tall and thin man wears a tight suit with clear longitudinal lines, he will look taller and thinner. A short and fat woman wearing a width-lined dress would appear spherical.

The relationship between elegance and fashion is very flimsy, and often the latest fashion innovations are far from being elegant.

Today, fashion is an overwhelming trend everywhere. It is an industry that affects people's tastes and their opinions about beauty, making them move and choose according to herd instinct.

Under the influence of fashion advertisements, promotions, and new fashion seasons, people choose the same styles and designs the fashion houses push rather than what fits their bodies or suits their personalities.

Most people wear the in-fashion clothes, looking the same and resembling no more than a herd of sheep.

Emily Post [4] said, "A woman who keeps pace with the latest designs of fashion houses is, by standards of elegance, no more than, a ewe moving relentlessly and without realizing the direction or distance it walks."

Every fashion season, almost all men and women become duplicate copies rather than wear what they like.

Anyhow, very often, many of us have had very good initial impressions and admired the elegance of people, but as soon as they started to talk we changed our minds after discovering the clear contradiction between external elegance and deficient internal potential.

An elegant person does not continue to be so without other personal characteristics, such as being a good speaker, tactful, and refined with broad knowledge.

---

3 Confucius (551-479 B.C.), a Chinese teacher and social philosopher whose teaching deeply influenced East Asian life.

4 Emily Post (1872-1960): An American author.

Types of Clothing

In most of the world's regions, clothes are classified into formal, informal, and casual. (With casual wear fewer rules are applied, therefore, it will not be part of our discussion).

- **Formal wear for men:**

For decades, the most prevalent formal clothing has been the suit. It is, generally, a set of garments consisting of trousers, a jacket (of the same color and fabric), and sometimes a vest, in addition to a shirt and necktie.

Due to its various designs and colors, as well as its elegant and practical elements, the suit has become popular and widespread internationally.

It is worth mentioning that some countries, for certain events, require that the suit should be of a specific design and color, and that some clothing accessories are required.

Previously, the first commemorative photographs of the Lebanese government, for example, showed the President of the Republic, the Prime Minister, and all the ministers wearing white suits.

A white suit is also required when a new ambassador presents his credentials to the President of the Republic (unless he is dressed in the national costume of his country).

Similarly, ambassadors who present their credentials to European kings and heads of state are required to wear Morning and Frock coats (unless they are wearing the national costumes of their countries).

In Oman, while it is possible not to put the Janbiya (Omani and Yemeni dagger) into the belt when wearing the national costume, it is compulsory when the event is formal.

— Things to consider:

" National costumes could be considered formal wear at every time, everywhere, and at all events. It is an international norm in all countries. "

· Men are expected to take off their coats indoors.

· Under the jacket, it is not advisable to wear a shirt with short sleeves; one to two centimeters of the cuff tip of the shirtsleeves should appear under the jacket's sleeves.

· The flaps of the two jacket pockets should always cover the pockets, rather than be pushed inside them.

— Supplementary and accessory items:

In addition to his wedding ring (if married), a man may only wear one more ring.

The suit handkerchief, whose color traditionally matches the color of the necktie, is no longer necessary, although some still use it to give an elegant impression.

It is no longer desirable to use a golden or silver pin to hold the necktie to fasten it to the middle of the shirt.

Cufflinks, of various colors, are still used with double-cuffed shirts, but using the attached buttons is most common and does not contradict the requirements of elegance.

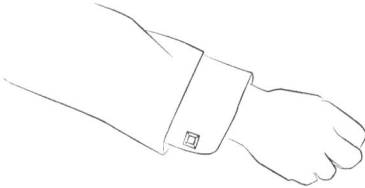

Previously, golden watches were used for night activities and events, while silver ones were used for daytime. Now the prerequisite of color is no longer binding.

While watchbands were once made of leather only, today they are made of leather, metal, and other materials of various colors. Nevertheless, multi-colored watches and bands, most often used by young people, are still inappropriate for men.

No rule specifies the number of decorative buttons[5] on a suit sleeve's cuff. Most commonly there are three or four, and once in a while, there are five. The number of suit jacket buttons is usually subject to fashion trends; they are one, two, three, or four. Men often wear gloves to prevent cold, but they should not shake hands with anyone while wearing gloves.

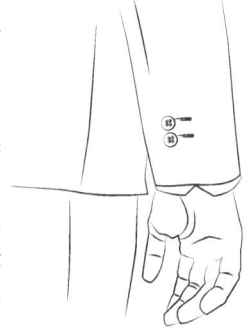

- **Types and elements of men's formal wear:**

Men's formal wear is usually classified as:

1. Suit Jacket.
2. Morning Coat / Morning suit (Bonjour in French).
3. Frock Coat / Evening suit (Frac in French).
4. Black Tie, including:
   - Dinner jacket / Dinner suit.
   - Tuxedo / Smoking.
   - White dinner jacket / White dinner suit.

---

5 Historically speaking, the decorative buttons were first used on military suits and were fixed on the upper side of the cuff. Some say that as Napoleon Bonaparte (others say the Russian Caesar Peter the Great) had noticed the dirt of the sleeve's cuffs of his soldiers suits due to wiping noses, he ordered to fix big copper buttons on suit cuffs so that to hinder this bad behavior. Over time, those buttons have become smaller, fixed of the lower side of the cuff, and used just for decorative purposes.

1. Suit Jacket:

A suit with a jacket is the most common suit in most countries of the world and has several styles and colors. Its elegance lies in the care for details that reflect the impressions about the wearer looking good.

▷ Styles of the Suit Jacket:

► One Button Suit:

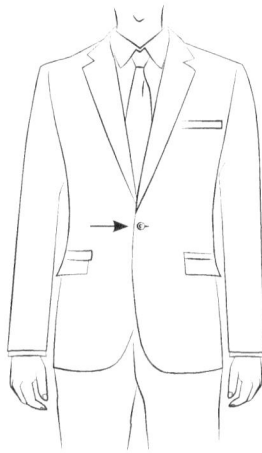

- A single-breasted suit.
- A traditional type that could be considered modern as well.
- Although not so common, today it could be worn at daily events as well as formal events and meetings.

► Two Button Suit:

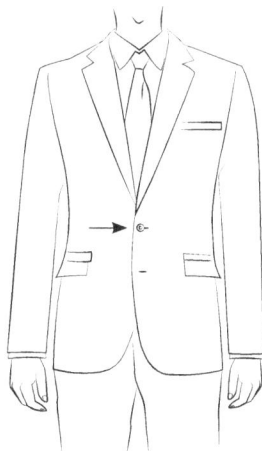

- A modern option suitable for daily use.
- A practical choice.
- Compared with the single-button suit, more suitable for those who are tall.

► Three Button Suit:

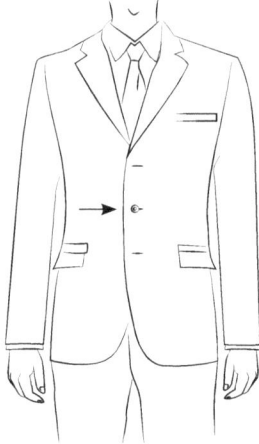

- One of the timeless classic suits.
- Suitable for employees, executives, and businessmen.
- Practical and suitable for job interviews.
- Suitable for special events as well as formal evenings.
- Could be worn whenever a Tuxedo or Frock is not compulsory.

► Four Button Suit:

!! Old-fashioned and no longer used. Therefore, it is not recommended.

► Double-Breasted Suit:

- The jacket of this type of suit has overlapping two front flaps.
- On its front flaps, it has two symmetrical columns of buttons.
- It was popular and worn at the most formal events from 1950 to 1965 and again from 1980 to 2000.

- **Fastening/ unfastening the jacket:**

When standing, the suit jacket should remain fastened to allow the suit to look better with a clearer silhouette.

When sitting, the suit jacket should be unbuttoned to allow the wearer to sit more comfortably and prevent wrinkles.

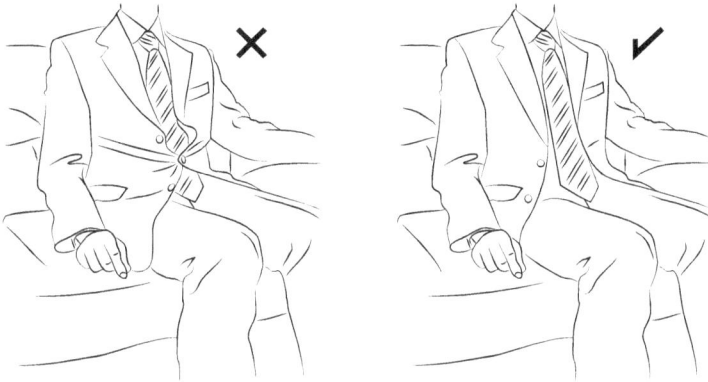

In this vein, the rule of "Sometimes, Always, Never,"[6] stipulates that:
- The upper button is sometimes closed.
- The second button is always closed.
- The lower button is never closed.
- If the suit is two-buttoned, only the top button is closed.

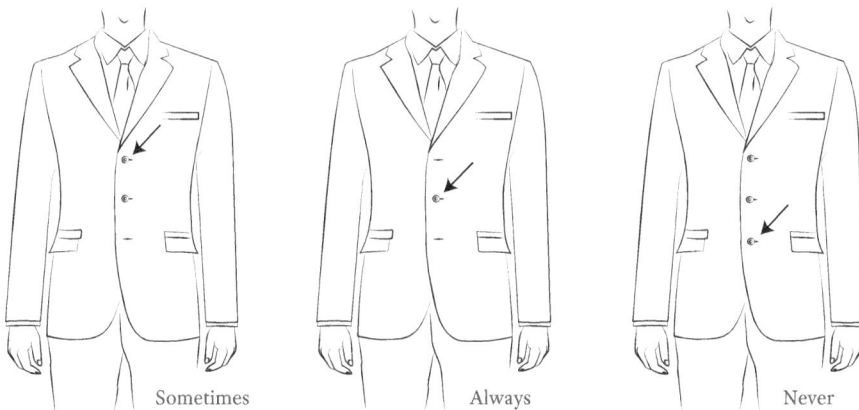

Sometimes   Always   Never

---

6 The "Sometimes, Always, Never" rule goes back to around 1900. The British King Edward VII (1841-1910), who was unable to close the lower button of his jacket or vest due to obesity. The entourage followed their king in leaving the lower button undone, and this behavior continued and has become an internationally adopted tradition.

- **Colors of formal Suit Jacket:**

  Traditionally, black was the only color for a formal suit jacket.

  Later, dark blue became common for formal suit jackets in all evening and daytime events.

  Since then, it has also become possible to wear a dark gray formal suit jacket, but only during the day.

  Other colors are not suitable for formal wear even if dark.

- **Suit fit shape:**

  If a suit does not fit well on someone's body, it would be inappropriate and would give a negative impression.

  When choosing a suit, it is important to take into consideration the measurement standards.

  Measurement standards take into consideration one's height, arm length, and width of the shoulders, waist, chest, etc.

- **Jacket length:**

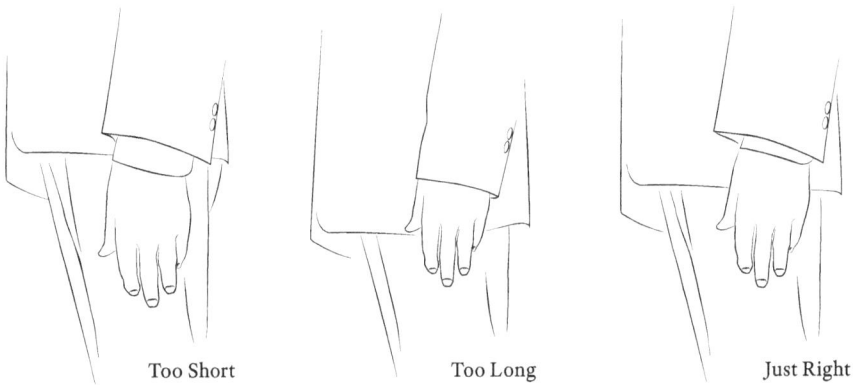

| Too Short | Too Long | Just Right |

  The proper length of the jacket depends on a person's height.

  When standing, the jacket's low end should reach the middle of the thumb.

  If shorter than that, the jacket will look short.

  If longer, it will look like a coat.

- **Jacket sleeve length:**

  To know the proper length of the sleeves, the wearer folds his arm towards his chest. Then, about one to two centimeters of the shirtsleeve cuff should appear outside the jacket sleeve. The sleeve shouldn't be tight, otherwise, wrinkles will appear and it will look as if the hand is stuck inside.

  The sleeve should not be wide, otherwise the hand will appear as if it is hanging.

- **Jacket shoulders:**

    If the shoulder measurement is too wide, wrinkles will appear in the chest area.
    If the shoulder measurement is too narrow, the person will look stuffed inside his jacket.

- **Jacket waist & chest:**

Too Small   Perfect Fit   Too Big

    If the waistline is too narrow, the buttons will not close without creating wrinkles.
    If the waistline is too wide, its wearer will appear as if wearing an overcoat.

- **"V" shape of jacket lapels:**

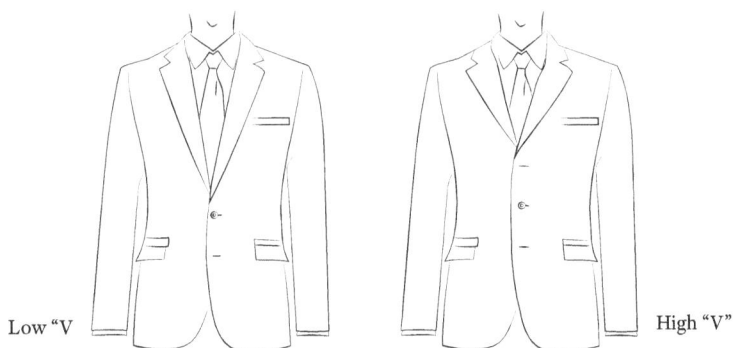

Low "V   High "V"

    An important design factor that affects the elegance of the wearer of the suit jacket is the "V" shape.
    The "V" shape refers to the space between the jacket's front lapels.
    The low "V" fits a tall man, as it widens his chest.
    The high "V" fits a short man, as it makes his torso appear taller.

· **Jacket lapel types:**

Notch Lapel   Peak Lapel   Shawl lapel

Generally speaking, there are three common jacket lapel types:
- **The peak lapel:** A formal jacket lapel positioned close to the collar and forming a peak that points upward.
- **The notch lapel:** Where the collar and lapel meet to form an oblique V shape.
- **The shawl lapel:** A lapel that is continuously curved, often made of satin or silk. Most often used in a tuxedo or smoking.

· **Suit jacket vents:**

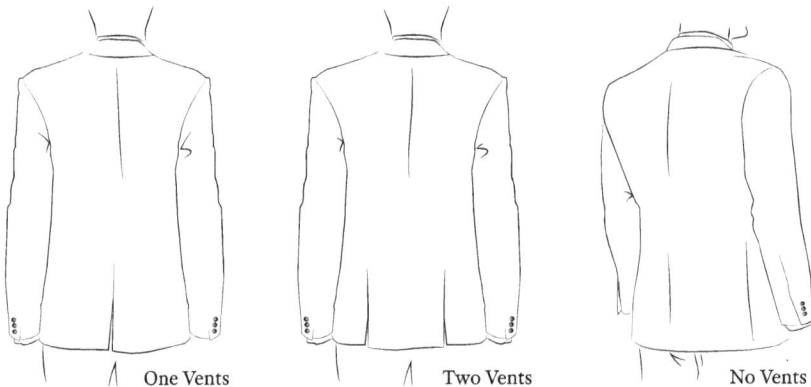

One Vents   Two Vents   No Vents

The suit jacket may or may not have a vent (or slit) in the lower back portion.
The three options for vents are:
- **No vent (ventless):** When one puts his hands in the trouser pockets or sits down, the jacket creases in the back. It is usually an Italian style.
- **Single vent:** When one places his hands in the trouser pockets, it exposes the backside. It is usually an American style.

– **Double or two-sided vent:** When the jacket wearer sits or puts his hands in his pockets, the flap comes up preventing the jacket from creasing and keeping the backside covered. It is usually an English style.

· **Trousers length:**

Too Long   Too Short   Just Right

The optimal length of trousers is about three to four centimeters above the ground. It should reach the top edge of the shoe heel with a slight/half break over the shoe top.

· **Trousers waist:**

Attention should be paid to how the fabric of formal trousers does not stretch, as do some types of jeans, for example.
If the waist of the trousers is too wide, the back of the fabric will be folded and hanging like curtains.
If the waist of the trousers is too narrow, small folds will appear, especially at the seams.

· **Formal suit jacket shirt:**

❝ *Traditionally, the color of a suit jacket shirt is white.* ❞

By evolution, it has become possible to wear a light gray shirt with a black or dark gray suit.
It has also become possible to wear a light blue shirt with a dark blue suit.
Although other light colors are more vivid, they are not formal.
The shirt's collar is supposed to protrude about 1.5 cm higher than the jacket's collar.

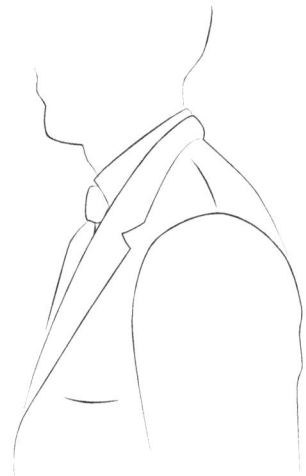

2. The morning coat (the bonjour, in French):

The morning coat (the bonjour) is one of the European male's daytime styles, only worn for formal events.

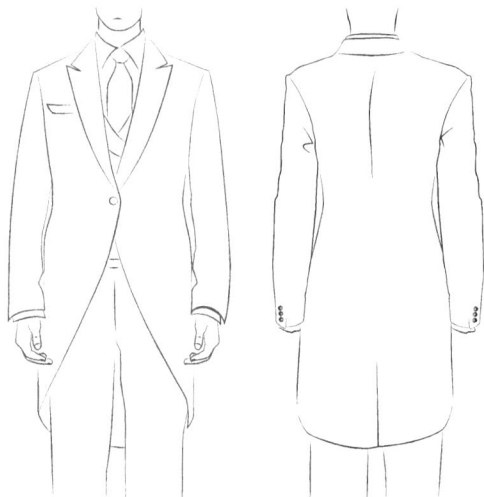

- It is cut away at the front to form knee-length tails at the back.
- It is black or grey single-breasted.
- Its full dress consists chiefly of, a morning coat, waistcoat, and striped trousers.
- The most formal option is a black morning coat with a matching black waistcoat.
- The waistcoat is traditionally either black or grey. Now, there has been a change and other options exist.
- The waistcoat matches the coat material.
- The waistcoat may be either single or double-breasted with or without lapels.
- The most formal shirt could be a turn-down collar.
- The shirt could be single-cuffed or double-cuffed.
- The trousers are usually either grey or grey striped vertically in black lines.
- The trousers can be black, but their color should be brighter than the jacket.
- Neckwear is obligatory in the form of a necktie, traditionally either grey or black. Now, all colors are worn.
- A plain or patterned handkerchief made of linen, cotton, or silk is used.
- The handkerchief matches the color of the tie.
- The handkerchief may be inserted or folded into the front breast pocket of the morning dress.
- The shoes should be a traditional black Oxford type and highly polished.
- Stockings should be black.

> **Optional Accessories:**

- A pocket watch with a chain.
- Boutonniere, a single flower, such as a rose or carnation, on the lapel.
- A white walking stick or tightly rolled umbrella.
- Lemon, grey, or white gloves.
- Grey or black medium top hat.

* Note:
Clerics as well as diplomats and others who wear the national costumes of their countries are exempt from wearing, the morning dress.

3. The evening coat/Frock coat (Frac, in French):

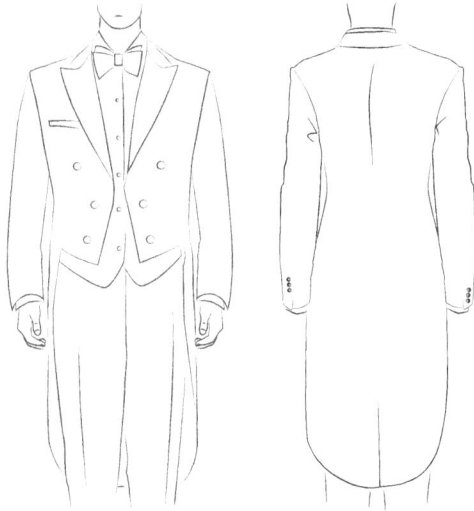

— **Other elements and accessories:**

– White shirt with winged collar (rolled or folded) and often with pleated fronts.

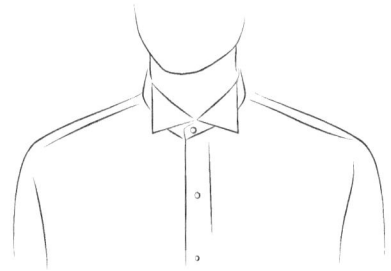

– The frock coat was worn at the end of the 18th century in England.
– It is number one in the classification of formal dress.
– Traditionally, it is worn for formal events after 7 p.m.
– A frock coat is characterized by a knee-length all around the base.
– It does not have the cut-away front, which gives morning coattails at the back.
– It is a fitted, long-sleeved coat with peaked lapels.
– The traditional color of a frock coat was solid black, but later charcoal grey became an acceptable alternative.

* Note:
Formally, frock coats worn with waistcoats and striped trousers are still worn as an alternative to morning coats (bonjoures) at certain daytime events. In particular, this style is appropriate for weddings.

– Bow tie or cravat (ascot).
– Waistcoat, usually double-breasted with peaked lapels.
– Uncuffed trousers, silk strips of satin on both sides.
– To prevent the top of the trousers from showing underneath the waistcoat, braces (suspenders) are worn.
– Black stockings.
– High top hat *(optional)*.

– White or grey gloves *(optional)*.
– Black shiny shoes.

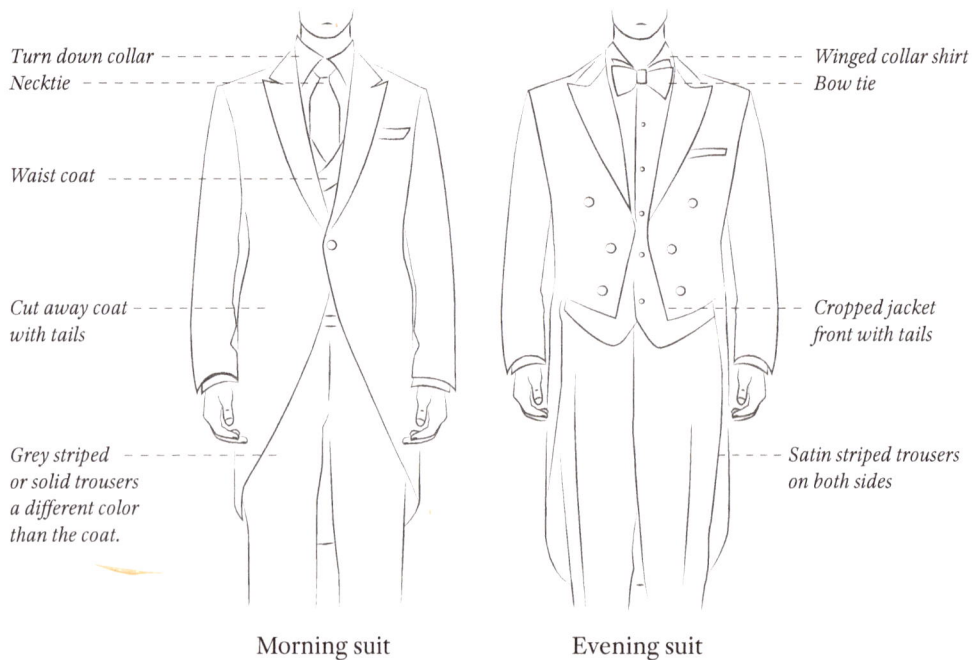

Turn down collar - - - - -

Necktie - - - - - - - - - -

Waist coat - - - - - - - - -

Cut away coat - - - - - -
with tails

Grey striped - - - - - - -
or solid trousers
a different color
than the coat.

- - - - - Winged collar shirt

- - - - - Bow tie

- - - - - Cropped jacket
front with tails

- - - - - Satin striped trousers
on both sides

Morning suit   Evening suit

* **Note:**

1. The designs of the frock coat/frac (evening suit) witnessed many developments, especially in the Victorian era. Therefore, it is difficult to capture all of them, as the matter requires many pages and illustrations. Therefore, only the most important design is approached.

2. Boys do not wear tailcoats (morning coats and frock coats) until they are about eighteen

4. "Black Tie" Suit:

It is worth mentioning that the phrase "black tie" does not refer to the color of the tie but rather the type of formal wear used for a certain event (in fact, colorful ties with matching cummerbunds are very popular). The types of this formal wear include:

- **Dinner suit / Dinner jacket.**
- **Tuxedo / Smoking.**
- **White dinner suit/jacket.**

So, when an event is called "Black Tie," wearing one of the aforementioned suits is obligatory. However, the white dinner suit is only worn when the event is held in the open air.

— 4.1. Dinner Suit (Dinner Jacket):

· Typically, a dinner suit does not follow the traditional path of a jacket matching the trousers.
· The jacket is trimmed with satin on the lapel.
· The necktie used is the usual one (not a bow tie).
· The suit is usually worn in the evening at formal and social events.

Among the best options:
· Black jacket and gray trousers.
· Gray jacket and black trousers.
· Dark burgundy jacket and black trousers.

— 4.2. Tuxedo/Smoking:

· In many European languages as well as Russian, Arabic, and Turkish, the term "Smoking" indicates a "Tuxedo."
· In English and Brazilian Portuguese, the term "Tuxedo" indicates "Smoking."
· Tuxedo is named after Tuxedo Park in New York and was first worn in the 19th century (exactly 1887).
· It appeared among the aristocratic classes in Britain and the U.S.
· At first, it was worn in cigar-smoking sessions and some parties, so its name was indeed associated with smoking.
· A Tuxedo/smoking is a stylish evening black tie suit.
· Traditionally, it is worn after 7 p.m.
· It is worn for formal events and social functions.
· It is the most famous suit in the history of formal men's elegance.

" *The tuxedo is sometimes called a penguin suit because it matches the bird's black body and white chest.* "

- **Components of a Tuxedo/ Smoking Suit:**

- A tuxedo refers to an ensemble of matching black jacket and trousers.
- Typically, it comes with a satin facing on the lapels of the jacket, pocket flaps, and sides of the trousers.
- Some modern tuxedo options have minimized the use of satin to a thin trim on the lapels, pocket flaps, and down the pant legs.
- The jacket is most commonly black and single-breasted.
- The jacket can have one or two satin-covered buttons, depending on how tall the wearer is.
- The lapels are either of shawl design or peaked.
- The black smoking jacket can be replaced with a white jacket if an evening event is outdoors.
- The shirt is double-cuffed with pin buttons.
- A tuxedo may have a low-cut waistcoat (mostly of the jacket color), in the "V" or "U" shape.

- The neckwear is a traditional silk black bow tie matching the lapel facings.
- The cummerbund (a sash worn around the waist) is black.
- The trousers have stripes along the outer seams and are worn with suspenders.
- Black shoes. They were traditionally made of patent leather, but are now polished Oxford instead.
- Black stockings (silk or fine wool).

  * Note:

No hat, gloves, or stick are used with a tuxedo. Generally, boys do not wear tuxedos before they are about fifteen.

· **Key differences between Tuxedo and Suit:**

Bow tie ----------

Satin shawl / Peaked lapel ----------

Waistcoat / Cummerbund ----------

Satin covered buttons ----------

Trouser stripe ----------

---------- *Necktie*

---------- *Any lapel style*

---------- *Waistcoat/no waistcoat*

---------- *Standard buttons*

Tuxedo   Suit

Regardless of some exceptions, the primary physical differences between a tuxedo and a suit are:

▷ **Tuxedo**

– Satin facing on the lapels and pocket flaps.
– Satin covering the jacket button/s.
– Satin side stripe down the legs of the trousers.
– Waistcoat (traditionally, the same color as the jacket).
– Double cuffed shirt.
– Pin buttons for the shirt.
– Bow tie (traditionally black).
– Cummerbund.
– Black patent leather shoes.

▷ **Suit**

– No use of satin.
– Usually, single cuff shirt.
– Usually, plastic buttons for the shirt.
– Necktie (various colors).
– Black leather shoes.
– Leather belt.

— 4.3. White Dinner Jacket/Suit:

- The white dinner jacket goes back to the 1930s.
- It is also called the "Tropical Black-Tie" suit.
- It comes in white and light cloth to be worn in warm climates. It is ivory in color rather than pure white.
- Its models are either single- or double-breasted.
- It has self-faced lapels rather than silk-faced lapels.
- The shirt has a classic pleated-front with a soft turndown collar.
- The neckwear is the classic bow tie.

* Note:
If the event is during the daytime or outdoors, the white dinner jacket could replace the black jacket.

› **Some more etiquette tips to consider:**

▷ **Neckwear:** [7]

Neckwear, with its various knots and shapes, is one of the most important men's fashion accessories.

- It gives men's wear an aesthetic touch.
- It is the first thing that catches the eye, as it is in the middle of the suit.
- It is recommended to choose it carefully so it's compatible with the suit's type and color.
- With morning coat/bonjour, traditionally a black or gray necktie is used. Now all colors are worn.
- With Frock coat/frac a bow tie or an ascot tie is used.
- With smoking, the black bow tie is used.
- With the White Dinner Jacket/Suit, the black bow tie is used.
- With other suit types, the necktie is used.
- Nowadays, neckties of all colors are used.
- However, dark ties are still recommended for formal events and workplaces.
- Bright neckties are suitable for young people and informal events.
- The necktie length may land below the belt buckle by no more than two centimeters.
- The back part of the necktie should not appear.

---

7 Necktie: The first appearance of the necktie was in the 17th century, in France, was during the reign of King Louis XIII. He hired mercenaries from Croatia who wore embroidered fabrics around the neck as part of their traditional costume. These pieces impressed the king, who ordered to add them to the mandatory uniform of the royal gatherings, in honor of the Croatian soldiers, and gave them the name "Cravat," which is still used in France now. The patterns of neckties in Europe developed and multiplied so much that the forms we know today did not appear until after 1920.

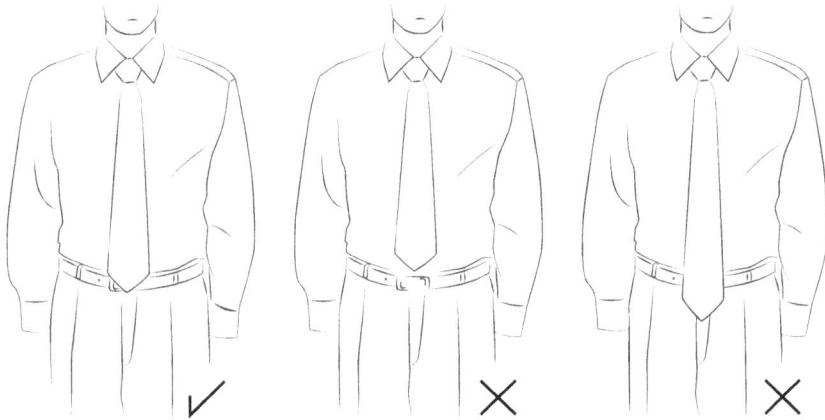

The necktie length may land below the belt buckle by no more than two centimeters.

· Shoes:

With formal wear, traditionally black Oxford shoes, with laces, are used. Today, the laces are no longer binding in formal shoes as they were in the past.

Contrary to formal shoes, casual shoes may have some metallic accessories, such as gold, silver, or bronze buckles.

· Stockings:

The stocking length should be appropriate so that any part of the leg does not appear.

In formal and informal wear, stocking color should always be compatible with the color of the trousers (the same color but not necessarily the same color tone).

Men's Informal Wear

In many regions, dress codes for men's informal attire are, in one way or another, less formal than the Suit Jacket but not as informal as the casual wear. Therefore, regardless of the innumerable casual wear options, informal wear can be:

– Jacket and trousers (not necessarily of the same color).
– A shirt, symmetrical with the jacket as much as possible.
– With or without a necktie.

– Shoes, which can be black, brown, web maroon, or firebrick, depending on the color of the trousers.

*   *Note:*
· *It is not appropriate to wear a striped jacket and a striped shirt at the same time.*
· *In all cases, it is untactful to wear shoes without stockings, as some adolescents do.*
· *The men's informal wear colors are not so confined or restricted. Nevertheless, they should not be too bright·*

Women's Formal Wear

While almost all people know what men's formal wear is, they very rarely have the right answer when they are asked about women's formal wear.

Their answers usually refer to dozens of designs, components, colors, etc.

Although several dresses could be, in one way or another, considered formal women's wear, such as a ball gown, cocktail gown, dinner dress, and long to full-length skirts (for some events), there are no strictly specific women's formal wear.

In this regard, etiquette stipulates that women's wear should be "decent" and "suitable." However, the words decent and suitable and what they mean are controversial and have prolonged, abstract definitions. The debates about this could start but never end.

Such concepts are subject to the customs, traditions, and cultural heritage of each region and people. Their indications might even vary in the same country from one place to another. Hence, what is decent and suitable in Brasilia, for example, might not be so in New Delhi or Beijing.

Furthermore, what is suitable and fits women at day events might be completely different at night events. While a woman may wear a long gown to an opera, it would be out of place to put on the same wear for lunch at a restaurant.

Some might wonder why men's formal wear is specific, while women's formal wear is not. Why are women able to choose whatever they deem appropriate for this or that event? Why is it that everything seems left to their discretion and taste?

The answer is as simple as the following: A man, young or old, tall or short, fat or thin, and with whatever features, can wear the same formal suit and fit in. While a woman should wear what fits her age, physical appearance, color, and features.

An older woman would look strange if she put on a young woman's wear. Some designs do not fit tall women; others do not fit short ones. Some women are unable to wear skirts; others cannot wear pants. Therefore, contrary to males, a woman must choose this or that wear with certain designs, sizes, and colors.

› Etiquette tips:

- National or popular costumes could be considered formal wear for all events.
- A woman is supposed to know from her own experience the type and design of clothes that fit her.
- She should carefully select the styles that fit her age. "People have no respect for an old person who goes to excesses."[8]
- Expensive and lavish clothes do not necessarily generate elegance. The important thing is to choose the right wear, regardless of its price. An "overdressed woman is like a cat dressed in saffron."[9]
- The golden rule in the use of jewelry and make-up is simplicity; otherwise, the result would have the opposite effect.

---

8 Nigerian proverb.

9 Egyptian proverb.

- For example, a woman who puts on more than three rings, several bracelets, necklaces, etc., does not give the impression she is elegant, but rather the opposite.
- Dangling earrings are suitable for evening events, while in daytime it is more appropriate to use simple golden, silver, or pearl earrings (one bead in each ear is enough).
- Diamond ornaments (natural or artificial) are more attractive and display light reflections in the evening, while in the daytime they lose their aesthetic characteristics.
- Therefore, it is not advised to wear them during the day, especially in workplaces.
- Necklaces vary so much in their components, colors, sizes, etc., yet elegance requires simplicity.
- The use of golden or silver brooches on the breast of jackets or blouses may add an extra beautiful touch, but their absence does not negate elegance.
- Elegance requires certain harmony in the structures, components, colors, and sizes of rings, bracelets, necklaces, and earrings used for this or that event.
- The shoe color should be compatible with that of the bag and belt colors.
- A woman should not put on her jewelry while participating in a charity event, so as not to damage the feelings of people in need.

- Women's handbags at formal events are usually small, contrary to the ones that might be carried in offices and workplaces where they could be large or medium-sized.
- For formal events, women are advised to wear closed shoes with heels[10] that do not exceed seven centimeters; shoes that are open in the front or back are not formal.
- For all formal or informal events, and in all places and times, women's stockings are binding, "It is a must." Stockings are supposed to be of neutral color.
- Women can wear gloves at formal and informal events; the best colors are white, beige, and light gray, with no trimmings or the fewest trimmings possible.
- At receptions and cocktail parties, a woman should take off her gloves and keep them in her bag, so she can hold a glass and eat.
- Women can wear fur and coats indoors unless seated at banquet tables.
- When a woman invites guests to her house for lunch or dinner, she should not wear a hat, even if all invited women wear hats.
- Women may not lift their hats during banquets, parties, or public places, unless the size of the hat is a source of discomfort for others, for example, the audience in a cinema, theater, or opera.
- Women should not wear large hats in crowded places.

---

10 Development of high-heeled shoes: High-heeled shoes were originally worn by men. As early as the 10th century, many horseback-riding cultures used heels on their boots and shoes. The Persian cavalry, for example, wore a kind of boot with heels to ensure their feet stayed in the stirrups. The first recorded instance of a high-heeled shoe being worn by a woman was by Catherine de Medici in the 16th century (queen of France from 1547-1559, by marriage to King Henry II). She stood about 150 centimeters but wanted to appear taller at her wedding. In the early 17th century, men, including King Louis XIV of France (1638-1715), wore them to imply their upper-class status. Authorities even began regulating the length of high heels according to social ranks.

Orders, Decorations & Medals

"Your deeds are your medals."[11]

What prompted me to address this issue is the link between formal clothes on one side and orders, decorations, and medals on the other side.

It is familiar to see, in some formal events, a person putting on an order, decoration, or medal, or perhaps just attaching a rosette to a suit's lapel. Here arises a set of questions about these things, their types, degrees, forms, etc.

· **Significance of orders, decorations, and medals:**

Orders, decorations, and medals are awards conferred by the highest official authorities to one or more people (the case with medals), as a sign of gratitude for a great service or action, whether national, cultural, social, military, etc.

· **Types of orders, decorations, and medals:**

There are different types of orders, decorations, and medals. They are:
– National or foreign.
– Civil or military.

· **Classes of orders, decorations, and medals:**

The classes of orders, decorations, and medals vary widely and differ from one country to another.

——————— 11 The author.

- ## Honor system of orders, decorations, and medals:

Orders, decorations, and medals do not have one unified international honor system.

Each country has its own honor system that includes classes and privileges or the orders, decorations, and medals.

Each country has an honor system and relevant laws and procedures, which determine who is entitled to confer the orders, decorations, and medals, to whom, and under which conditions.

- ## Granting rules of orders, decorations, and medals:

Kings and heads of state usually grant orders.

Kings, heads of state, and governments usually grant decorations.

National orders, decorations, and medals are awarded for life.

A special patent (certificate/document) is given for each order, decoration, and some kinds of medals.

Some kinds of medals can be awarded to a person or group of people, as in the case of sports teams, artistic bands, military units, etc.

Based on the principle of reciprocity, orders, and decorations could be awarded to senior officials and dignitaries of friendly countries.

When an order or decoration is awarded to a foreigner, it would be a recognition of services outside their home country, strengthening friendships and consolidating relations.

The acceptance of a foreign order or decoration must be made after getting the consent of the authorities of the state to which the recipient belongs.

On high official visits, orders and decorations could be exchanged if the visit is at the level of a head of state or a prime minister.

- ## An order

" *An order is generally the highest honor a citizen may receive for a career or service of outstanding distinction in their country.* "

Generally, the head of state confers the orders and is typically the "grand master" of the order who grants its membership.

Orders may have several classes of membership.

Orders have a variety of studs or scarves of rank and distinction.

The scarves are often referred to as "orders."

The studs typically are made of precious metals with enameled or jeweled designs.

· A Decoration:

A decoration is an award conferred by a head of state or head of government for heroism, meritorious achievement, or distinguished service.

Decorations do not normally denote membership.

An individual may be awarded a decoration for specific categories or types of service, civil or military.

Decorations usually take the form of crosses or medallions and other shapes of gold, silver, bronze, or enameled metal suspended from a ribbon.

· A Medal:

A medal is an award given by a head of state, head of government, or other high dignitaries (depending on the honor system of each country).

A medal is usually awarded to recognize the recipient's participation in a military, civil, or other significant event.

A medal can also be awarded to all who participated in an event.

· Wearing orders, decorations, and medals:

Orders could be necklaced or scarved. Necklaces and scarves end with medallions.

Scarves of full orders (with a scarf, ribbon, etc.) are worn around the right shoulder down over the right chest, down to the left side of the hip, and completed by a medallion.

Decorations are usually studs suspended from a colorful scarf/ribbon, and worn on the left chest.

Orders and decorations are supposed to be worn on formal dresses at national celebrations, events, and other formal occasions.

A decoration's rosette could be worn on a formal or informal dress, provided that it is not a coat. They are worn in the same manner as lapel pins.

The rosettes can also be worn on the decorations' ribbons.

A full order and decoration could be replaced with a stud, attached to a gilded chain or ribbon, and worn on the left side of the clothes or the left front of the jacket. The stud (without a chain or ribbon) can also be placed/fixed on the left front of the jacket or clothes.

• The order of placing the medallions on the chest:

The medallions, which may replace the orders and decorations, can be placed/worn on the left front of the jacket or clothes.

When placing/wearing the medallions on the jacket's left front, the order of precedence[12] should be considered.

The order of precedence starts with national medallions from the right, and then the foreign ones.[13]

According to their classes, the medallions are worn in sequence (the highest medallion first), from right to left and downward towards the left side of the hip.

Note:

Heirs may retain an order, decoration, or medal after the death of the holder, without having the right to wear it or enjoy its privileges.

---

12 The order of precedence of the orders and decorations is stipulated in the honor system of each country.

13 My late friend and colleague,, ambassador Dr. Tawfiq Salloum, was director of protocol and one of the most prominent diplomats and intellectuals of the Syrian Foreign Ministry. He told me the Ministry of Foreign Affairs was considering awarding a decoration to one of the ambassadors of the United Kingdom after completing his service in Damascus, but the British ambassador informed him that he would not be able to accept it, as the ambassadors of the United Kingdom are not allowed to accept foreign decorations and medals. It is a practice that goes back to the days of Queen Victoria, who did not allow her ambassadors to accept foreign decorations. She said, (according to that ambassador), "I do not accept my ambassadors to be leashed by other countries."

Section Four

Telephone Etiquette

*"Cell phone companies are a new version
of dominant superpowers."*[1]

The telephone has rapidly developed due to the improvement of communications technology, especially with applications like WhatsApp, Skype, Viber, WeChat, Messenger, Twitter, Facebook, etc.

❝ Some complain that recent means of communication have reduced contact among people and diminished social relations. Others argue these means have reduced distances and made places and people across the world closer to each other. ❞

Anyhow, cellphones have become almost indispensable in modern life. Telecommunication companies have become a new version of a superpower.

› **General etiquette tips:**

– Phones should not be misused; a phone should be used with a purpose and for certain valid reasons. The way a phone is used, to make a call or answer, plays an important role in forming a first impression.
– In phone calls (rather than video calls), the first impression comes through the tone of the voice. Although the recipient of the call does not see the caller, they sense the caller through the voice.
– For the reasons mentioned above, the voices of both the caller as well as the recipient should demonstrate clear friendliness.
– After the greeting, one should directly identify themselves unless certain their voice is familiar to the recipient.
– When answering a call or calling someone, a normal tone of voice should be used.

---

1 The author.

- A loud voice disturbs the recipient as well as the people around the speaker.
- Phone calls are expected to be brief.
- Slang words[2] or poor language should be avoided.
- Unless the caller and recipient are friends, the person who is calling should use proper titles for the recipient rather than a first name.
- While someone speaks on the telephone, they should never eat or drink.
- Voicemail messages should be brief and to the point.
- Generally, one should not call another at home before 9 a.m. or after 9 or 10 p.m.
- Similarly, calls should be avoided at lunchtime, unless a very important or urgent conversation cannot be postponed.
- A patient in a hospital should not be called. Instead, one can call a member of the patient's family or their friend.
- If one is certain a patient in a hospital can speak by phone, the call should be brief and no details about the patient's illness should be asked.
- On the street, one should make a phone call and respond in a quieter voice, without involving others in their affairs.
- To make phone calls or send messages while walking on the street, one should step aside to avoid colliding with anyone or object.
- If a phone call is interrupted (due to lack of reception, for example), the caller should call again rather than wait for the recipient to do so.
- When the recipient misses a call, text, or email, they should respond in an appropriate and timely manner, with an apology first if necessary.
- When speaking by phone, one should stop the music or turn down the TV.
- One should not text or check their phone when speaking with others.
- When the use of mobile phones is prohibited, as in theatres, cinemas, hospitals, fuel stations, aircraft, etc., one must keep the phone turned off.
- The "No Talk & Drive" rule is applied almost everywhere.
- If it is urgent to use the phone, one should drive to a safe area away from traffic.
- New vehicle technology comes with integrated hands-off and Bluetooth options. If a vehicle does not have this technology, the driver should be cautious and attentive to the road. Safety first!
- In social situations, such as dinners or dates, one should not be busy with phone calls. If there is something urgent, calls could be made away from the people around and kept as short as possible.
- Cell phones should be kept off or on silent mode at funerals.
- A video phone call is a face-to-face call and is almost like being in a meeting in person. Therefore, before making such a call, the caller should make sure the recipient is prepared for this kind of communication.
- For international calls, to avoid inappropriate timing, one should know the time difference between their country and the recipient. Furthermore, most countries have summer and winter changes to take into account.

---

2 Slang is informal language or specific words used by a particular group of people. You'll usually hear slang spoken more often than you'll see it in writing, although emails and texts often contain many conversational slang words.

– In most societies, the phone has replaced letters and is commonly used to send informal invitations between family and close friends.

– Formally, invitations are done in writing rather than by phone.

– In business, presenting a professional image on the telephone is very important. Speaking clearly, slowly, and in a cheerful voice leads to this end.

– It is essential to take good care of customers and anyone over the telephone and to make them feel well-informed and appreciated.

– When calling (whether in person or leaving a voicemail) a client or customer, one should always identify themselves properly by providing a name, workplace, and telephone number.

– If a recipient is responsible for answering multiple calls at once, for instance, at a business, they should ask the caller politely if they may put them on hold. But they should never leave the person on hold for more than a few seconds (the person may become upset and hang up).

– If a caller is irate or upset for whatever reason, the recipient should be patient and helpful, listen to what is said, and then refer the caller to the appropriate resource. They should never speak sharply or act rudely.

– When taking a message for a business, it is a good habit to repeat the information back to a client and verify the message is heard and transcribed accurately.

– When a boss is taking part in meetings, the secretary should not transmit phone calls unless it is an emergency. Instead, the secretary can inform their boss through a notepaper.

– Cell phones should be turned off and without vibration before a formal meeting.

Conversation and dialogue etiquette

"People who know little are usually great talkers,
while those who know much say little."[3]

The reader will notice that a good space has been devoted to this topic, as conversation is a large portion of our daily life. Also, it is a very important social and human art and practice.

Although it is argued that modern methods of digital communication (mainly social media) have greatly reduced the time available for people to talk, there is still much time for them to do that.

Conversation is the art and talent of expressing ideas and opinions elegantly, effectively, and politely.

The ultimate goal of any conversation is to communicate, enjoy, and benefit, through discussing and developing the various topics addressed.

— Topics to avoid

When meeting some people for the first time, it is advisable to avoid discussing certain topics that should be exclusive to friends:

- **Political topics:**

  Political issues are often complex, controversial, and have potential divergence of views that may lead to deep differences and sharp inconsistency. So, they should be avoided unless a good relationship has been established.

- **Religious topics:**

  Religious issues are sensitive and require a broad knowledge of religion's diversities. Therefore, it is not recommended to initiate

---

3 Jean-Jacques Rousseau (1712-1778), a Swiss francophone philosopher and writer whose thoughts and political philosophy largely influenced the French Revolution and contributed to the development of modern politics and education.

a conversation on such matters, as any misunderstanding could be grave.

If a religious matter is opened, everyone, regardless of their viewpoint, must demonstrate respect and should have moderate opinions, so as not to provoke anyone directly or indirectly.

- **Personal and family affairs:**

These are private and belong just to the relevant few members involved. Hence, it is not admissible for others to discuss such matters unless they are close to family, relatives, and friends.

> ## Etiquette tips:

It is important to mention some of the requirements to observe successful participation in any conversation to be compatible with etiquette.

Regardless of their sequence, which may seem logical or not, the priority is to highlight and know these requirements:

▷ **First impression:**

One should do their best so others get a good idea about them at the first meeting. First impressions generated about anyone last long and are not easy to change. In addition to clothes, one's speaking style, self-confidence, tactfulness, etc., are vital in forming the first impression about a person. Ali bin Abi Talib[4] said, "Man is hidden under his tongue."

▷ **The other partner:**

Before getting involved in a conversation with others, it is necessary to know who they are. A discussion with distinguished people culturally, socially, politically, and otherwise, differs from a discussion with ordinary people.

▷ **Interruption:**

It is inappropriate to interrupt others and not let them complete what they have started. Even if the interruption is done by using nice words such as "Sorry," "Excuse me for interrupting you," or "A moment please," this does not change anything. Interruption sometimes equals imprudence.

▷ **Giving up speaking:**

It is incompatible with etiquette to take all the time to talk without giving others the possibility to speak. The person who would silence the others with the power of their lungs and booming voice, is no more than a noisy person. Actually, during conversation, there is often enough space for all to talk. Therefore, it is not bad to give up speaking and wait for a while.

▷ **Brilliance:**

To be a brilliant person is to be differentiated and to be able to catch the attention of others. No one can be brilliant and attractive if they speak without knowledge like ignorant, naïve people. As long as a person is ordinary in their conversation, and provides no additional value,

---

4 Ali bin Abi Talib (601-661): The fourth Caliph, cousin, and son-in-law of Prophet Muhammad.

the recipients would assess them in return as an ordinary person, who is not entitled to be among the "brilliants."

Brilliance does not depend only on the subject discussed or on one's presentation, but also their knowledge and education. It is a matter that requires "knowing something about everything; and everything about one thing."

Let us imagine how embarrassing it would be if a dignitary, a diplomat, a businessperson, a professor a politician, etc., is to inaugurate an art exhibition and has no idea about any of the art trends or schools.

▷ **Wisdom:**

It is important to think and behave the same as wise people do, i.e., to try to know all aspects of any matter under discussion.

Nevertheless, during a conversation, one is supposed to talk normally to be more convincing. Otherwise, the result will be a failure. Thoughts should be presented smoothly without complications, to be received and interacted with.

▷ **Provocative topics:**

It is natural to look for the companionship of others, to be pleased, to benefit, and to exchange knowledge. Therefore, it is inadvisable to talk about provocative issues that would annoy others. Normal people do not look for quarrels and conflict.

It might be better to approach a controversial subject with much care or even leave some of its details for specialists.

▷ **Provocative answers:**

It is not convenient to reply with some kind of short and concise answers to someone who asks. Phrases such as "I do not know" or "I cannot answer" are rather provocative answers, especially if accompanied by expressions or gestures of indifference. Such expressions and the like are not acceptable unless accompanied by an explanation such as saying, "I do not know, because I did not go to the place yet" or "I do not know. I forgot to ask about this matter."[5]

▷ **Preciseness:**

If an idea could be presented by using ten words, it is better not to utter twelve. One should be brief and precise, without going too far in details. Otherwise, the others would be pushed to neglect him and his debate. Probably, this is why it is said, "The smarter you are, the less you speak."[6]

▷ **Matters of interest:**

Life is full of topics and issues to handle and talk about. Yet, it is wise to choose to talk about things of common interest.

Lord Philip Chesterfield[7] advised his son to speak when he had the chance but recom-

---

5 The French politician and diplomat Charles Maurice de Talleyrand (1754-1838) said, "A diplomat who says "yes" means "maybe;" a diplomat who says "maybe" means "no;" and a diplomat who says "no" is no diplomat."

6 Syrian proverb.

7 Philip Dormer Stanhope, 4th Earl of Chesterfield (1694-1773), a British statesman, diplomat and a man of letters. His book on the "Art of Becoming a Man of the World and a Gentleman" was published in (1774). It comprises a thirty-year correspondence in more than four hundred letters to his son.

mended he stop when he felt others were not pleased and had no interest.

What is the importance of talking, for example, about opera, arts, ballet, skiing, surfing, and similar topics, in a rural society, where most people have no access to or even the possibility to think about such things?

Such topics will only cause them to think the speaker is either showing off or presenting themselves as superior. In both cases, they are a big loser.

▷ **Personal interests:**

It is inappropriate to focus on subjects related to one's children, hobbies, trips, photos, and other personal things. What is worse is to involve others in such subjects and even to be upset by those who show a lack of interest.

▷ **Lack of interest:**

The person who appears absent mentally, does not show interest in what others say, and maybe even yawns in front of them, deserves to be classified as "lukewarm."

It is better not to care and leave them contemplating their daydreams.

▷ **Listening more than speaking:**

It is wise to remember what Epictetus[8] said, "We have two ears and one mouth so that we can listen twice as much as we speak."

Hence, it is always advisable we listen double the time we take for speaking.

This leads other people to positive impressions of us.

▷ **Patience:**

Even if you are talking to people who have limited skills and knowledge, you need to understand you have something good to receive and to offer. So, one should neither be bumptious nor ignore them. One should be patient and listen to people with respect and interest.

A Sudanese proverb says, "Patience is the key to solving problems."

▷ **Being a judge:**

In any intense argument between others taking sides, it is not wise to back one and stand against another, but rather act as referee or judge to whom the others may look to help resolve a conflict or misunderstanding. Taking this position, one can carefully examine and summarize the different viewpoints, focusing on the points of convergence and helping end the argument in a way everyone can feel like a winner.

▷ **Challenging ideas:**

It is impermissible for anyone to underestimate others' ideas, claiming their point of view is the only correct one. This method is the fastest way to win enemies.

Companionship is not a gathering to challenge the other's ideas.

Marcus Aurelius[9] said, "Everything we hear is an opinion, not a fact. Everything we see is a perspective, not the truth."

▷ **Correcting mistakes:**

Joining others to chat and socialize does not mean one is a member of a drafting

8 Epictetus (55-135 AD), a Greek Stoic philosopher.

9 Marcus Aurelius (121-180), a Roman emperor from 161 to 180 and a Stoic philosopher.

committee that has a mandate to scrutinize every word.

When someone is corrected in the presence of others, they might be upset, clinging to an opinion and considering such a correction as criticism.

Talking about others' professions:

Companionship of others necessarily means the presence of several people who belong to different professions.

During the conversation, it is recommended to avoid going through the details of the others' work, the problems of their jobs, or to consult them.

The lawyer there is not coming to hear the details of the lawsuit of one against another; the doctor, likewise, is not there to diagnose someone's illness. Along these lines, it is not fair to criticize others' professions or talk negatively about them.

▷ **Ridicule and sarcasm:**

It is advised to avoid direct or indirect ridicule, sarcasm, and using puns and phrases with double connotations.

It is important to try creating a humorous and delightful atmosphere, but using a sober style and valuable ideas that do not compromise character.

▷ **Loud voice:**

Desmond Tutu[10] said, "Don't raise your voice, improve your argument."

A loud voice is not a privilege. It rather bothers listeners and shows a lack of confidence.

Furthermore, the loud voice reflects an aggressive attitude whether it is intended or not. Hence, it is always advised to use a natural voice with a natural tone.

Jalal Al-din Rumi[11] said,

> ❝ *Let the meaning rise, not the sound, for what makes the flower grow and bloom is rain, not thunder.* ❞

▷ **Speaking quickly/slowly:**

It is important to remember that, sometimes, the speaking style is more important than the subject itself. One who speaks quickly might mix up their ideas and consequently confuse the listener. Meanwhile, talking too slowly is like holding one's horse and inhibiting its march.

▷ **Praise and flattery:**

All people, regardless of their age and gender, like praise, flattery, encouragement, and appreciation. Nevertheless, such things are a double-edged sword and could be negative if used at the wrong time and place. Praising or flattering a person who has a political, administrative, or financial rank, for example, might be interpreted as an attempt to get closer and earn their friendship.

---

10 Desmond Mpilo Tutu (1931-2021) is a South African Anglican cleric, theologian, and human rights activist. He was the Bishop of Johannesburg (1985-1986) and the Archbishop of Cape Town (1986-1996).

11 Jalal Al-Din Rumi (1207-1273), was a 13th-century Persian poet, Islamic scholar, theologian, and Sufi mystic originally from Iran. His poems have been widely translated into many of the world's languages and transposed into various formats. Rumi has been described as the "most popular poet" and the "best-selling poet" in the United States.

▷ **Pleasantry:**

One who is committed to joking every time and everywhere would certainly lose the privilege of being considered a respectful person and might be looked at as a clown. It is not harmful to excite humor with wittiness, a touch of joy, and a joke, but when jokes and pleasantries become the dominant feature of a conversation, the result would certainly be reversed.

It is advisable to avoid kidding with anyone before being fully acquainted and knowing the nature of their reactions.

▷ **Giving advice:**

Giving advice arbitrarily does not make anyone a philanthropist.

It is preferable to offer advice only to those who can consider it, keeping in mind that not all people are willing to accept and appreciate advice.

▷ **Frequent questions:**

It is recommended not to ask so many questions about all matters. Otherwise, one would certainly look naïve, with little knowledge and education.

▷ **Frequent subject:**

There is a person who has nothing to talk about but one issue, or a specific event they always repeat whenever and wherever.

They assume that others should listen whether they have enough time or not and whether they are in the mood or not.

For example, they frequently talk about how straight, courageous, and competent they were as an employee, director, soldier, etc.

They expect others to praise their exceptional deeds and wisdom!

▷ **Missed words and phrases:**

When failing to hear something said, it is better not to ask for repetition, so as not to disturb the speaker. The person speaking might feel what they are saying is not of interest to some people, and others who will be obliged to listen to repeated things as well.

▷ **Hiding some facts:**

There is no need to say all the facts one knows about a certain matter unless the recipient has the right to know them.

Participating in conversation is not like being a witness in court. In any case, one should always speak honestly about whatever subject is discussed.

▷ **Talking about oneself:**

If appropriate, one may speak briefly about themselves, but as short as possible, so as not to appear to show off. In companionship, other people might not care about all the aspects of someone's life and the things they have achieved in their career.

The conversation's time available is supposed to be shared among all present.

▷ **Last speaker:**

When required to give an opinion on a complicated issue, it is better to be the last speaker. First, you can explore the views of others. Secondly, you can gain enough time to revise one's thoughts thoroughly. Thirdly, you can take advantage of others' lapses and weaknesses.

▷ **Flexibility:**

It is recommended that one should not try to give too firm an opinion on dialectical issues and cling to it.

Also, one should avoid sticking to absolute convictions that might not be true. One may discover, through dialogue, other aspects of the truth. The German philosopher and writer Friedrich Nietzsche[12] said, "The enemy of truth is not lies, but firm convictions."

▷ **Sayings, proverbs, terms, and phrases:**

Being acquainted with some sayings, proverbs, familiar phrases, and expressions, which are abundant in heritage, culture, and social resources, enables one to look knowledgeable and educated.

▷ **Foreign expressions:**

During conversation, one should not assume all people present are competent in foreign languages. Therefore, it is not preferable to use, very often or even from time to time, foreign words and expressions. Such behavior might display oneself as showing off, and some people will not be able to follow what has been said.

▷ **Foreign language:**

It is improper to talk to another person or a friend in another language not known by all other people present. Others may think there are secrets, that they are not privy to knowing.

▷ **Scorning women's beauty:**

To criticize a woman's performance could sometimes be forgivable, but criticizing or underestimating her beauty is enough to make her an opponent. She will never forget such a mistake and will certainly avail herself of whatever chance to retaliate.

▷ **Arguing with an angry person:**

Before arguing with an angry person, it is better to let them calm down first. Actually, they might respond in a very negative and unreasonable way.

▷ **Arguing with a fool:**

Naturally, dialogue, discussion, and debate with the wise, no matter how different opinions are, remain useful. Yet one should not undermine friendship in case of disagreement. On the contrary, arguing with any fool is a waste of time, and may lead to disastrous results. "Except foolishness, every disease has a remedy."[13]

▷ **Anger:**

Certainly, calmness goes along with balanced, sober, and sound thinking. The first moment anyone loses their temper, they begin to commit mistakes and waste all these privileges. Maybe this is why it is said, "Calmness is the master of values."[14]

▷ **Insulting others:**

Insulting others is the fastest way to gain their enmity. Therefore, one avoids insulting others, directly or indirectly, and tries, to win the others' friendship.

▷ **"He" and "She":**

During the conversation, it does not correspond to politeness and etiquette, to use "he" or "she" to refer to a third person

---

12 Friedrich Wilhelm Nietzsche (1844-1900), a German philosopher, cultural critic, poet, philologist, whose works have influenced Western philosophy and literature.

13 Abu al-Tayyib al-Mutanabbi (915-965), the greatest Arab poet.

14 An Arab proverb.

present among other participants. The right way, which implies respect, is to mention his/her name or to say my/our friend.

▷ **"He" and "I":**

To highlight modesty and politeness, one is supposed to mention the other's name before referring to themselves. For example, "Flavia and I did that" or "Paulo Leão and I met yesterday." This sequence does not diminish one's position.

▷ **Lifting barriers:**

It is not wise to address those who are older or higher in rank by using their first names, or just by the second-person pronoun "you." It is better to maintain some lines and not lift barriers.

▷ **Hatred:**

Psychologically, the worst thing for an enemy is to show that person they are not taken as an enemy. No matter how much one hates another, one should try hard when meeting them to conceal hatred and contempt. Otherwise, undesirable reactions might happen.

Buddha[15] said, "Hatred does not cease by hatred, but only by love."

▷ **Hostility:**

Regardless of one's opinion on a certain issue, disagreement with others should not lead to hostility. Anyhow, when arguing it is advisable to maintain respect and avoid personal accusations and criticism because such behavior would inevitably lead to conflict.

Dr. Martin Luther King Jr.[16] said, "Time is always right to do what is right."

▷ **Swearing:**

Swear words should never be used. One is supposed to be sincere without resorting to an intercessor.

One who swears without justification compels others to doubt. One can emphasize a certain point, by saying, "Believe me" and the like, no more.

▷ **"One's tongue is one's horse":[17]**

This implies that one should refrain from talking about issues unknown to them, so as not to be involved in matters that they have nothing to do with. One's tongue is not just an organ to chatter.

▷ **Gossiping:**

Actually, any direct or indirect observation or comment towards an absent person could be explained negatively, and may reach the absent person, who, in return, will feel contempt or disrespect. Positive or constructive criticism can be displayed gently to a friend directly, with an emphasis on friendship.

---

15 Gautama Buddha (563-483 BC), one of the most important Asian thinkers and spiritual masters of all time. He contributed to many areas of philosophy, including epistemology, metaphysics, and ethics.

16 Dr. Martin Luther King, Jr. (1929-1968), an American Baptist minister and civil rights leader.

17 Arab proverb

The Virtue of Silence

"Only he who knows how to speak can be silent."[18]

Although silence can be physically identified as the ceasing of vocal performance, it includes a special dynamism that qualifies it to be classified as a virtue. Therefore, it is wrong to think silence is always a static and negative trait in the behavior of people. It is a language by itself, an effective means of expression, and "it is a conversation."[19]

Furthermore, let me quote Pythagoras, "If you're asked: What is the silence? Respond: It is the first stone of the wisdom's temple."[20]

- **Some considerations:**

For those who do not meet the conditions of the conversation, and do not know all aspects of the subject discussed, "silence" is a prerequisite and a necessity.

· Silence is a technique used by educated and competent people, who resort to it especially when they are uncertain about some details. "Silence is a true friend who never betrays."[21]

· It may be considered that silence requires a higher competence than the ability to speak, and the percentage of those who are endowed with the advantage of silence

18 Jean-Paul Sartre (1905-1980), a French playwright, novelist, screenwriter, political activist, biographer, and literary critic. He was known as a representative of "existentialism" and a leading figure in 20th-century philosophy. He was awarded the 1964 Nobel Prize in Literature, but he refused to receive it.

19 Ramana Maharshi (1879-1950), an Indian Hindu "sage" (wise man).

20 Pythagoras (570-495 BC), a Greek philosopher and mathematician. His political and religious teachings were well known and influenced the philosophies of Plato and Aristotle.

21 Confucius (551-479 BC), a Chinese teacher and philosopher whose teachings deeply influenced East Asian life.

is really small compared to those who cannot close their mouths.

· It is necessary to distinguish between the silence of wise people (which is a positive and an interactive one) and the passive silence of naïve people.

· It is necessary to note as well that silence does not mean staring at a speaker with indifference and without any facial expressions. This does not comply with etiquette and politeness.

· As most people talk about things and later discover they should have remained silent, languages often have an expression along the lines of, "If speech is silver; silence is golden."

—Silence, as an art of etiquette, enables you:

1. To get the opportunity to listen.
2. To think deeply about what is going on.
3. To take enough time to analyze what has been said.
4. To focus on and choose the right reactions and words.
5. To choose the right time to speak. "Be silent, if you choose; but when it is necessary, speak – and speak in such a way that people will remember it."[22]
6. To make use of the other speaker's shortcomings. "A wise man learns at the fool's expense."[23]
7. To have a kind of control over the other speaker, by resorting to eye glances loaded with unspoken meaning.

8. To perplex the other and keep him confused and bewildered about the interpretation of the real intention of the silent peer.
9. To compel the other, through silence and some gestures, to reveal what the listener has in mind.
10. To stir the anger of the other who may consider silence as a hidden attack. This increases the speaker's weakness and can prompt them to reveal something hidden.
11. To avoid involvement in harsh debates that might lead to a misunderstanding or conflict. Publilius Syrus[24] said, "I often regret that I have spoken; never that I have been silent."
12. To strip and dismantle the speaker's ability to continue their speech, especially if speech is the only weapon.
13. To avoid the consequences of giving embarrassing answers one might not have the right to give. Silence implies more than one answer with different interpretations.

In brief:

Silence is an art, and speech is an art, but most important is choosing the right timing. One is supposed to be selective. Silence is not always good, and speech is not always bad.

Silence out of context is retroversion, and speaking out of context is a waste of time.

---

22 Wolfgang Amadeus Mozart (1756-1791), an Austrian who was a prolific and influential composer of the Classical period, and is considered among the greatest composers in Western history. Despite his short life, his rapid pace of composition resulted in more than 800 works of virtually every genre of his time.

23 A Brazilian proverb.

24 Publilius Syrus (85-43 BC), a Latin writer of Syrian origin, best known for his sententiae (brief moral sayings, such as proverbs, adages, aphorisms, and maxims).

The Virtues of Apologizing and Forgiveness

"Let us forgive each other — only then will we live in peace."[25]

During their lifetime, all people are vulnerable to behave, talk, or comment in a way that might be offensive to others. Such a thing can happen anywhere: at home, in public, at work, etc. In this vein, apologies are essential to clear the air and get back on the right track.

The art of a sincere apology is one of the greatest human skills.

Apology is an effective treatment for misunderstanding, insensitivity, and bluntness.

** " *Apologies are not meant to change the past but are the best way to mitigate the damage.* " **

Apologizing is like superglue to fix broken relationships among people.

Apologies often can repair fractures with simple words like "sorry," "excuse me," "forgive me, I did not mean to disturb you," and many other similar words and phrases usually reduce misunderstanding and heal some wounds.

Apologizing does not always mean you're wrong and the other person is right. Instead, it means you value your relationship with others more than your ego.

> **Etiquette tips and the right way to apologize:**

While apologizing to someone we have hurt, we should be honest and mean it.

---

25 Leo Tolstoy (1828-1910), a Russian writer who is regarded as one of the greatest authors of all time. His notable works include the novels "War and Peace" and "Anna Karenina."

· When we are at fault, the first thing to do is to admit the matter. In fact, denying a mistake is a bigger mistake.

· It is necessary to accept responsibility for the mistake and remorsefully express sincere regret for the damage done. It is better to address the situation immediately and apologize promptly.

· The right words are important because if we make an apology with an excuse, it won't do any good.

· It is best to apologize in person and say "I'm sorry" face-to-face. This helps the other person notice the body language and hear the tone of voice.

· It might be necessary to give the other person a brief cool-down period, but not much time should pass. Otherwise, they will think they're not cared about.

· Worse yet, ignoring what happened and not mentioning it again is the most damaging way to handle the situation.

· It is necessary to allow the other person to express their feelings without turning the conversation back around to explain what happened. The goal here is an apology and asking for forgiveness, not an explanation.

· Nevertheless, one should not be surprised if the apology is not received as it is desired. A longer time might be needed to get over the hurt. Saying, "I am sorry," (and other similar phrases) is not always a miracle and immediate problem eraser.

▷ **Some considerations:**

· Apology and forgiveness, as supreme virtues, are required from both men and women.

· Apology and forgiveness are virtues required from all people regardless of their age, status, and rank.

· While apology is an act of courage, forgiveness is an act of strength.

· It is said that "the first to apologize is the bravest. The first to forgive is the strongest."[26]

· While holding a grudge doesn't make one strong, forgiving doesn't make one weak.

· Holding a grudge makes one bitter, while forgiveness makes them free.

· Mahatma Gandhi[27] said, "The weak can never forgive. Forgiveness is the attribute of the strong."

· Apology and forgiveness should be constant attitudes and not just occasional acts.

· Both the virtues of apology and forgiveness require high understanding and patience.

---

26 Anonymous.

27 Mahatma Gandhi (1869–1948) was the leader of the Indian independence, employing non-violent civil disobedience.

Correspondence
Etiquette

"Never write a letter while you are angry."[28]

Correspondence is part of most people's daily communications in the form of letters, messages, emails, social media messages, and texts. Correspondence is one of the important fields of etiquette observed through writing style, proper expressions of politeness, subject matter, and neatness of the correspondence, including a traditional envelope.

Most of today's correspondence is electronic, though, as we send endless e-mails. Unfortunately, we have lost touch with the practice of old-fashioned correspondence and resort to quick and brief ways of writing.

We should occasionally send a written letter, particularly to older relatives and friends without a computer. In addition to technological considerations, older people probably have fond memories of letters and would cherish handwritten correspondence.

In this chapter, I remind readers of the proper forms of correspondence to be familiar with, including the social letter, thank-you note, and business letter, keeping in mind that correspondence could be considered a mirror that reflects the personality of its writer.

An elegantly written correspondence creates a gentle feeling when received. Meanwhile, bad correspondence is:

1. Written carelessly.

2. Written on paper that does not fit the envelope.

3. Written with spelling and grammar mistakes.

4. Written in a poor format without regular margins.

28 Chinese proverb.

▷ Writing a Social Letter:

Handwriting should be done neatly with a pen rather than a pencil.

Naturally, the recipient will be interested in the news about mutual friends, family, and others. It is nice to update the recipient about the sender's life.

It is advised to include an amusing story or incident that is appropriate.

The recipient will appreciate being asked about their own life.

A bit of reminiscing is always nice; for example, "Today, I was thinking about the last good and joyful vacation we spent together."

If there is a photo or two to include, it can bring a smile to the recipient.

It is always advisable to use real stationery rather than a page ripped from a notebook. Otherwise, the recipient will get the impression that he is simply written to as a chore.

If a mistake is made, one should start again with a fresh sheet. It is improper to scratch out words or make a mess of the page.

▷ Writing a business letter:

Business letters can be used to apply for a job and recommend someone for a job. They can also be used as legal cover letters, letters of complaint, and daily correspondence.

There is a proper and universally accepted form to follow for such kinds of letters, with some slight variations.

In most business letters, the sender should stick to the topic at hand until the last paragraph.

Before the closing sentence, the sender can add a brief personal note, such as "It was nice to see you again at the weekend," or "Please make sure you call me directly if you have any questions."

▷ Thank-you Note/letter:

Thank-you notes should be written when receiving a gift or flowers, an invitation to spend a weekend or have dinner, when taken to the theater or concert, or receiving some kind of favor.

A thank-you note is supposed to be short, specific, and personal.

As in the other kinds of letters, a thank-you note should be done neatly with a pen rather than pencil, and written on quality stationery without a mess or mistakes.

▪ The most difficult parts of a correspondence:

For many, the first and final parts of a correspondence are usually the most challenging.

When the introduction of the correspondence is completed, it can be easier to insert the subject of the correspondence, which should be clear in the mind of its writer.

In the conclusion of the text, the writer sometimes finds it difficult to maintain the main idea or information, like painters who frequently hesitate on how to finish a painting.

A correspondence's conclusion can either steady its content or scatter it.

- **Some basic principles to follow:**

  · Any written letter should be clear.

  · Regarding font and ink,[29] modern pens with their various specifications, sizes, and colors have replaced old pens.

  · Today's pens are mostly dispensable, ready for writing, and do not need to be filled with ink.

  · Although computers compose most letters now, some are still written by hand.

  · If not typewritten, letters are usually written with blue or black pens.

  · Some high dignitaries, entitled to sign and write notes in other colors such as green for example, can write their correspondence in blue or black as well to avoid giving the impression of superiority.

  · The pen should not be pressed against the paper while writing. Otherwise, an extra line could be created and make the writing look unclear and confusing to the recipient.

  · Deletion and correction should be avoided so the letter would not appear sloppy.

  · Even in typed official correspondence, some words of courtesy can be handwritten, close to the place of signature, to add intimacy and respect to the addressee.

- **Correspondence elements:**

  Any correspondence consists of several elements, such as name, address, date, salutation, subject, body (content/text), complimentary closing, signature, cover, or envelope.

▷ **The heading:**

1 **The sender's address:**

  · Traditionally, the sender's address is written at the top right corner of the correspondence. However, some may prefer to have it on the top left corner, preceding the date and the recipient's address.

  · Some correspondence may begin with the sender's workplace and address in the middle of the upper quarter of the page.

2 **Date:**

  · The date of the correspondence should be fixed under the sender's address.

  · Any date should include the day, the month, and the year.

  · Until recently, there were many ways of forming dates, like using names rather than numbers.

  · Today's two common ways of dates are: Indicating day and year by numbers with the month's full name:
  "04 September 1996" or September 4, 1996.
  To write only in numbers: "04/09/1996" (using slashes instead of commas).

  · For documentation and archiving, it has become important to record the number of the correspondence directly before the date, on the same line.

  · It is worth noting that it has become common to have the address, telephone, and e-mail numbers listed in the form of a footnote at the bottom of the correspondence.

---

29 Until recently, pens were filled with ink, using multiple types of writing blades.

2 The recipient's name and address:

Usually, the recipient's name and address come on the left-hand side of the correspondence directly under the date (after skipping one line).

4 Salutation:

It is important to bear in mind that the salutation generates the first impression about the correspondence and its sender.

· Formal salutation is usually "Dear Sir," or "Dear Mr./Mrs.," or "Dear Madam," followed by the recipient's full name.

· A correspondence addressed to a friend can be started with various greetings and phrases, such as "Dear," "Dear brother," and "Esteemed friend."

· If you know the person well, you can use the first name only: "Dear Jonathan."

· When you do not have a name to use, you can use: "Dear Sir or Madam."

· In casual/informal correspondence, you can use: "Hello" or "Hi."

· In group correspondence, you can use: "Hi All" or "Dear Nof, Rose, Sulafa, Bayram."

· In business correspondence, you can use: "To whom it may concern."

· When writing to a woman, a man is not entitled to start his correspondence by saying "My dear" or "My dear lady/madam" or the like. The woman's full name should be mentioned.

· If she is a friend or relative, a man could start his correspondence with phrases that include her first name, such as saying, "Dear Gabriela" or "Dear Mrs.Lina."

· The titles of persons or dignitaries, whether civilian, military, religious, etc., should not be ignored. You should write, for example, "Dear Dr. Sidney..."

▷ Body of the correspondence:

1 The subject

The subject is usually one sentence containing a short description of the purpose or reason of correspondenc$^{e.}$

2 The content:

This part includes:

1. An introduction.
2. The main content or subject of the correspondence with details.
3. The conclusion that ends the correspondence.

The various types of content in the correspondence are innumerable. It can be personal or official business. It can be about social affairs, greetings, condolences, recommendations, thanks, love, congratulations, etc.

There is no general rule, but writing styles can vary based on the subject itself.

The writing style should be clear and straightforward, with well-organized paragraphs. It should stay away from either vulgarity or platitude.

3 The complimentary closing:

Any correspondence is usually concluded by words and phrases of courtesy.

Words and phrases of courtesy come in all languages and cultures. Generally, words and phrases of courtesy are chosen according to the relationship between the sender and recipient, as well as their status and rank.

In correspondence, the sender should choose appropriate words. The most common closing words used now are "Sincerely yours," "Faithfully yours," "Respectfully yours," "With my/our best regards/wishes," "Please accept my/our highest considerations/esteem," and so on.

▷ Signature:

The full name is usually written without abbreviations. However, some people may choose to have their first name abbreviated.

In personal correspondence, to add a sense of modesty and courtesy, it is not necessary to mention the title, position, or profession.

In public and official letters, the full name as well as the title is required.

▷ Envelope:

Attention should be paid to this aspect, as the envelope can be symbolically considered as the clothing that gives the first impression about the sender.

Whether the correspondence is formal, informal, or personal, depending on its purpose and event, there are numerous formal and informal envelope sizes, colors, and designs.

Full names and titles should be inscribed on the envelope without abbreviations.

The addresses of both the sender and recipient should be written clearly.

Most public and private units/authorities have inscribed names and addresses on their envelopes.

When correspondence is addressed to someone at their home, words and phrases such as "Private" or "To be opened personally" on correspondences should be avoided.

Words like "Private," "Confidential," and "To be personally opened," might imply a lack of confidence, and that there is a suspicion that the correspondence could be opened before reaching the recipient concerned.

Words and phrases, such as "Private" or "To be opened personally," could be written in some official or public correspondence for a specific reason. In this case, the secretary is not entitled to open it, unless the person to whom it is addressed permits or asks for that.

The postal stamp is usually fixed at the right top of the envelope.

* Note:
If a person mistakenly opens an envelope addressed to a colleague, they must immediately transfer it to them in another envelope and write, "With my apologies, I opened this letter by mistake" with their signature.

• Etiquette of email correspondences

Regarding modern and electronic means of communication, the details related to the form, nature, and style of email and messaging are important. This includes both the rules of etiquette and how this means of communication reflects the traits, personalities, and professionalism of the people using them.

▪ Why email correspondence is different?

Electronic correspondence is characterized by speed and flexibility.

Email messages are the fastest, cheapest, and least vulnerable to interference correspondence.

Unlike letters, email messages do not require paper.

Paper correspondence includes the details about when it was sent. It becomes a record.

When an email correspondence is sent, it is assumed to be directly received. The recipient can inquire about additional matters or just respond directly. Unlike phone calls, any email message could be sent with no need to pay attention to time differences between one zone and another.

Email messaging provides vast possibilities, including conducting chatting and conversation.

Although a telephone call transmits speech, voice, tone, mood, etc., and allows many words, it does not provide official documents that could be consulted again, as email correspondence does.

■ **Email correspondence should have the following elements:**

— **Professionalism:**

To be professional, email correspondence should have proper and correct language, format, spelling, etc.

An email carried out professionally would inevitably create good impressions for the recipient, confirming the professionalism of the sender.

— **Effectiveness:**

Email correspondence should have understandable, clear, and straightforward content.

If some parts are obscure or vague, confusion among recipients might happen.

— **Safety against Consequences:**

When an email sender knows they bear the responsibility for any mistake in corre-

spondence, they will be more careful to do everything properly.

> **Etiquette tips:**

1. **Preciseness:**

When sending an email to inquire or ask for something, the question should be clear and specific. For example, it is not logical to ask a company that makes microwaves of various types, models, and sizes, about a product, without specifying the type of microwave.

2. **Quick reply:**

The email sender expects a quick answer to their correspondence.

Per etiquette rules, an email should be answered within the same working day or 24 hours. If more time is needed to answer, the receiver should reply with whatever short note to assure the sender their email has been received and that it will be answered as soon as possible.

3. **Brief messages:**

The sentences used in email messages should be as short as possible. One should expect that long email messages could be ignored, keeping in mind that, for some people, reading this type of text is more difficult than reading texts typewritten on paper.

An email with long sentences could be tiring and appear as an article. The recipient might be reluctant to complete reading it.

4. **Correct grammar, spelling, and punctuation:**

Sending an email full of grammar, spelling, and punctuation mistakes, would certainly create a bad impression. Lack of punctuation or misuse may alter the meaning of a sentence or all of the text. This could certainly lead to a misunderstanding.

Examples showing the difference between a mistaken punctuated sentence and another correct one:
- Learn how to cut, marinate, and cook friends! (misleading)
- Learn how to cut, marinate, and cook, friends. (correct).
  Or:
- Let's eat grandpa! (misleading)
- Let's eat, grandpa. (correct)
  Note:

By using a computer program with auto-correct, it has become easier to have flawless email correspondence.

5. Clear formatting and specific paragraphs:

If reading on the screen is harder than reading papers, paragraphs should be clearly defined and organized. If appropriate, they should have clear numbering.

6. Responding to all questions:

In a reply email, all questions asked by the other side should be answered. If questions are ignored, some repeated questions are to be expected. Thus, the time of both parties involved is wasted.

An email sender is supposed to imagine what a recipient may ask and try to explain things in advance as much as possible. The recipient would appreciate that.

7. Personal touches:

Although there are formulas for dealing with familiar email content and topics, it is good for one to add some personal touches that reflect their character.

For example, it is enough to use the recipient's name more than once or to end an email with "Have a great day" or other similar phrases.

8. Unnecessary files:

Unnecessary files confuse the recipient and waste time.

Long files increase the storage and overload on the receiving computer.

Long files may increase the possibility of containing viruses, especially if the sender does not have a good anti-virus program.

9. Terms of importance and primacy:

Words and phrases such as "very important" and "urgent" should not be used unless there is a real need.

The overuse of "very important" and "urgent" will cause them to lose their meaning, and they will not receive attention when they are indeed required.

10. Using uppercase letters:

It is not necessary to use all uppercase letters in an email message to draw the recipient's attention.

The sender might appear to be screaming and receive undesirable replies.

11. Including previous thread of emails:

Some people do not like others including the previous thread of emails with a reply, arguing that it prolongs the loading time of the correspondence.

Others find it saves the recipient's time and effort while searching for the origin and subject of the correspondence.

Regardless, including the previous thread of emails reduces the recipient's storage.

12. Responsibility disclaimers:

Most private and public establishments, usually add some phrases at the end of their emails, such as "Make sure there is no virus" or "The company does not allow its employees to use defamation, sexual and racial discrimination phrases" and similar closings.

Such phrases reduce legal accountability if an employee intentionally or unintentionally sends viruses, causing disruption or even damage to the recipients' systems.

Such phrases reduce accountability if there are words of defamation or racial discrimination within an email.

Nevertheless, any phrases that go against laws, etiquette, and politeness should be avoided.

13. Re-reading email text:

Taking the burden of proofreading emails before sending them reduces spelling, punctuation, and grammar errors.

Reading emails again may remind the sender of a certain missed idea and limits the possibility of embarrassment for the sender or confusion for the recipient.

14. Abbreviations:

Abbreviations are not ideal in corporations and business correspondence, but they are used.

The sender should be sure that the recipient knows the abbreviations used. It is inappropriate to use English abbreviations such as "LOL" (laughing out loud) unless among friends.

Some common email abbreviations/acronyms include:

Word/phrase	Abbreviation
Message	MS
End of message	EOM
Please	PLS
Thank you	TY
Best regards	BR
Yes / No	Y/N
Laughing out loud	LOL
I love you	ILY
By the way	BTW
Text	TXT
No text	NT
Not work-related	NWR
Carbon copy	CC
To be forwarded	TBF
Blind carbon copy	BCC
Chief executive officer	CEO
Estimated time of arrival	ETA
Let me know	LMK
Work from home	WFH
No comment	NC
Why	Y
Oh my God	OMG
Action required	AR
Action by	AB
For your information	FYI
For your guidance	FYG
For your reference	FYR
As soon as possible	ASAP
Attention	ATT
For the attention of	FAO
Please find the attachment	PFA
Above mentioned	ABVM
End of day	EOD
End of week	EOW
Please respond	RSVP
Please reply by	PRB
Very short reply expected	VSRE
To be decided	TBD

As early as possible	AEAP
Leaving early today	LET
Real-Time	RT
Personal computer	PC
At your earlier convenience	AYEC
Too much information	2MI
For your information	FYI
Need your response	NYR
Need your response quickly	NYRQ
Need your response today	NYRT
Need your response - Next business day	NYR-NBD
No need to respond	NNTR
Reply requested or Reply required	RR
Not applicable	N/A
Check your email	CYE
In search of	ISO
Point of view	POV
In real life	IRL
Good game	GG
Good luck	GL
Good job	GJ
You're welcome	YW
Hope this helps	HTH
In a meeting	IAM
Sleeping	ZZZ
People	PPL
Out of office	OOO
Age/Sex/Location	ASL
Facebook official	FBO

15. Chain Letters:

Most email recipients immediately delete correspondence in the form of a chain letter. They may contain viruses, have unreliable information, or be apocryphal.

16. Notification of receiving:

It is not normal to ask for a notification of receiving an email correspondence. Such a request might disturb the recipient. If necessary, the sender may state they would be grateful if the recipient could reply.

17. Attachments:

Any file belonging to a third party should not be attached without permission. Otherwise, it could be considered a violation of property rights.

18. Confidential matters:

Confidential information should not be shared, i.e., an email should not include content that might lead to problems. In this case, it is possible to comment for example: "The information transmitted is intended only for the person or entity to which it is addressed and may contain confidential and/or privileged material."

19. Active voice:

To be more intimate, it is preferable to use active voice sentences rather than passive ones. A sentence like "What you have asked for will be sent to you" is very formal while a sentence like "We will send you what you have asked for" is more intimate.

20. Neutral gender:

It is more compatible with etiquette rules to use neutral language regardless of the recipient's gender.

When writing, for example, "Clients, you can find the details in the link ..." the words "Clients" could apply to both males and females.

21. Viruses spreading:

Chain letters and deceptive messages often contain viruses. Therefore, one should not send them and contribute to the spread of viruses.

A message with a statement such as "A virus will delete everything on the computer" is probably a deceptive message with viruses. If a recipient sends it to others to warn them, they contribute to spreading viruses.

22. "Spam":

Email spam, also referred to as junk email, is an unsolicited message sent in bulk by email.

Spam messages might include viruses. They should be deleted.

Replying to "spam" and advertisements implies:
- That the recipient's mailing address is correct.
- The recipient confirms that his mail is "Live" and ready to receive such things.

23. "CC" or "BCC":

"CC" (Carbon copy) is used when copies of a message are sent to one person or more.

"BCC" (Blind Carbon Copy) is used when copies of a message are sent to a certain group of participants.

"BCC" indicates that a recipient is supposed to know that other copies are directed to all other people in the same group.

The "BCC" procedure maintains the privacy of the group members.

24. Formatting or Font:

When your document comprises many pages of plain text, it can be very hard for your reader to find the important ideas within. You can improve the appearance and readability of your document by changing the appearance of the text.

Sending an email correspondence by using a certain formatting or font might not appear on the recipient's screen as the sender desired. The message or file transmitted in a certain version of format, font, and color might not be compatible with the recipient's computer programs.

Sending an email message with a file created in "Word 2010," for instance, might have formatting, font, and color differences when a recipient has a "Word 2008" version. It might not be possible to even open the file at all.

25. "HTML" messages
(Hyper Text Markup Language):

HTML is a way to code a document (made of ASCII text) that lets an HTML reader (such as a web browser) know how to render certain types of information.

HTML emails have everything plain text emails don't have: color, style, images, and sometimes multimedia.

The "HTML" link may include a page, image, or video. The "HTML" link is often in blue and underlined.

When inserting the "HTML" link in an email correspondence, it should be done correctly, so that the recipient can open it.

Section Five

Theater Etiquette

"Theatre is life, cinema is art,
television is some furniture."[1]

There is not enough space to address everything related to culture and its different aspects, including theaters. Yet, I must say there is no doubt the cultural aspects reflected in writing, art, theater, singing, music, dance, folklore, etc., are vital to forming a clear idea about any group of people's identity.

"Through culture and through the critical outlooks it promotes, that man usually discovers the mechanisms of events and regains the strength to recover his humanity. Culture, after all, provides the ideas and the ideals, which enhance man's freedom, consciousness, and beauty.

In this context, the theatre, through example and participation, can teach us how to rebuild and recreate and how to engage in the dialogue for which we all thirst. The theatre must stay alive because without it the world would grow lonelier, uglier, and poorer."[2]

Undoubtedly, most people like to go to theaters, opera houses, and concerts. Hence, this chapter reminds us of the proper decorum to follow at theaters. When we talk about theatre, we mean in this context, as it is well known, any place where plays, operas, classical music concerts (and even movies occasionally) are performed (which requires observance of specific etiquette rules). This differs from the places where youth music

---

1 Anonymous.

2 Excerpts from Saadallah Wannous' speech on the World Theater Day 1996. Saadallah Wannou (1941- 1997) is an award-winning Syrian playwright and editor who gained international fame.

and singing parties are held, in which the rules of etiquette are almost absent.

› Etiquette tips

As going to the theater is a special event, the audience is supposed to dress for this occasion. Although formal attire was once expected when attending theater performances, casual attire has become acceptable now (it is more comfortable). Nevertheless, casual attire does not mean sloppy attire.

– Wearing too much perfume or aftershave or deodorant and eating breath mints should be avoided.

– All audience members must arrive at the scheduled time.

– By being on time, one shows respect for the actors and fellow theatergoers.

– In fact, by entering a theater, after the start of the performance, one would disturb the spectators who must let them pass to reach a seat.

– In theaters' balconies and cabins, women sit on the front seats and men sit behind them.

– A spectator is supposed to go to the restroom before sitting down, or at the intermission. Leaving a seat during the performance is not only disruptive to people in the same row and nearby rows but also for the actors.

– Any cough drops or candy should be unwrapped before the show begins. The only sound the audience should hear at a performance should come from the stage.

– Men should take their hats off so as not to block another person's view.

– Women can wear low hats (not high ones).

– Any woman should take off her hat if a spectator behind her asks. She must meet this request without showing any resentment.

– A spectator should respect the space of people on either side and try to stay within the boundaries of their chair without taking both armrests.

– A spectator should stay awake. Snoring, or leaning one's head on a neighbor's shoulder when sleeping is unacceptable.

– One should keep their shoes on.

– One should do their best not to fidget. Otherwise, they would be very distracting to people sitting nearby.

– One should be interested. Musicians often complain about some audience members who make noise and show a lack of interest during concerts.

– Unless asked to sing along by those on stage, the audience should refrain from singing, humming, or whistling the tunes.

– Eating potato chips, pretzels, or any other crunchy snack during a live performance is impermissible.

– Furthermore, it is preferable to delay eating candies or some dry sweets until the end of a performance. The theater is not a place to eat.

– Mobile phones should be kept on silent mode, or preferably off, as they might affect the audio devices and amplifiers. No phone calls should be answered during the performance.

– It is preferable not to even check mobile phones during the performance; the light of the phone screen will bother people sitting nearby and distract their attention.

– Once the performance begins, the audience should keep silent, and not whisper or make comments, no matter how content they are.

– Singers or musicians should not be accompanied by chanting, fingers tapping on the seats, or feet striking the floor.

– A spectator should curb coughing as much as possible during the performance; otherwise, one should leave the showroom.

– In classical concerts, applause is expected only at the end of songs, not at the end of each segment, as some may do.

– A spectator is supposed to be appreciative. They can show appreciation by clapping at the appropriate times; and standing at the end of the show when others stand.

– Negative comments and criticism should not be said loudly during intermission. It is not tactful to hurt the feelings of any actors, musicians, or people who might know them.

– Note:

– Usually, children less than 10 years old are not allowed to attend opera performances and classical symphonies, unless such activities are especially dedicated to them.

– In "youth" and non-classical singing parties, it is no longer possible to talk about silence and quietness. Applause in all manners, including whistling and shouting, has become a dominant characteristic of these activities.

Museum and Art Gallery Etiquett

"Art aims to represent not the outward appearance of things, but their inward significance."[3]

There is no doubt that visiting a museum, or an art gallery is a remarkable cultural experience, which gives one the chance to enhance their knowledge, interest, and pleasure.

Museums and art galleries are special spaces, where visitors should tread as lightly and carefully as they can, to prevent mishaps.

Here are some helpful etiquette tips and rules on how visitors can best conduct themselves when going.

> **Etiquette tips:**

The most important basic rule is to see with the eyes and not with the hands. To ensure the preservation of exhibited pieces, any touching, poking, or prodding of sculptures, paintings, or photographs may lead to physical damage, even if not immediately seen.

Hands contain oils that corrode surfaces, lessen the life expectancy of the piece, and may lead to destruction. The museum and gallery are public places, and visitors should always respect each other's presence.

– A visitor is required to take a step back and not stand too close to the exhibited pieces, giving everyone a chance to view them.

– The visitor does not need to spend too much time in front of any piece to understand it.

– The visitor is supposed to minimize their time, and if so interested in a certain piece, come back to it for another viewing.

– To create a comfortable environment and avoid the disruption of a stress-free atmosphere, one is required to turn off their camera's flash and not take photos of every single piece.

---

3   Aristotle (384-322 BC.): a Greek philosopher and scientist.

- It is good to remember that museums and galleries are not the places for photo shoots. Therefore, the visitor should avoid making the art pieces backdrops for photos. This might offend other visitors.
- Relatedly, taking selfies should be avoided.
- To have ample opportunity to take in the art on a sensory level, the visitor is required to keep their phone on silent mode, avoid taking a call in the middle of viewing an installation, and minimize any phone conversation.
- It is impermissible to walk around with food and drink as a spill may cause damage.
- To respect other visitors, one should try to use an indoor voice and avoid making loud noises by talking, laughing, singing, and whistling.
- In addition to being quiet, the visitor should not give negative critical comments, even if they have a bad impression of what is exhibited.

In an art gallery:

- The visitor should not insist on the exhibiting artist or painter, if present, giving an extensive explanation about any exhibited works.
- Many artists believe viewers are free to form impressions and ideas by themselves; artists are not necessarily teachers or social reformers.
- If there is a visitor's book, those who wish to record some comments should be objective. Still, one can convey whatever opinion gently.
- It is not appropriate to ignore or throw away invitation cards, posters, brochures, booklets, and other exhibition publications.
- If a visitor wants to buy a price-tagged artwork, they should not bargain, even if that is a prevailing tradition in the society. Any art should be bought at the artist's listed price. It is the reflection of the artist's thoughts, emotions, and effort rather than a beautiful piece of furniture.

Dance Etiquette

*"Dance is two thinking feet and
a wisdom teaching waist."*[4]

It is worth mentioning that dance is the oldest kind of art and a basic component of any culture.

It is a symbolic and aesthetic performing art form that depends on the use of selected sequences of human movement.

Recently, some kinds of dance no longer have the same restrictions and procedures that prevailed in previous periods. Today, it is enough for some young people to meet in a hall, restaurant or house, to dance the way they like, in a noisy atmosphere of loud music.

Notably, the oriental Belly Dance (an Arabic dance) has become a hobby, a profession, and a trend in many non-Arab regions, especially in Latin American countries.

Regardless of globalization, popular and folkloric dances that distinguish regions should be preserved, developed, and enriched to maintain cultural diversities.

› **Etiquette tips:**

Giving a bow is the only kind of greeting exchanged among dancing partners at the beginning and end of each dance.

– A man asks a woman to dance, not vice versa.

– The invitation to dance is not an invitation for acquaintance and conversation.

– A man should accompany his dance partner to the place where she sits at the end of each dance and thank her for being his partner without prolonged conversation.

– A girl or woman's acceptance to dance

---

4 Dr. Afif Othman (Born, 1956), a Lebanese university professor and researcher in philosophy and human sciences.

with someone does not justify persistence to ask for further companionship.

– If a girl or woman responds with manners, she should be dealt with in a civilized and decent manner as well.

– It is inappropriate for men and women to dance only with one partner throughout all dances.

– The man who is untrained in certain dances is advised not to dance rather than dance badly. It is not tactful to impose himself on a partner.

– If a man is not competent in a certain dance while still accompanied by his partner, he should try to follow quietly, so as not to disturb her and others.

– Man is expected to avoid putting his hand on the dress of his dance partner if his hand is sweaty.

– In "waltz," a man should not squeeze his partner's waist, but gently touch it with his palm.

– A girl or a woman, who accompanies her friends, husband, family, or others to a dance floor, should expect that someone might ask her to dance.

– Before asking a woman to dance, a man should ask the permission of any male who is accompanying her.

– At the end of the dance, he returns with her to her table and gives her a simple bow before returning to his place.

– Refusing to dance with someone (without clear justification), might be considered an insult and disregard for the person.

– A girl or woman may sometimes have an excuse not to dance or just not be in the mood. She should provide a convincing reason for her refusal.

– It is bad and insulting behavior if a girl or a woman refuses to dance with someone who asks and then accepts another's invitation.

– If a man asks a woman to dance and she declines but promises to be his partner in the next dance, he should not ignore her when the next dance comes.

› **Etiquette for "Ballrooms":**

In addition to dancing, ballrooms are places for fun ad entertainment.

Those not in the mood for fun, delight, and smiling are not advised to go to a ballroom.

– The more formal the dance, the more formal the outfit. Therefore, men and women dress accordingly.

– Usually, invitations and announcements include a dress code to follow.

– When arriving at a ballroom, the man accompanying a woman precedes her until the women's dressing area. Naturally, it is impermissible for men to enter.

– Similarly, the man goes to the men's dressing area to put on his coat and hat and adjust his garments.

– After a while, the man returns and waits at the door of the women's dressing area to accompany his partner to the ballroom.

– At the ballroom, she joins the women's group and he joins the men.

– At ballrooms, "Floor managers" control and organize dances and assist with the selection of dance partners for strangers who do not know other participants.

– It is inappropriate for a stranger (who is a first-time participant) to move directly toward a woman and ask her to dance with him. It is the task of the floor manager to arrange that.

– The man should start the first dance with the woman whom he accompanied to the ballroom.

– Any dance partner should inform the floor manager if he/she is unable to continue a dance. There should be a good reason for that.

– The dancing on a floor is done along a counterclockwise direction, known as the "Line of Dance."

– This applies to traveling dances (which move on the boundary along the line of dance) including the Waltz, Foxtrot, Tango, Quickstep, and Viennese Waltz, as well as Polka and other dances.

– Latin (including Samba, Cha-cha-cha, Rumba, Salsa, Paso Doble, etc.) and Swing dances are almost stationary (dancers stay in the middle of the floor) and have no line of dance.

– In case a partner leaves the ballroom or sits before the dance ends, the floor manager should find an alternative partner.

– At the end of the dance and before parting, the gentleman thanks his partner. This "Thank you!" is not due to a favor but to politeness.

– When the dance comes to an end, tradition requires the gentleman to give his arm to the lady and take her back to her seat.

– Although accepting the blame is especially a nice touch for the gentleman, a dancer should not blame his partner for the missed execution of figures.

– Regardless of who is at fault when a dancing mishap occurs, both parties are supposed to smile and go on. This applies to the better dancer, who bears a greater responsibility.

– It often happens that the two partners dancing socially are not at the same level. In this case, the more experienced partner should dance at the level of the less experienced partner.

– The same principle applies to Latin and Swing followers, although to a lesser degree. Doing extra syncopations, footwork, free spins, etc. can be distracting and even intimidating for a less experienced leader.

– While soliciting teaching on the floor is not necessarily a flagrant violation, unsolicited teaching can be humiliating and takes the fun out of dancing.

– As the dance floor is not a place to teach or correct a partner, it is better to concentrate on the dances that both partners can do and enjoy.

– A dancer should be personable, smiling, and making eye contact with his partner.

– He should try to project a warm and good image on the dance floor, even if that is not his style.

– Once one asks or accepts a dance, it is important to be outwardly positive, even if he does not feel exactly enthusiastic.

– Before the start of a subsequent dance, men line up in a queue and one by one proceed toward the women.

– Each man proceeds, with his arm bent, toward the woman he wishes to dance with or who shows a desire to be his partner.

– At ballrooms, there is no need for men to be in a hurry; exchanging partners is to happen in the coming dances.

– Dance etiquette strongly encourages everyone to dance with many different partners. This is to ensure a diversity of partnerships on the floor and give everyone a chance to dance.

– Dance etiquette rules are against asking the same partner for more than two consecutive dances.

– Dance etiquette requires that one should avoid declining a dance under most circumstances.

– According to tradition, the only graceful way of declining a dance is either not knowing the dance, the need for rest, or if someone else has already promised to dance.

– He who declines a dance cannot dance the same song with someone else.

– When declining a dance, it is good form to offer another dance instead: "No, thank you, I'm taking a break. Would you like to do another dance later?"

– Usually, after almost an hour of dancing, all couples go to dinner.

– At the dinner table, each man takes care of the woman with whom he first came to the ballroom.

– After dinner, all the dancers go back to the ballroom, enjoying themselves with new dances.

Borrowing Books
Etiquette

"The reading of all good books is like a conversation with the finest minds of past centuries." [5]

Despite the skeptical and perhaps pessimistic attitude of some people concerning the future of books, and the overwhelming trend of electronic versions, the pleasure of reading traditional books remains a need and probably an obsession for many.

> **❝ Borrowing or lending a book is always a treat, especially when it is a good one. ❞**

It is a joy for friends to get the chance to talk about it.

Unfortunately, lending a book to someone can be risky. There's always that nagging question of whether the borrower is going to treat it well or give it back at all.

In my opinion, books are meant to be shared and enjoyed. I'm not one of those who believe that books should be kept on the shelf to stay in perfect condition.

› **Etiquette tips:**

– If the lending time is unlimited, the borrower should inquire about when to return it to its owner.

– A borrowed book is supposed to be read and returned to its owner within a reasonable time. That is usually about 15 to 25 days.

– After 25 days, if one is keen to complete the reading of a borrowed book, they should ask permission for additional time.

– The owner of a borrowed book should not be forced to ask for the return of a book.

– A borrowed book should be given back in the same condition as when it was borrowed.

---

5 René Descartes (1596-1650), a French philosopher, mathematician, and scientist. Dubbed the father of modern philosophy.

– It is important to remember a borrowed book is a friend's property that should be taken care of and treated as such.

– A book borrower must not bend pages or corners.

– A book borrower must never write any notes on the book of a friend or from a library.

– The margins in books are designed for aesthetics and framing, not as a space for personal notes and comments.

– Writing in the margins ruins the book and distracts future readers.

– A book borrower has no right to lend a borrowed book to another person without asking permission from the owner.

– When an author gives a book as a gift to someone, they expect it will be read, and the reader will later express an opinion about it.

– It is a big affront for an author to see their book neglected on someone's table without being browsed or read, especially if it's been signed.[6]

– If there are any critical viewpoints or negative comments, one should try to express them politely so as not to hurt the author's feelings.

---

6 George Bernard Shaw (the well-known Irish novelist and playwright) went to a bookstore that sells second-hand books at a cheap price. He saw one of his books that contains some of his plays and when he opened it, he was amazed to see that this copy which he presented to one of his friends and had written on it and signed: "To my dear friend who values the free word, with the warmest regards from George Bernard Shaw." Bernard Shaw bought this copy and wrote under the first dedication: "George Bernard Shaw renews his greetings to the friend who values the free word well." Then send the copy back to that friend.

I personally went through a similar experience. I was standing, by chance, next to one of my diplomatic colleagues who, for some reason, opened his desk drawer. I saw my book entitled "Public Relations and Protocol" that I had presented to him one year earlier. After asking for permission, I joyfully took the book to discover that this diplomat did not even bother himself to browse it and untie some of its sticky papers (due to a publication default). I felt resentful and even offended, especially as the book was supposed to be useful and important to him in his work.

Playing Cards Etiquette

"Holding aces doesn't ensure a win.
Right moves do."[7]

Playing cards is not a bad hobby if practiced among friends and family casually for some entertainment. Otherwise, it would be a waste of time and a vulgar habit.

Anyhow, the following etiquette rules are not concerned with betting games and do not deal with casino, poker parlors, or other game etiquette, but rather with playing among friends for diversion.

- **Playing cards' symbols and letters:**

There are four symbols used for playing cards, the heart, the spade, the club, and the diamond. They originally represented the pillars of the economy and the state in the Middle Ages societies:

- The **heart** symbol (♥) represents the church.

- The **spade** symbol (♠) represents the military.

- The **club** symbol (♣) represents agriculture.

- The **diamond** symbol (♦) represents the merchant and business class.

There are also four letters used for playing cards, A, K, Q, and J:
– "**A**" is an abbreviation for the card designated as "Ace," which represents the number one. It is regarded as the strongest card in the deck.

——————— 7 Anonymous.

A ♦ A ♥ A ♠ A ♣

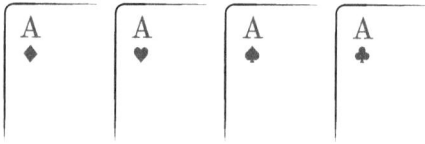

— The letter "**K**" represents the King card.

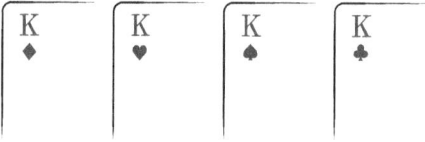

K ♦ K ♥ K ♠ K ♣

— The letter "**Q**" represents the Queen card.

Q ♦ Q ♥ Q ♠ Q ♣

— The letter "**J**" represents the Jack card, which can be understood to mean "man" or "companion."

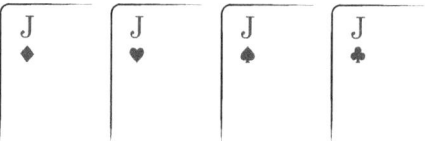

J ♦ J ♥ J ♠ J ♣

Furthermore, a standard deck of cards contains only two joker cards, and many games exclude them. Games that utilize jokers often employ them as wildcards or placeholders—a powerful card that can be used in place of any other card. In essence, they are distinct cards that serve different roles. That is why Jokers are seldom seen in many popular card games.

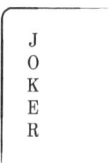

J
O
K
E
R

Playing with friends is for entertainment, straightness, and clarity. It must not let the casual atmosphere affect the game to a point where it causes confusion or allows for easier cheating.

— The game environment should remain amicable, and not full of stress and tension.
— The players are expected to play with amenities and accept win-in-loss results.
— The player should be patient and accept his partner's mistakes silently.
— The winner/s should not express a lot of joy and the looser/s should not show discontent.
— The host should urge the guests to play first. He is supposed to give them priority and refrain from playing at the beginning.
— Although the casual atmosphere allows conversation, the focus should be on the game being played.
— Too much conversation causes distraction. It is very frustrating for one player to play while everyone else is distracted.
— Decks (playing cards) should not be old, worn out, crimped, or marked.
— Decks should be with symmetrical backs.
— Players should all be sitting about the same space away from the center of the table and unable to peek at each other's hands.
— Dealing cards (distributing cards) should not be at a slow or inconsistent pace.
— Distributed cards should not be touched until the dealer finishes dealing (the last card dealt out). The only exception is if the cards are dealt sloppily and there is a mistake in distributing an equal number of cards for each player.

– Before dealing, the dealer asks the player on his left to cut the cards into two piles. Cutting should be done with only one hand.

– After the cut, the dealer should not peek at the bottom card.

– Players should wait and not start playing until all players have their cards organized.

– Any statements about bidding, passing, or whatever speaking that is part of the game should be loud, clear, and direct.

– Making any strange gesture, nod, signal, or statement should be avoided. It may be misunderstood as some sort of signal.

– Playing cards should not be played violently, tossed off-handedly, or carelessly onto the table.

– Some players may lean far back and spin the cards to the table from a distance. It is a common improper move.

– During the game, hands should be kept above the table.

– Similarly, cards should never be held under the table.

– It is improper to peek/look at the playing cards in the hands of the other players.

– It is improper to give advice to players or to criticize any of them during the game.

– It is improper to praise other players (opponents or partners).

– It is improper for players to ask about previously played cards. It is better to pay attention without having to ask.

– No spectator should go around the table looking, making remarks about the score, and trying to give this or that player some advice.

– No spectator should make guesses or bets on who is winning or what will happen, distracting players, or drawing players into side conversations.

Section Six

Religious Places
Etiquette

"My concern is not whether God is on our side; my greatest concern is to be on God's side, for God is always right."[1]

❝ Every person has personal religious opinions and beliefs, which often come from where they were born or grew up. Regardless of one's theological views, all religions and beliefs must be respected at all times and everywhere. ❞

All places of worship in the world have sanctity; therefore, when they are visited, one must adhere to the obligations of the devout believers and behave among them as if they believe what the devout believes, regardless of personal convictions or religious beliefs.

One's behavior must be appropriate and consistent with the traditions and rites of the places they are visiting, rather than the traditions and rites common to their religious community.

When visiting India, for example, nobody is obliged to visit a Hindu temple; but upon entering one, they must abide by the etiquette of that temple and respect its rites without showing surprise or disapproval. Negative behavior will upset believers whose reactions might be strong.[2]

---

1 Abraham Lincoln (1809-1865), an American statesman and lawyer who served as the 16th president of the United States.

2 Once, I visited a temple in New Delhi and noticed some people feeding rats. There, they consider all beings created to be respected and left to live their own way; and there is no justification to remove or hurt rats, as the right to live is sacred to all creatures without exception.

This behavior might seem odd to those with values similar to mine. Yet, in conformity with etiquette, I showed full respect.

Clergy are formal leaders within established religions. Their roles and functions vary in different religious traditions but usually involve presiding over specific rituals and teaching their religion's doctrines and practices.

In all functions and gatherings, it should be remembered that the clergy have a degree of authority and precedence in protocol.

According to denomination, status, and occupation, the specific names, titles, and roles of clergy vary according to each religion and even each sect.

Generally, Christianity has a wide range of formal and informal clergy positions, including *pastor*s, *deacons, priests, bishops, archbishops, patriarchs, cardinals, and the Pope.*

Traditionally, Islamic religious sheikhs, who have many titles, play a prominent role within their communities or nations and their religious leadership may take a variety of formal and non-formal shapes, providing religious rules to the pious as well as resolving ordinary matters (even the most minor and private ones).

In Islam, a religious leader is often known formally or informally as an *Imam, Qadi, Mufti, Sheikh Aqil, Mullah, Hujjat Al-Islam, and Ayatollah.*

In Judaism, religious leaders have many positions and titles. *Rabbi, cantor, and Gabbai* are the three main types of Jewish clergy.

Buddhist clergies are often collectively referred to as the *Sangha* and consist of various orders of male monks (originally called *bhikshus*) and female monks (originally called *bhikshunis*). Buddhist clergy have many names, titles, and roles that vary according to country and community.

Hinduism is an Indian religion and culture widely practiced in India and parts of Southeast Asia.

Scholars regard Hinduism as a fusion or synthesis of various Indian cultures and traditions, with diverse roots and no founder.

Hindu priests (identified as *Pundits or Pujaris* among devotees) are known to perform services often referred to as *Puja.*

Although proper etiquette can vary depending on which religious site is visited, there are some general rules most major houses of worship share.

I have put together a list of behaviors to follow in places of worship of four major religions: Christianity, Islam, Buddhism, and Hinduism.

> ## Etiquette tips:

– All people, regardless of their beliefs, should respect clergy from all religions, sects, or communities.

– All worship places require men to take hats off, wear conservative clothes covering shoulders and legs, and avoid tight clothing, short shorts, sleeveless tops, and shirts with slogans or advertisements.

– Women are required to wear modest clothes that cover shoulders (such as sweaters and shawls) and to cover knees (such as pants, skirts, and dresses).

– In mosques, in addition to covering their head and hair, women should also wear ankle-length skirts or dresses.

– In mosques and Hindu and Buddhist temples, men and women are required to take off their shoes before entering.

– In almost, all worship places, one should ask permission before taking pictures and filming, especially if the place has statues and paintings.

- If cameras are permitted, the flash, which can damage old art, should be turned off.
- Cell phone ringers should always be turned off before entering religious spaces.
- Visitors should refrain from loud or inappropriate conversation. Worship places are just for worship and meditation.
- If the visitors are in large groups, they should avoid a religious ceremony, so as not to upset believers.

> ### More detailed etiquette tips:

- Although church visitors are generally not required to take off their shoes, in Ethiopia, visitors are expected to remove shoes.
- When seated in Greek Orthodox churches, visitors should refrain from crossing their legs.
- In Hindu temples, upon entering, it is proper for visitors to remove leather, including shoes, belts, jackets, etc. Although not a steadfast rule, it is a sign of respect.
- In Buddhist and Hindu temples, only the right hand is used to handle donations (or anything else) given to another.
- In Buddhist temples, everybody should stand when monks or nuns enter.
- In Buddhist temples, when pointing something out to a fellow visitor, the right hand with an open palm is used.
- It is improper to turn one's back to Buddha statues. Therefore, visitors can turn around only when they are a few feet away from such statues.
- Moreover, statues of Buddha and monks should not be touched.
- In mosques, visitors should pay attention to signs at the entrance.
- Some mosques have separate designated entrances for men and women.
- If a visitor misses the sign, they should still notice that men and women are gathering at different entrances and proceed accordingly.
- Although taking pictures inside mosques is generally allowed, it is impermissible to do that during prayer.

Funeral Etiquette

"Fame lives on after death." [3]

Regarding funerals, customs, traditions, and attitudes vary according to different cultures and religions. Therefore, no common etiquette (concerning procedures, clothes, flowers, etc.) prevails everywhere. Each society, and even various groups within some communities, may have different practices for funerals.

In this chapter, etiquette, and procedures for funerals include memorials, which is a service held without the body present. Perhaps an individual or family has chosen cremation, or the deceased may have died in military combat (as a soldier or civilian) or in another country, etc. Nevertheless, the memorial service itself is usually more informal than a traditional funeral. Although proper funeral etiquette varies widely, most of us sense general guidelines to consider.

> **Etiquette tips:**

– Whether one should attend a funeral depends on the kind of relationship one had with the deceased or the bereaved, such as being a family member or close friend.

– With a less familiar relationship, one's attendance is optional. They can choose to stay home and write a condolence note instead. A printed sympathy card with a handwritten line or two to personalize the message is appropriate as well.

– Other options are sending flowers or donating in memory of the deceased to a charity designated in the obituary.

– Generally, for a wake, viewing, or visitation (where the casket is present, whether open or closed), it is not obligatory to attend unless there's an important connection.

– A mourner should express deep sorrow and sympathy.

– Mourning periods vary from one place to another. Women's mourning periods usually depend on the degree of kinship with the deceased.

– Regarding clothes, it can be tricky to determine both what is respectful to the deceased and bereaved and what is comfortable.

– Men who do the duty of consolation should wear formal or dark professional attire, with an appropriate black or dark necktie.

– Women can wear dark pants, skirts (at the knees or below), blouses, jackets, sweaters, or dresses.

– Today, as the current "anything goes" trend is spreading, casual clothing has become a more acceptable dress code in many places and situations. Therefore, most funerals don't require formal clothing or the most somber colors. The truth is somewhere in between:

– A fairly simple conservative dress with neutral, dark, or muted colors and respectful silhouettes is acceptable.

– Avoiding bright colors, prints, and anything flashy or glittery, prevents offending the bereaved.

– Women can wear minimal jewelry and stick with simple accessories. A funeral is not a time to show off the swankiest jewels.

– Keep in mind that there is always quite a bit of variation concerning the culture and traditions of the deceased person's family, region, heritage, and religion. For example,

in addition to black, white is also the color of mourning in Ethiopia.

– The mourning color in some parts of Ghana is black and red. People there may also perform some dances at such an event.

– In some Brazilian areas, alongside black dress, purple is considered a mourning color.

– In Papua New Guinea, a woman covers herself in light clay from head to toe when mourning the loss of her husband. Derived from this practice, the country's mourning color is grey, the color of clay.

– According to different places and cultures, the funeral flower arrangements (wreaths) and colors vary widely.

– Although white flowers reflect joy, love, and happiness in most of the world, they might additionally reflect sorrow and death in many countries.

– White flowers are certainly more common at funerals than brightly colored ones, but that doesn't mean there's no place for other colors in a funeral arrangement.

– It is worth mentioning the Japanese never offer a bunch of four flowers or four pieces of any item. According to the Japanese language, the number 4 is pronounced "shi," which also means death.

– Moreover, the Japanese consider odd numbers to be more positive than even ones, even regarding flowers.

– Lilies, carnations, pink orchids, and purple tulips (and others) are common choices for funerals.

– Many of the most popular sympathy flowers are chosen based on their symbolic meanings, such as forget-me-nots[4] that convey everlasting affection, or violets that represent a young life cut short.

---

4 forget-me-nots (Scorpion grasses), is a genus of northern hemisphere flowering plants in the family Boraginaceae.

– Wreaths used in funerals are almost circular, reflecting the completeness of the life cycle.

– Similarly, floral wreaths placed on mausoleums of the Unknown Soldier and the Martyrs' Monuments are circular.

– If someone is in doubt about proper flowers for funerals, the local flower provider is likely to offer a variety of arrangements.

– If there is a memorial register to sign, it is good to write some brief comments.

– If someone is walking on the street or driving their car, they are expected to stop until a funeral procession passes.

– In cemeteries, one should take into consideration the sacred nature of the place and not tread on graves, smoke, chatter, or laugh.

– In funerals and cemeteries, cellphones should be turned off or kept on silent mode.

Section Seven

Gift etiquette

"A gift given without hesitation
is as good as two gifts."[1]

❝ In all societies, there are events and occasions such as feasts, holidays, birthdays, weddings.. Therefore, it is common to exchange gifts as part of the social and cultural customs accompanying such functions. ❞

Gifts might express interest, love, friendship, gratitude, and other values and concepts. Hence, it is important to give the right gift, in the right way, at the right time.

It is important to know some of the rules of gift etiquette and some related concepts and differences in this regard, to make the gift stand out while being suited to the occasion and, most importantly, treasured by the recipient.

> **Etiquette tips:**

– The nature and quality of gifts are subject to the cultural and social heritage of each society and region.

– The type of gift usually corresponds to the kind of relationship between persons, such as friends, lovers, husbands, colleagues, etc.

– The nature of the gift varies according to the receiver's age. A gift presented to a grandparent or a father is different from that presented to a friend or son.

– The type of gift varies according to the status and rank (whether functional, social, or scientific). A gift presented to a business owner or boss is not the same as that given to a colleague or one of the employees.

---

1   Latin proverb.

- The nature of the gift is supposed to correspond to the occasion. It is not appropriate to present a medal, for example, for a couple at their wedding party.
- The type of gift varies according to the religious, civil, or military status of the people to whom they are presented. It is odd to present a sword as a gift to a Christian clergy, for example, while it would be a beautiful gift for an army officer.
- The value of a gift is supposed to be linked with its nature and symbolic significance rather than its price (although some societies still think differently). Otherwise, it could be a kind of statement about one's wealth.
- It is inappropriate to give a valuable gift to someone unable to give something equivalent in return; that would embarrass them.
- When a gift is sent to a foreigner in another country, it is supposed to be, as much as possible, typical of the sender's country.
- It is not permissible to present a gift to a foreigner that is typical or symbolic of the recipient's own country. It would be strange to give a souvenir that embodies the Sphinx to an Egyptian friend.
- The gift is supposed to be joyful to the person to whom it is offered; therefore, the gift must be selected to suit the recipient's taste and inclination as much as possible. Otherwise, the gift will be glanced at and then stuck on a shelf and forgotten. Those who care about archeology, for example, will be happy with a gift that embodies something historical or antique rather than a modern item.
- It is one's duty to remember the others' occasions and give them gifts, as they do towards the gift-giver.
- As the wife remembers the occasions that belong to her husband, he should not forget the occasions that belong to her, such as her birthday and their wedding anniversary. He is expected to present her with appropriate gifts. Such initiatives strengthen family bonds.
- The father should remind, encourage, and enable his children to offer a gift to their mother on Mother's Day.
- Without the consent of her husband, a man must not present jewelry to a married woman; otherwise, it would be considered a serious breach of friendship and magnanimity.
- When someone receives a gift, they should not present it to another person later. This is not fair to anyone involved.
- The gift should not precede its time, such as sending in October, a gift for New Year's Day. It is normal to send it between the middle of December and New Year's Eve.
- The price label should be removed before presenting a gift to anyone. Likewise, the price should not be mentioned directly or indirectly in front of the person to whom the gift is given.
- Some companies offer samples of their products to their customers. It is impermissible to present them to others as gifts.
- At various events in most countries of the world, flowers are among the beautiful gifts exchanged among friends, lovers, etc.
- A bouquet of flowers could also be a good solution for those uncertain or unable to choose a suitable gift.
- It is necessary to take care of the way a gift is wrapped, making it look neat and elegant with sufficient touches of beauty.

– Gift bags should be carefully selected. Their designs and decorations are supposed to correspond to the occasion.

– In many countries, it is tactful to open the gift in front of its presenter immediately after receiving it. This allows the recipient to thank the gift-giver and show appreciation. While in other countries, gifts are not opened upon receipt.

– By receiving a gift, one should thank the sender in writing or by telephone. This should be done on the same day, if possible.

– In many countries, if a group of people visits someone on their birthday, wedding anniversary, promotion, etc., and each one or couple brings a gift, the receiver is supposed to take the gifts and give thanks without opening them. Otherwise, they might embarrass some of the group members based on their gift choices or gift values.

– Generally, in Western and American countries, gifts are immediately opened upon receipt in front of those who present them, whether as individuals or as a group. There is nothing wrong with that and no embarrassment may take place, as all gifts are usually symbolic and simple.

– In countries such as China, Japan, Korea, Malaysia, and East Asian countries, people give and receive gifts with both hands.

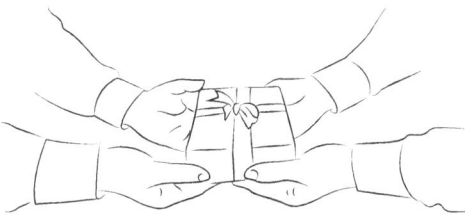

– In countries such as China, Japan, and Korea, it is impermissible to present a gift composed of four pieces, as the number four itself indicates death.

– The most unwanted gifts in China are all types of watches because the phrase "giving a watch as a gift" in the Chinese language is identical to the phrase "participating in a funeral ceremony." Therefore, giving a watch to anyone means wishing them death.

– It is possible and even necessary to present someone with a gift in the form of a small coffin. The coffin in China is associated with job promotion and therefore a coffin indicates wishes of success.

– In China, it is forbidden to give a green hat as a gift to a man. Such a gift is considered an insult as it indicates that his wife is cheating on him.

– In most countries of the world, number 13 is a presentiment or foreboding. Therefore, gifts composed of thirteen pieces are supposed to be avoided.

– In most countries of the world, black-colored covers are avoided in wrapping gifts, as black represents grief and sorrow.

– In Japan and Korea, gifts in the form of a knife must be avoided as they might suggest suicide.

– Purple is the color of solace and death in several countries such as Italy, Britain, and Thailand, so it must be avoided in gift covers and bags.

– In Vietnam, napkins and handkerchiefs as gifts are avoided as they symbolize sad farewell.

– In Switzerland, Germany, and many other countries, red roses are only presented or exchanged among lovers; they symbolize love and passion. In such countries, while cloves and some kinds of lilies are symbolic of mourning and funerals, knives, scissors, and umbrellas are symbolic of bad luck.

– For religious reasons, it is not permissible to present alcoholic beverages as gifts to some people in Islamic countries.

– In Armenia, gifts are offered on New Year's Day but not on Christmas, which is a purely religious holiday.

– Some countries do not prevent their officials and dignitaries from accepting simple gifts. Nevertheless, if the value exceeds a certain limit, it must be submitted to an accredited body to be registered and become public property.

Section Eight

Women's Etiquette

"Women are made to be loved,
not understood."[1]

" *Despite the diversity of cultures and the differences in related traditions, women have already obtained the privilege of special treatment.* "

A set of related principles of etiquette and politeness has become common and familiar in almost all countries.

The statement "Ladies First"[2] has become so popular it is essentially a golden rule, according to which many behaviors are based. It implies women receive precedence and preferential advantage in various situations.

---

1 Oscar Wilde (1854-1900), Irish poet and playwright.

2 It is common to hear the expression "Ladies first" and use it without knowing its origin for certain. Some say it comes from a story that took place in Italy, when a couple decided to get married. Due to social circumstances, their relatives didn't approve of their marriage. They planned to take their own lives by throwing themselves from a mountain into the sea. The man decided to jump first because he couldn't stand to see his lover drowning before him. When it was her turn, she decided not to jump and returned home. Therefore, after the incident men decided to play it safe and the term "Ladies first" arose. Another story says that during the Middle Ages, knights and men would throw their coats over puddles of mud to allow women to pass to the other sides safely. While doing so, they'd say, "Ladies first."

> **General etiquette tips:**

– Women precede men in entering the doors of public places and houses.
– Men hold the doors open for women.

<u>It is civilized and tactful behavior to open the car door for a wife and other women, to help them get both in and out. Above all, it is a sign of respect.</u>

– Furthermore, when getting out of the car, a man helps a woman by offering his hand.
– It is the man's duty to take off his wife's coat and leave it at the cloakroom.
– At parties and banquets, it is the duty of the husband or nearest man to help his wife or nearest woman take off and put on her coat, not vice versa.
– At parties, dinners, and banquets, men pull chairs out and back to allow the women or girls next to them to sit at the table.
– In restaurants, waiters typically begin serving food and drink to women before men.
– In places where smoking is allowed, it is the man's duty (if he smokes and has a lighter) to light the woman's cigarette (if she smokes), never vice versa.
– According to etiquette, women should never be asked their age. (Even if the man is a notary or a judge, it is better to ask when she was born than how old she is!) Robert Frost [3] said, "A diplomat remembers a woman's birthday and forgets her age".
– Since women always have something positive in their character, men should focus on and emphasize that part as much as possible.

– It is unwise for a man to express hatred or to criticize some of a woman's negative qualities. Such actions are unlikely to be forgiven.
– In the event that a woman is provoked by a certain word or behavior perpetrated by a man, it is the man's responsibility to apologize and clarify any misunderstanding without engaging in lengthy discussions.
– Unless an emergency situation occurs, a man should never hold a woman's handbag, even if he just wants to help.
– On stairs, the woman precedes the man by one or two steps when ascending, while she stays behind the man in the same manner when descending.

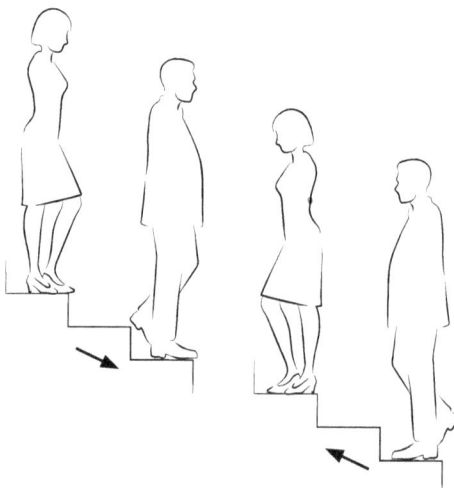

– These behaviors are to protect women in the event of stumbling, slipping, or falling. A man should be ready and able to help if necessary.
– Accompanying a woman on the sidewalk along the street, the man stays on the side

---

3 Robert Lee Frost (1874 – 1963) an American poet who was the only one to receive four Pulitzer Prizes for Poetry. He was known for his realistic depictions of rural life and his command of American colloquial speech.

closest to the road to protect her from imminent dangers. Once upon a time, it might be a runaway carriage, but now it would be splashes and other unpleasantries from the road.

– A woman suffering from fatigue and exhaustion appreciates any simple aid offered by a man.

– It is good to remember that some women are affected by the fluctuations of their hormones, which affect their mood. Knowing that could explain some reactions and behaviors.

– If a woman seeks to be alone and does not want to talk to others, she should be given that possibility.

– If a woman is depressed, a man should do his best to communicate and encourage her.

• How to Be a Lady

› Etiquette tips:

– A lady is supposed to be gracious. When being introduced to someone, she never just says "Hello." On the contrary, she is required to offer a kind greeting like, "It's a pleasure to meet you," or "How are you today?"

– She gives compliments with sincerity and only when she means it. She does not say things just to say them. Insincerity is easier to read than one thinks.

– A lady offers help when seeing someone in need. For example, she offers her seat to the elderly, people with special needs, or a parent with small children.

– To show gratitude for specific actions or generosities, she follows a good rule of thumb to say "please" and "thank you." These are basic golden words, which can make the world a happier and more polite place. Good manners never get old.

– She says, "Yes, please" or "No, thank you." She does not say, "Yeah" or "No."

– Being a lady and acting lady-like does not mean being snobby.

– She should do her best to be kind, gracious, and confident while not talking or behaving in a way that may lead others to think of her as a braggart. There is nothing as refined and attractive as humility.

– It is unbecoming for a woman to frequently post photos on social media about herself and family, businessmates, or friends. A real lady does not do this unless there is a significant reason or a special event.

– She must be well acquainted with table manners and all relevant details.

– At the dinner table, women might have some extra challenges:

– If she wears lipstick, [4] she can blot it on a tissue in the ladies' room before being seated at the table.

---

4 History of lipstick: During the ancient Sumerian civilization (dating back to the Chalcolithic and Early Bronze Ages (4500-1900 BC), which was the earliest known civilization in the historical region of southern Mesopotamia (now southern Iraq), men and women were possibly the first to invent and wear lipstick, about 5,000 years ago. They crushed gemstones and used them to decorate their faces, mainly on the lips and around the eyes. In the modern era, Estelle Winwood (1883-1984), an English stage and film actress who moved to the United States in mid-career and became celebrated for her wit and longevity. She was the first woman to wear lipstick in one of her movies in 1916 to look scarier. She said in 1960, "I think I've done more for women all over the world by being the first person to use rouge on my lips in public."

- She puts her handbag on her lap under the napkin (usually the handbag is small at dinners) rather than hanging it on the chair back, which could obstruct wait staff and other passersby.
- After receiving an invitation, she RSVPs (please reply) promptly and does not ask for exceptions, for example, to bring an uninvited guest.
- She always promptly sends a detailed thank you note to anyone who has shown her hospitality.
- She never arrives empty-handed, as bringing a small gift shows appreciation for the host's preparation.
- If a man knows it is etiquette to remain standing until the woman next to him is seated, she must sit as promptly as possible and not leave him standing too long.
- When at the dinner table, at a wedding, or spending time with family and friends, a woman is not supposed to make phone calls but rather engage in conversation, building relationships, and friendships.
- She must avoid talking with a mouth full or using rude or shocking language, especially at the table. Language and the way of talking are a representation of one's mind and heart.
- She should discard chewing gum before a dinner, meeting, or interview. And if she is chewing gum in public, she should make sure not to smack it.
- At receptions, cocktail parties, dinners, and other events, she should moderate her cocktails and always try to have water between drinks if she can.
- If she has had too much to drink, she should excuse herself and leave.
- It's unbecoming to spread gossip and air someone else's dirty laundry, especially via social media.
- A lady's word is her bond. She always keeps her promises and warrants a respectable reputation purely by the consistency of her word.
- If dating a gentleman, she should have respect for him and not behave with entitlement by ordering the most expensive thing on the menu. If he wants to treat her to a fine bottle of wine, he can order it or offer her the selection.
- When dating, she has to be a good listener and conversationalist, putting her phone away and being present. A lady is not boring, rude, or dismissive.
- On the job as well as in outdoor events, there are general rules regarding appropriate attire, jewelry, makeup, tattoos, and other grooming details.
- A woman's appearance is important not only in making the right first impression but also in building long-term relations that rely upon mutual respect and understanding.
- As women have a more complicated dress code than men, they should, when attending any event, dress tastefully and appropriately for the occasion. Women face greater scrutiny about what they wear than men.
- As elegance requires minimalism, a lady does not wear revealing clothing. Showing excessive cleavage or wearing bare-midriff tops suggests she is not dressing for herself, but rather, to attract men.
- While it is quite acceptable to wear pants, skirts or dresses bring out elegance, and femininity and display a woman's curves better than pants.
- When wearing a skirt, dress, or any other garment, she should make sure it does reach higher than the knee.
- She must not try to squeeze herself into clothes that don't fit.

– Today, women can choose either wedge heel shoes or pump shoes for formal use (including the workplace), although wedge heels are still considered more elegant and more formal.

– However, very high heel shoes are not advised (5 to 7 cm is a good and comfortable option).
– Formally, a woman wears closed shoes. Yet in the workplace, she can wear slightly open shoes, but her toes should not overhang.
– Furthermore, if she feels wedge heels or pumps are uncomfortable, some carefully chosen flat shoes are just as good.
– She must always wear stockings or pantyhose (usually of neutral color) rather than go to work bare-legged.
– Her hair should be kept neatly styled and clean, avoiding dramatic or severe styles that can be distracting or project an unprofessional image.
– She must not wear excessive makeup. Makeup is to accentuate beauty, not to cover it up.
– For lipstick, she is supposed to use shades that match her skin color.
– As lipstick options are plentiful, she can choose what looks good for her by testing different shades.
– Women's eyebrows should be neatly trimmed and shaped.
– According to her experience, a woman can apply the proper eye shadow that suits her complexion and skin tone.

– When getting a manicure, a woman's hands should be neat with short and trimmed nails.
– She should not fall prey to the latest nail trend.
– The nail polish should be neutral as much as possible. It is better, for example, to wear a neutral shade of nail polish, avoid using embellishments, and rely on soft pinks rather than purple, yellow, and bold reds.
– Fingernails should not be to a distracting length. Otherwise, the attention will be focused on the shiny nails rather than a woman's personality.
– A woman should avoid over-scenting with perfume (especially to mask body odors). Over-scenting can be just as offensive as unpleasant body odor.
– Regarding wearing jewelry, modesty is important. Too much jewelry, especially on the job, or several different styles demonstrates its owner's poor taste.
– It is worth mentioning that a woman's facial jewelry (such as nose rings) is still inappropriate while on the job. Therefore, they should be removed.
– Regarding tattoos. Unless a woman works in a tattoo parlor or belongs to a "garage band," tattoos should be covered.

- **Sitting down and standing:**

– For a woman, the right way to stand is to combine her legs, with one a bit in front of the other so that no space appears between the top inner parts of the two thighs (if wearing pants).
– When a woman sits, she should keep her legs combined, unlike a man who can sit with his legs slightly apart. Good posture and leg position while sitting are crucial.

– If a woman sits in a low armchair, she does not put one leg over the other one but rather keeps her knees close to each other and legs parallel.

– She can also use what is called the "Cambridge cross" putting one foot behind the other and crossing her ankles (ankle-lock position).

– When a woman sits down crossing her legs (leg-over-leg cross position), no matter what she wears, both legs should go back a little, unlike a man who can keep his knees slightly open without extending his legs too far.

▪ **Getting in and out of a car:**

Regardless of what she wears, when a woman gets in a car after opening its door, she sits on the side of the seat and then lifts both legs combined towards the inside of the car.

(This procedure is not required from a man who can lift his legs inside the car one by one.)

Similarly, a woman gets out of a car while the legs are combined.

The Elderly Etiquette

"With age, the faults of early childhood reappear."[5]

Showing respect toward the elderly, in all cultures is a moral, social, and even religious duty. Furthermore, the elderly have life experience and should be listened to and learned from.

" The wisdom of older people can truly enrich our lives. "

Even if we don't agree with some of what they're saying, it is good to at least listen and we may come away with an important nugget of knowledge for the future.

› **Etiquette tips:**

– Being gracious to everyone, regardless of age, shows one's true character.
– The elderly should be addressed properly with the name they prefer.
– Unless they say otherwise, they should be called Mr. or Mrs., followed by their last name.
– Shaking hands when meeting an elderly person for the first time or hasn't been seen in a while, is a simple yet friendly gesture that shows good manners.
– When talking with the elderly, one should keep their voice as clear as possible,

———————— 5 An African proverb from Burundi.

use proper language (without slang), and be willing to speak louder if it's clear the person can't hear well.

– When approaching or greeting the elderly, eye contact and a smile should always be made. This shows acknowledgment of their presence.

– The elderly might talk some nonsense, yet one should listen with interest, be gentle, and display respect.

– Some very elderly people might act or behave oddly. It is impermissible to ridicule them or appear indifferent.

– Older people generally feel happy to receive help from others and often expect such an initiative.

– When an elderly person approaches a building entrance, it is courteous to hold the door and allow them to enter first. Such simple and tactful behavior makes them happy and will be appreciated.

– When there is a stair, the elderly might need help. They should be given a hand of support.

– The elderly might sometimes find it difficult to follow directions. They should be asked where they are going and gently helped or guided.

– Most elderly face some problems with technology tools and often need help.

– Help could be provided by explaining a technological complexity in simple terms.

– If the elderly cause something to fall, they should not be blamed or looked at with pity. Things could be corrected. It is OK to pick it up and hand it back silently.

– It is natural that some elderly people have memory loss. They need to be given enough time to recall things rather than being urged to remember.

– Some elderly may suffer from hearing, sight, and speech difficulties, so one should be aware. Others should not ask for repetition of words or sentences.

– It is worth remembering that elderly people can be melancholy or distressed by loneliness; they generally feel happy when meeting others. Therefore, it is a responsibility to welcome and engage with them.

– In formal or informal functions and gatherings, the elderly should be given a kind of precedence.

– Usually, there should be priority seats for the elderly in public transportation.

PRIORITY SEAT

– Unfortunately, in some countries, there are still no such seats in public transportation. In this case, young people should remember to offer their seats.

– Similarly, in some countries, there is no lineup/queue priority or preference for elderly people in public places or public transportation stations. Young people should remember to offer their seats there as well.

People with Special Needs Etiquette

"Correction does much,
but encouragement does more." [6]

Due to certain inherent or acquired shortcomings, some people are unable to make use of full physical, behavioral, or mental skills. They are people with special needs.

Within the framework of their potential and abilities, they are people who have the same rights and responsibilities as others.

Governments, civil society associations, and international organizations usually have special programs and plans to take care of them and make the most of their capabilities.

People with special needs are not the responsibility of only their families, but the responsibility of all people, anytime and anywhere.

Many countries have provided the necessary environment and infrastructure to integrate people with special needs within their communities. However, many others have not yet done what is required in this regard. People with special needs in such countries can suffer quite a bit, as there are no preferential wheelchair ramps, seats, lifts, walking routes, or toilets in public places including banks, commercial centers, and public transportation.

It is worth mentioning that the proportion of people with special needs in any society is not small. It is estimated that 10 percent of the world's population has some kind of disability, and many of them live in developing countries, wherein they almost do not enjoy the necessary integration and

---

6 Johann Wolfgang von Goethe (1749-1832), German poet, novelist, playwright, and philosopher.

are unable to live and exercise their life at a decent standard of living.

Among them, there are talented people and even geniuses, who only need an opportunity, and perhaps some training and rehabilitation. The product of their creativity and skills would then be realized.

One should acknowledge their differences as they would acknowledge anyone else's uniqueness as "normal." One should not talk down to people with special needs.

▷ **Terminology Tips:**

– Several terms are outdated, such as "disabled," "handicapped," "crippled," or "retarded." These terms presuppose the lack of ability or inferiority of people with special needs. This is not true and such terms are offensive. They should be avoided entirely.

– Saying someone is "disabled" means that they are completely and physically unable to do anything. This is wrong and not the case.

– It can be said that someone "uses a wheelchair" rather than "is handicapped in a wheelchair."

– Saying that someone "has a visual disability" shows that they are healthy and capable but have a specific disability in eyesight.

– One should put the "person" first and say a "person with a disability."

– For example, saying a "person with Tourette syndrome," or a "person who has cerebral palsy" is best.

– It is impermissible to call a person with a mental disability "crazy," "mad," "insane," or "an idiot." Other similar expressions do not reflect the real case. "Insane," for example, means that someone is completely mindless, and this is not always the case for people with mental disabilities.

– Mental disabilities have so many degrees and types, some of which are noticeable and some which are not apparent.

– The following table shows which words and phrases to avoid and which to use:

AVOID	USE
affected by (name of the condition) victim of (name of the condition) suffers from (name of the condition)	He/she has has (name of the condition)
confined to a chair wheelchair-bound	uses a chair
mental patient insane mad	a person with a mental health condition
the blind	a person with visual impairment a person who is blind or partially sighted
able-bodied	Abled non-disabled
Spastic	a person with cerebral palsy

manic depression manic depressive	a person with bipolar disorder
mentally handicapped retarded backward	has a learning disability
Mongol mongoloid mongolism	a person with Down syndrome

It is worth mentioning that in the presence of people with special needs, it is acceptable to use phrases that include reference to vision, hearing, and movement like "see you later," "I have to walk there," "I would rather run to join my colleagues," "She spoke loudly, yet I did not hear anything."

Such phrases generally do not bother those who lack some of the capabilities mentioned.

› **Etiquette tips:**

– Some people with special needs require certain treatment, but they are principally normal people and should be dealt with on this basis.

– People with special needs should not be stared at. This behavior is insulting and lacks the minimum amount of politeness. It is annoying to them and their relatives and presumes they are strange.

– If a certain person with special needs is slow in motion or reaction, other people should be patient and not complain. Such a

– person has real reason to be so.

– When meeting a person with special needs, it should not be assumed in advance they need help. A person with special needs is accustomed to their condition and knows how to act in general.

– It is recommended to ask for permission from a person with special needs before assisting them.

– Any kind of help should be conducted the way a person with special needs decides. It is important to remember that any help should be offered without pity.

– A person with special needs might refuse an offer of assistance. This should be understood and accepted.

– One should speak with a person with special needs naturally, just as they would with anyone else. There is no need to resort to a louder or slower voice unless required.

– Speech should be directly addressed to the person with special needs and not through a third person.

– It is impermissible to ask a person with special needs any questions about the cause of their condition or anything similar.

– It is inappropriate to give a person with special needs advice about the treatment of their condition.

– To greet a person with special needs, one is expected to gently shake hands, even if he has a prosthetic hand (unless they appear to dislike a handshake).

- **Behavior towards a person with hearing impairment (partial or total):**

When speaking with a person using a hearing device in one or both ears, one's voice should be normal.

Louder voices can confuse the reception of the hearing system of someone using a hearing device.

When a person has a hearing impairment in one ear, one should sit next to the sound ear to be heard.

While talking to a person with a full hearing impairment, the movement of the lips should be normal; otherwise, they would be confused.

To enable a person with a full hearing impairment to read lips and interpret facial and eye expressions, the speaker's face should be in the light.

It is permissible to pat a person with hearing impairment gently on the shoulder or wave a hand, to draw their attention.

One should be patient, as they might have to repeat words so a person with a hearing impairment can read lips.

When talking to someone with a hearing impediment through an interpreter of sign language, visual communication should be maintained with the recipient rather than the interpreter.

A person with hearing impairment can become less social; therefore, they should be encouraged to participate in social life and family activities.

A noisy atmosphere or many people speaking at once could cause a person with hearing impairment discomfort or lead to reactions counter to what is intended. That should be understood and accepted.

Complete hearing disability coincides with at least some disability in speaking.

To communicate with a person with a complete disability in hearing and speaking, one can resort to sign language or writing if lip reading has not succeeded.

- **Behavior toward a person with partial or full impairment to speaking:**

When a person with speaking impairment expresses themselves, they should be given enough time to complete sentences without interruption.

When the person is doing their best to speak, they should be left to continue without the interference of someone else on their behalf. It is not necessary to claim understanding of what they have spoken if what they uttered is not clear.

If the person is not understood, they can be asked to repeat themselves as long as the request comes without any resentment, contempt, or sarcasm.

If the person is not understood, despite repetition, they can be asked to write it down.

- **Behavior toward a person with vision impairment (total or partial):**

Usually, the other senses of a person with visual impairment work very efficiently and perhaps more acutely than other people's senses. Therefore, a person with vision impairment generally speaks with appropriate volume and tone.

Still, when talking to a person with visual impairment, it is preferable to reduce noise, because they depend on hearing ability to understand.

It is not appropriate to knock on the table in front of them, for example. This might distract and confuse them.

If the person is on the street, due to the noise of cars and passers-by, they should be spoken with from a little closer distance.

When talking to a person with vision impairment, one should introduce themselves and, if possible, provide the names of the other people present.

In a room or hall, it is preferable to describe the place to them, as much as possible.

A person with visual impairment is usually proficient in walking on the street and moves freely with a white cane or a special dog.

▷ When guiding a person with vision impairment, one should:

· Introduce themselves and ask the person if they need assistance.

· Not insist upon trying to help if the offer of assistance is declined.

· Give them an arm (preferably folded) to hold or let them put their hand on one's shoulder.

· Lead them by half a step.

· Their hand should not be held. Otherwise, they might lose their balance.

· Inform them in advance when approaching a pavement, corner, curb, steps, stairs (say whether they go up or down), or a door.

· Guide them, on stairs, to find the handrail and locate the edge of the first step before proceeding.

· Use words such as "straight ahead," "turn left" and "on your right."

· Not point and say, "Go that way," or "It's over there."

· Mention any potential hazards ahead.

· Not grab their cane or a guide dog's harness. They are part of his privacy.

· If they sit and put their cane aside, one should not change its place unless they say to do so.

· Not pet, feed, or distract a guide dog. It is not a pet; it is a working companion on whom a person depends.

· By walking alongside them on the street, on the opposite side of the dog.

· When seen off, a person with visual impairment should not be left in the middle of a yard or open place. Instead, they should be escorted to the nearest wall or the side of a building.

· Usually, a person with partial visual impairment is unable to read some signs, indicators, or instruction boards. They need help if those signs are not lit or written in bold and clear letters.

▷ To help a person with visual impairment sit on a chair:

· Hold their hand and place it on the chair's arm and the chair's back.

· Move their hand to the chair's seat to let them know its depth and enable them to have a complete idea of the chair.

▷ To help a person with visual impairments to get into a car:

· Hold the person's hand, putting it on the car's door handle.

· Tell them if it is the front or rear door.

· Put their hand on the edge of the car's roof (when the door is opened), to let them know its height before getting in.

- **Behavior towards someone using a wheelchair:**

- **Talking to a person using a wheelchair:**

  – Do not approach them too closely.
  – Do not lean too much toward them.
  – As much as possible, do not put a hand on the wheelchair, as it is part of that person's own space.
  – When the conversation is long, one is recommended to squat at the eye level of the wheelchair user. Otherwise, the wheelchair user would be forced to raise their head for a long time toward the speaker and would become physically tired.

- **To help someone using a wheelchair who wants to descend a steep slope:**

  – Hold the two handles of the wheelchair's back.
  – Turn the wheelchair backward.
  – Draw it while moving backward down the slope.
  – Hold the wheelchair firmly to avoid sliding.

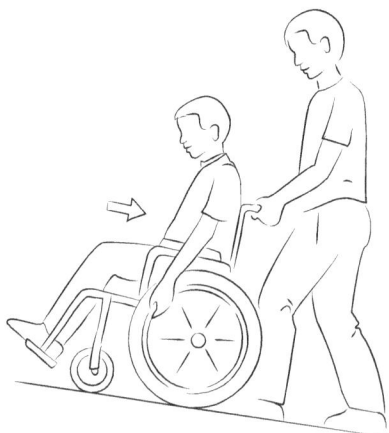

- **To help a person using a wheelchair ascend a slope:**

  – Hold the two handles of the wheelchair's back.
  – Push the wheelchair upward.
  – Hold the wheelchair firmly to avoid sliding.

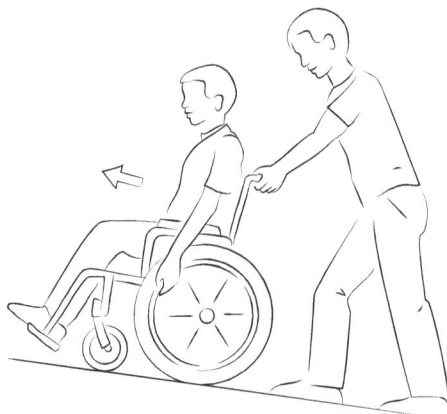

- **To help someone using a wheelchair ascend steps or stairs:**

  ▷ **One-person help:**

    · Regardless of how many people are giving help, the most important thing to remember is to be careful so the chair user will be safe.
    · Use the safety belt to prevent them from moving and causing an accident.
    · Place the back of the manual wheelchair against the first step.
    · Grasp the wheelchair handles firmly and press the rear wheels against the step.
    · Put your left foot on the first step and your right on the second step.

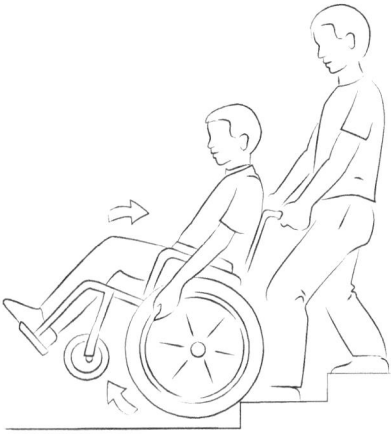

- Bend your upper leg and kneel a little.
- Tilt the chair so the front wheels rise from the ground.
- Pull the wheelchair up slowly and steadfastly while the front wheels are up the entire time, even when reaching the last step.
- Repeat this and remember the best way to help them climb stairs is to move the chair one step at a time.
- When passing the last step and being at the top of the staircase, the chair is gently tilted forward so the front wheels safely touch the ground.

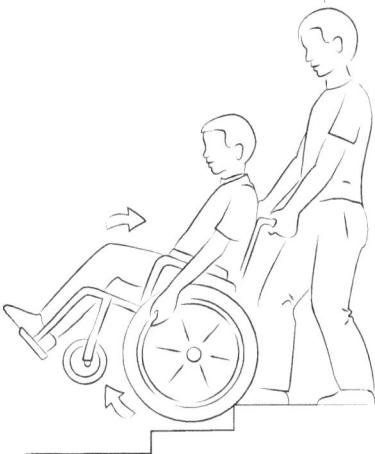

▷ **Two-person help:**

- The strongest person should be the one behind the wheelchair grasping the back handles, while the other is in front.
- Place the back of the manual wheelchair against the first step.
- The stronger person's foot should be a step above and be ready to lift the wheelchair by the handles.
- The other person should be standing in front of the chair holding on to the frame just above the chair's front wheels, avoiding any removable parts.
- They tilt the wheelchair backward and make sure only the rear wheels of the wheelchair are on the ground.
- Simultaneously, the two helpers lift the chair and roll it up so that the rear wheels rest on the first step.

- The same is to be done for the other steps that follow.
- The two helpers should make sure that after every step, they stop and find their balance point before moving to the next step.
- When passing the last step and being at the top of the staircase, the chair is gently tilted forward so the front wheels safely touch the ground.

▷ **Multiple people help:**

· To climb several steps in a single movement, it is essential to have the help of several people.

· The chair must be lifted by the frame, as the helpers move up the stairs.

· In this case, they can climb several steps at a time.

▪ **To help someone using a wheelchair descend steps or stairs:**

▷ **One-person help:**

· Grasp the wheelchair's back handles firmly and carefully move back the chair close to the edge of the first step.

· Put your right foot on the second step and move back with your left foot to keep your balance and control the chair movement.

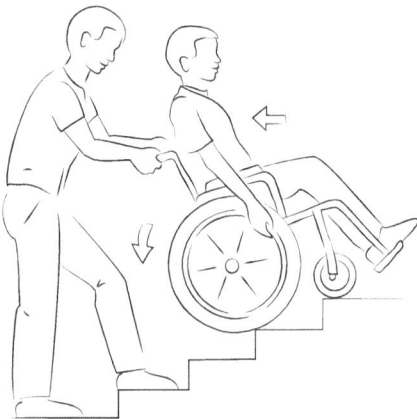

· Tilt the chair so that the front wheels rise from the ground.

· Slowly and steadfastly draw the chair and let the rear wheels rest on the second step.

· Go down further by repeating the same process and moving down one step at a time, while the front wheels are up until reaching the last step.

▷ **Two-person help:**

· The first person stands behind the chair holding its two back handles, tilting it down slightly so the front wheels rise from the ground.

· The second holds the chair frame close to the front wheels and raises the chair.

· Simultaneously, the first one slowly and steadfastly pushes the wheelchair while the large wheels move down the step.

· The second person moves backward, just holding and raising the chair (close to the front wheels).

· Both should try to synchronize, as much as possible, their movement down the steps so the chair user would be safe.

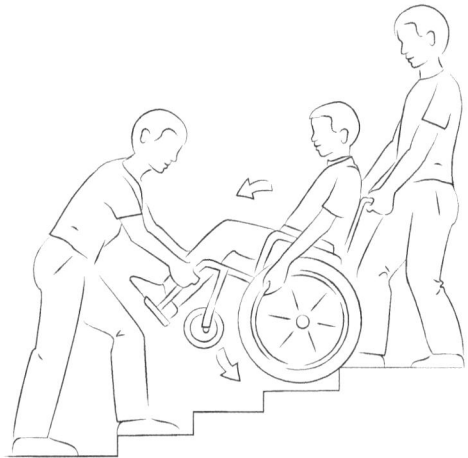

▪ **To help a person using a wheelchair at the elevator:**

· To enter the elevator, precede the person using the wheelchair.

· Keep pressing the "open" button on the control panel.

· Ask the person using the wheelchair to enter.

· When sure the person in the wheelchair has entered, press the required floor button.

- **If a person falls from their wheelchair:**

▷ **One can help by:**
- Asking people to stay away for a moment.
- Asking the person about the proper way to help.
- Behaving according to what they say to avoid hurting them physically.

- **Behavior toward a person with an invisible impairment:**

Some people might have conditions that one cannot see, for example, heart disease, cancer, asthma, or Alzheimer's. Do not look impatient.

It is not easy to know when someone has an invisible impairment unless they say so or make a request to indicate it. For example, they might ask to sit in a chair instead of standing in the queue.

People with invisible impairments should be dealt with carefully, kindly, and with respect.

People with invisible impairments should be given preference.

Some people have other kinds of invisible impairments, such as epilepsy.[7]

A person with epilepsy might suddenly suffer an epileptic seizure that makes them unexpectedly and temporally ill.

During an epileptic seizure, there is nothing to be done except prevent the person from hitting their head on something solid. For this reason, one should try to cushion the person's head, and try to turn them on their side.

Furthermore, there is no need for CPR (cardiopulmonary resuscitation) and they should not be given anything to drink or to eat.

When an epileptic seizure ends, such a person will be exhausted and confused about what has happened.

They should be treated with the utmost care until they regain strength.

- **Etiquette and behavior toward children with special needs:**

Many people do not know how to interact appropriately with children with special needs. Some even feel afraid.

People should remember children with special needs are sensitive and need care and affection.

These children need much care and attention to acquire skills and language.

They need social interaction to develop mental and physical abilities.

It is not easy for children to express their feelings and emotions.

The most important task is to make them feel they are like the other children.

A child with special needs requires encouragement, kindness, and tenderness, but not pity.

It should be remembered that a child with special needs usually conceives their ideas about themselves through how others treat them. If people act kindly, gently, and respectfully, they will feel appreciated for whom they are and will reciprocate that appreciation toward others.

---

7 Some intellectuals, including the Russian writer Fyodor Dostoevsky (1821-1881) had epilepsy.

Children with Down syndrome often can independently move, go up and down stairs, eat, go to the bathroom, and change clothes.

Children with Down syndrome can express their feelings, and, in most cases, can integrate into society.

What children with Down syndrome need from others is no more than a person who is patient and gives them proper opportunities.

> **Etiquette tips:**

– Maturing and developing the ability to acquire skills might be a bit slow among some children with special needs.
– A child with special needs should be listened to without complaint.
– A child with special needs should be given enough time to express themselves how they like, even if some of what they say is not understood.
– A child with special needs should not be dealt with indifferently.
– Lack of effort to integrate a child with special needs may push them to socially withdraw, retreat, and become a reticent child.
– While growing up, a child with special needs, like other children, needs to be encouraged to follow and do what is positive. Meanwhile, adults can correct their mistakes carefully and respectfully.

– One should address a child with special needs using a normal voice and wait for their reaction.
– One should expect and accept that some reactions of children with special needs could be inappropriate.
– When meeting or receiving a child with special needs, one should introduce themselves, shake hands, and smile to make them feel confident and safe, especially if they respond to physical contact.
– Calmly and naturally, the child can be asked their name. If they do not respond, one should not insist but rather ask their companions.
– If someone has their children accompanying them, they are expected to ask them to behave kindly and help them break any barriers of fear they might have of a child with special needs.
– To avoid causing any child to feel lonely and alienated, children should be encouraged to play with children with special needs.

• **Behavior toward children with autism.**[8]

Autism is usually characterized by:
– Impaired social interaction.
– Impaired verbal and non-verbal communication.
– Restrictive and repetitive behavior.

---

8 According to the Great Britain's National Autistic Society, the specific pattern of abnormal behavior first described by Leo Kanner is also known as "early infantile autism." Kanner made no estimate of the possible numbers of people with this condition, but he thought that it was rare (Kanner, 1943). Over 20 years later, Victor Lotter published the first results of an epidemiological study of children with the behavior pattern described by Kanner in the former county of Middlesex, which gave an overall prevalence rate of 4.5 per 10,000 children (Lotter, 1966).

▷ Children with autism can have the following traits:

- Live in their own repeated world.
- Have difficulty acquiring language and communicating even with their parents.
- Do not interact socially and try to avoid others.
- Cannot differentiate between dangerous and safe things.
- Need a safe environment provided for them.
- Do not know how to protect themselves.
- Can have trouble understanding words.
- Here are some guidelines for interacting with children with autism:
- They should be addressed with simple sentences, as much as possible, without choosing new words. You should use a consistent tone of voice, facial expressions, and gestures.
- It is necessary to know sounds, expressions, and gestures that attract their attention and learn to use them without too much repetition.
- The children should not be exposed to new situations without their parents. New situations cause tension, and possible screaming or outbursts.
- The children's routine should not be interrupted or broken; this may cause tension, anger, and screaming.
- One should not ignore them and try to understand them as well as possible. Ignoring or neglecting them may cause their annoyance and anger.
- Despite their condition, they are still children and need guidance in how to learn and mature.
- Develop ways to encourage them to socialize, be cheerful, and laugh.
- Attention should be paid to their tactile senses.
- Many of them have hypersensitivity to light, sound, touch, taste, and smell.
- The simplest physical contact, such as touching or hugging, might upset them.
- Some children with autism are talented in activities that depend on repetition, such as playing music, painting, and sculpting.

Patient's Etiquette

*"There are no incurable diseases
- only the lack of will."* [9]

Sickness is a provisional and interim case that everybody is vulnerable to experiencing. This chapter will not address the "doctor- and nurse-to-patient etiquette," but rather the visitor's behavior toward a patient and a patient's behavior toward others.

› **Etiquette tips for visiting a patient:**

- Visiting a patient encourages and supports them, strengthening social bonds.
- A visitor should have their hands washed before and after visiting a patient, so germs aren't transported to or from the hospital.
- Most hospitals have visitation rules posted in or near the main lobby. The visitor can read them before visiting a patient.
- Visitors should offer support to a patient.
- Unless a visitor is the spouse, parent, or child of the patient, they should not exceed the time limit decided by the doctor or the hospital. It is usually about 15 to 20 minutes. This makes sure a visit does not interfere with a patient's need for rest.
- If a patient shows that they want to be alone, their wish should be respected.
- If, for any reason, doctors come to perform an examination, visitors should leave the room and wait patiently.

---

9   Avicenna (Ibn-Sina) (980-1037), An Arab-Persian philosopher and physician whose medical work Qanun was of great influence on medieval medicine in Europe until the 17th century.

- If a visitor feels the need to cry or is getting mixed emotions, they should step outside the room for a while, take deep breaths, and return when feeling better.
- A visitor should keep the noise down and walk quietly, especially if a patient is in a semi-private room with a roommate.
- It is important to remember the hospital is not a place for loud voices and booming laughter.
- If another patient is sharing the room, talking about matters of a personal nature should be avoided.
- Pity is unacceptable and has nothing to do with sympathy and the spirit of solidarity with the patient.
- Unless the patient asks a visitor to sit beside them on the bed, one should not do that.
- Kissing and hugging should usually be avoided, as the patient can be weak and could be more susceptible to harm from an illness, infection, or disease.
- The visitor's cellphone should be put on silent or vibrate mode.
- The visitor should keep their hands off all medical equipment. It is never permissible to touch or reset anything.
- As some patients may have allergies or adverse reactions to fragrances, a visitor should not wear overpowering perfumes or heavily scented cosmetics.
- At the hospital, a visitor is supposed to be as positive as he can and smile if appropriate. They should not share negative past experiences in the hospital.
- The patient should not be stirred emotionally. Any prompt feelings or excitement might hinder recovery and even cause the aggravation of a condition.

- The conversation should be light, avoiding business, politics, or anything that may hinder the patient's recovery.
- When asking about a patient's health condition, questions should be general and avoid going into details.
- A patient might not know a lot about their illness, or some details might embarrass them.
- Sending flowers to a patient is the most common choice, but they should not be large bouquets.
- It is recommended that flowers should be odorless (or artificial). Some people might have allergies or sensitivity to pollen and smells.
- Flowers can be replaced by other gifts such as chocolate, sweets, books, and magazines.
- Patients should not be called by phone unless permitted.
- Except for some special cases, hospital administrations prevent visiting patients who are in the intensive care ward. The health of the patients in this case is delicate and contact with visitors is prohibited.

- **Patient behavior:**

Regardless of the patient's health conditions, there are some expectations around their behavior toward visitors:

· No one expects the patient to be particularly cheerful in the hospital. If they do not feel like smiling, visitors, doctors, nurses, and therapists will understand.
· The patient may try to be calm and limit severe mood changes as much as possible.
· The patient should try to best tolerate physical pain as much as possible, so as not

to increase the anxiety of family, relatives, and friends.

· The patient should not involve all others in the explicit details of their illness and pain.

· The patient still should cooperate with the medical staff and do everything possible to participate in their healing.

· The patient must abide by the instructions of doctors, nurses, and therapists.

· The patient should not take advantage of their weakness to overburden those around him with requests.

· The patient should show full respect toward nurses and respect their competence. They are not babysitters.

· The patient is expected to thank and be grateful for those working at the hospital as well as visitors.

Etiquette Toward Misconduct

"Let him who is without sin cast the first stone."[10]

People, whether they are of standard intelligence or genius, young or old, are liable to have faults and misconducts. An Arab proverb says:

> **" He who belongs to Adam's lineage commits mistakes. "**

Here, I will not try to handle the ethical, legal, or philosophical aspects of this subject and the classification of people as moral, immoral, good, sinful, etc.

I would rather leave this complicated matter and all its tangled details to philosophers, reformers, and ethicists.

What is important to consider in this chapter is that all cultures generally urge tolerance, forgiveness, and good treatment of others' faults.

Abu Hayyan al-Tawhidi[11] said:

> **" He who enjoys tolerance and forgiveness can enjoy the other's companionship. "**

10 Jesus Christ, The Bible: Gospel of John 8:7.

11 Abu Hayyan al-Tawhidi (923-1023), an Iraqi thinker who was one of the most influential intellectuals of the 10th century. Historian Yaqut Al-Hamawi described him as "the philosopher of litterateurs and the litterateur of philosophers."

Similarly, Leo Tolstoy[12] said, "The closer people are to the truth, the more tolerant they are of the mistakes of others."

› Tips to consider:

- With goodwill, some obvious mistakes could be corrected, while some other hidden ones could sometimes be ignored, especially since "not every mistake is a folly," as Cicero[13] said.
- While handling another person's mistake, long arguments should be avoided.
- Attention to a certain mistake should be given without pushing the mistake beyond that incident. Otherwise, the offender might link the mistake with their dignity, trying to defend both instead of correcting the mistake.
- If the offender feels they are underestimated, they could be provoked and react in a hostile way.
- Blaming the offender does not usually lead to a positive result, so it should be avoided. To paraphrase the poet Bashar ibn Burd[14]: If you always blame friends, a day will come when you will not find anyone to blame.
- When addressing someone's mistake, it is possible to apply simple tactics, such as using the phrase "I have heard that you have done that, but I do not think that is true," or other similar phrases, instead of directly accusing anyone of committing this and that mistake.

▷ Suggested etiquette tips:

In the following phrases saying a person is "**wrong**," word choices range from severe to friendly.

1. That's wrong.
2. You're wrong.
3. No, that's all wrong.
4. You made an error.
5. You made a mistake.

— The expressions in 1 to 5 are very severe. However, you might still use them in emergencies or safety situations where correcting the matter quickly is more important than the relationship.

— Expressions 6 to 11 begin with a softening phrase:

6. I'm sorry to disagree, but...
7. I'm afraid you're mistaken in that...
8. Actually, I think you'll find that...
9. Actually, I don't think that's right.
10. I'm afraid that is not quite right.
11. I don't think you're right about that.

These expressions help allow the wrong-doer to appreciate your message without being offended.

— In expressions 12 to 16, by referring to the mistake as a glitch, bump, hiccup, hurdle, or slip-up, attention is drawn to the need to correct the mistake rather than just focusing on who made the mistake.

12. There's a slight hurdle for us to discuss.
13. This slip-up will take us just a minute to correct.

---

12 Count Lev Nikolayevich Tolstoy (1828-1910), usually referred to in English as Leo Tolstoy, a Russian regarded as one of the greatest authors of all time.

13 Marcus Tullius Cicero (106-43 BC.), Rome's greatest speaker, who was a politician, philosopher, writer, and orator.

14 Bashar ibn Burd (714-783), an Arab poet.

14. There are a few small bumps for us to fix.

15. Let's take care of a few hiccups here.

16. There's a minor glitch to correct.

Such expressions suggest that anyone could make this type of mistake and therefore it doesn't reflect badly on the wrong-doer and protect his ego.

— In expressions 17 to 20 you begin with a question, then expand with the correct information you wish to contribute.

17. Would you be open to a different approach to this problem?

18. Where did you hear that/find that information?

19. Why do you believe/think that?

20. I'm curious about that. Could we take another look at it?

When using these expressions, you may smile and make eye contact.

— The expressions 21 to 24 use the modifying verb "may" or "appears to be" or "looks like" to express the possibility of an error and suggest a second look at the problem.

21. Perhaps there may have been some confusion here.

22. This looks like an oversight.

23. It appears to be a mistake.

24. You may have made a mistake.

With these expressions, embarrassment for both parties is avoided.

Etiquette Toward Enmity

*"You should not have enmity with the crocodile
if you are living in the water."*[15]

In the case of enmity, differences among some people may reach a sharp point, to the extent that brusqueness and perhaps hatred may become deeply formed, habitual behavior. How could one behave in a situation like this when they meet an antagonist?

> **Etiquette tips:**

– Abuse should not be faced by counter-abuse or revenge.
– One should control their mood and temper, curb anger, and ignore the antagonist's presence. "Anger can destroy us individually," Seneca[16] said.

– When inviting some people to a banquet, the host should not invite people who are antagonists of other invitees, which avoids embarrassing or disturbing those attending the event.
– If invited to a certain gathering and getting surprised by the presence of an antagonist, one should be calm and not show discomfort.
– Etiquette often demands that one pretends to be pleased to see people they would like not to see, temporarily assuming the guise of friendship. Such mild "hypocrisy" is preferable to injuring the feelings of those who mistakenly bring antagonists together.

---

15 Hindi proverb.
16 Lucius Annaeus Seneca (4 BC-65 AD), a Roman Stoic philosopher, statesman and dramatist.

- One of the skills that could be resorted to is the ability to miss seeing one's enemy. It is not necessary to either socialize with the person or make a scene. It is better to look beyond and not greet them.
- Another tactic is to say, "Excuse me" and remove yourself as if called away.
- If one is obliged to shake hands with an antagonist, they are recommended to do only that. In this case, one would not have to make eye contact during the handshake, displaying implicit disrespect.
- If one is obliged to sit next to an antagonist, one should do so calmly. Showing some indifference is enough.
- If there are some inappropriate comments by an antagonist, it is better to ignore them as much as possible.
- In any case, it is important to remember that if a dispute or quarrel happens between two people at someone's house, it would be an unfortunate incident for both parties as well as an insult to the host.

Foreigner and Visitor Etiquette

"How nice when foreigners become friends and how awful when friends suddenly become foreigners."[17]

A foreigner is a person belonging to a foreign country. The person might be a visitor, a tourist, an immigrant, a refugee, etc.

› **Etiquette tips:**

The dweller's behavior toward foreigners:
- Foreigners are supposed to be well received and given a particular treatment in some situations.
- Traditions and customs of the foreigner's country should be respected, regardless of one's opinion about them.
- One should not be surprised at some behaviors of foreigners that seem unfamiliar.
- Foreigners' languages and accents should not be ridiculed. Some mistakes of this kind could easily be ignored.
- Political stands based on the foreigners' country should not be criticized unless the relationship has become close enough to allow such kind of disclosure.
- Any criticism is supposed to be against the government and not the people of the foreigner's country.
- It is impermissible to insult or disrespect the foreigner's feelings about their country.
- Excessive care of the foreigner, to the extent of giving up local customs and traditions to satisfy him, is not required.

---

17 Nagib Mahfouz (1911-2006), an Egyptian writer who won the 1988 Nobel Prize for Literature. He published 34 novels, over 350 short stories, dozens of movie scripts and five plays.

– Trying to create an environment for a foreigner that corresponds to their own country is undue care. It is preferable to present a foreigner with local kinds of food. That would be an additional cultural experience, which gives an idea about eating styles and cuisine that differ from what is familiar.

▷ The foreigners' behavior toward the dwellers:

It is important for a foreigner to remember that they are in a foreign country and to treat the local population with full respect.

It is expected that a foreigner will conduct themselves in an appropriate manner and utilize polite expressions such as "please" and "thank you," or their translatable equivalents, when necessary. Such phrases are remarkably concise and straightforward, yet their impact can be profound.

A foreigner should not assume that it is the duty of the local population to adapt to their own values and culture. It is advisable for them to adopt a slightly condescending attitude.

In all cases, a foreigner should adhere to the golden rule of etiquette: "When in Rome, do as the Romans do."

Section Nine

Police Etiquette

"Custom and law are sisters."[1]

All police and security forces, with their various agencies and organs, such as Public Security, Customs Officers, Military Police, Civil Police, Traffic Police, etc., have specific tasks, under relevant laws and regulations, to maintain the security and safety of people, enable them to conduct their life affairs, and preserve public order.

There is not enough space to elaborate on many details concerning police and security forces.

What is most important is to highlight some relevant behaviors that apply to police forces and citizens.

- **Behaviors of police towards citizens:**

· The police officer must not discriminate between people, regardless of their gender, race, status, or rank. While applying law and order, all police officers must observe the dignity of all people, regardless of their breaches or actions.

· All police officers should have the ability to endure intense contact with citizens, as well as the ability to implement laws effectively.

· At airports, border centers, and ports, which are among the most crowded public places, police officers should have the highest standard of professionalism.

─────────── 1 Slovak Proverb.

· Police officers should know how to deal with different types of visitors and foreigners from various backgrounds and cultures.

· If a customs officer discovers a minor, unintentional breach committed by a citizen or a foreigner, the police can gently warn them so such a breach would not be repeated.

· If the breach is deliberate, unjustified, and in clear violation of law, the police officer should certainly resort to the legal procedures and regulations without hesitation, but without violence or insulting the violator.

· Police officers are supposed to know the diplomatic immunities and privileges stipulated by international agreements and conventions.

· Diplomatic immunity does not mean diplomats are exempt from legal accountability if they commit a breach or violate the laws of the country where accredited.

· If a citizen violates any traffic rules, a traffic officer will require them to pull over before enforcing the relevant rules.

· The officer will approach and identify themself and tell the citizen the reason for pulling them over.

· The officer will ask for the driver's license, registration, and possibly an insurance card.

· It is no longer acceptable for some police and security officers to not respect the basic human rights granted to all people, such as their constitutional right to live in dignity, even if breaching the law. Means of handling irregularities, of all kinds, are stipulated in all national laws of all countries.

· None of the laws gives the right for any police officers, for whatever reason and pretexts, to disrespect, insult, or violate the human rights of people.

▪ **Etiquette of citizens toward police officers:**

Citizens are required to show respect for the police officers who maintain the state's prestige and authority.

In general, people should help the police and security forces fulfill their duties.

If any police officers commit a mistake, it should be considered as an individual action, rather than as a general practice.

The person who commits a traffic breach and is signaled by an officer to pull over is required to:

– Turn off the engine and wait until the officer approaches.

– Stay inside the vehicle.

– Turn on the dome light (car interior light) if it is dark.

– Roll down the window all the way.

– Show driver's license or vehicle registration when asked by the officer. It is not necessary to reach for it without being asked first.

– Keep hands visible and placed on the steering wheel.

– Avoid any suspicious behavior.

– Respond to questions politely without being combative.

– Accept comments without being engaged in discussions and objections.

Secretarial Etiquette

*"A successful boss needs
a talented secretary."*[2]

In any workplace, secretaries are important staff members. Their job is linked with significant tasks that are no longer limited to making and responding to calls for the boss or arranging meetings and appointments. Many executive and priority functions are now the responsibility of a secretary.

Although the scope and content of a secretary's duties depend on the status of their bosses, they hold positions of great responsibility.

A chief executive's secretary would naturally hold wider responsibilities than one who works for the head of a department.

To be successful, a secretary in today's workplace must have good manners and possess the right skills and understanding of the workplace policies and procedures.

Anyhow, in this connection, I will not talk about the various secretarial assignments and responsibilities, but rather about the secretary's behavior concerning etiquette, especially when in contact with clients and other important visitors.

› **Etiquette tips:**

– Practicing a few common rules of business etiquette can help a secretary create the most positive impression of a supervisor and company. A secretary's conduct directly affects a supervisor's credibility as well as that of the workplace.

---

2 The author.

- Simple manners in the workplace are not always noticed but bad manners certainly are. To get ahead and stay ahead, simple courtesy can make a secretary stand out.
- Whether face-to-face, on the phone, or in emails, a secretary should always know when and how to say please and thank you.
- A secretary must adhere to the workplace dress code. If there is no such code, the secretary should maintain a respectable appearance and know how to choose conservative (formal or casual) and neat attire. A secretary should set an example for the rest of the staff.
- A female secretary should avoid tight or revealing clothing as well as short skirts. Inappropriate dress is a call for others to overlook her skills.
- A secretary is required to keep proper makeup and hair.
- According to the workplace dress code, a female secretary might be required to wear flat, closed-toe shoes. However, in all cases, she should avoid sneakers or flip-flops.
- A secretary should pay attention to personal grooming and hygiene.
- To appear professional, a secretary should have proficiency in answering phone calls, distinguishing voices, and remembering names as well as important dates and events.
- To maintain a professional workplace environment and be productive, a secretary must possess basic communication skills, including telephone or in-person conversations. A secretary must rely on professional expressions, write and respond to emails efficiently,
coordinate schedules, and prepare correspondence.
- A secretary must know the order of precedence and position of everyone they communicate or deal with.
- At all times, a secretary has to smile and greet visitors in a friendly, courteous, appropriate, and professional manner.
- In addition to complete knowledge of table etiquette, a secretary should know how banquets are held. A boss may invite people to dinner from time to time and assign a secretary to arrange that.
- A secretary must manage her emotions carefully, especially anger, in order to always appear calm, polite, and respectful.
- For business etiquette purposes, a secretary is required to create a positive first impression by maintaining a clean and well-organized workspace.
- A secretary should not leave papers or magazines scattered throughout the work area.
- A secretary must keep all personal items and confidential files out of the visitors' sight.
- A secretary must be frank, and sincere and maintain the secrets of their boss and workplace.
- A secretary should have the spirit of service and the ability to help and lighten the work of their boss.
- A secretary should show initiative and not wait idly for the orders of their boss.
- With a boss, a secretary should have friendly but impersonal relationships.
- With co-workers, a secretary should be kind without having too many personal relationships.

- In case the boss has no time to meet others, for whatever reason, the secretary should find the proper way to apologize to clients, employees, and others.
- The secretary, who says to someone "The boss does not want to meet anyone," or "The boss has important work," does not recognize the etiquette boundaries of a secretary.
- Professionally, a secretary apologizes by saying, for example, "The boss would like to meet you, but they're busy with a meeting that could take a while. May I take your phone number to have them call you later?"
- Any unprofessional comments by a secretary would hurt the boss and show the inexperience of the secretary.
- If a boss is in a meeting that has taken much time at the expense of other scheduled meetings, the secretary should recognize possible ways to help end the meeting. One tactic is to enter the meeting room and give the boss a written note.

Workplace Etiquette

"Doing little things well is a step towards doing big things better."[3]

Due to the requirements of modern life and all its social, economic, and administrative aspects, offices in public and private, businesses, banks, and other places have become a main feature of people's daily lives.

Everywhere, a large portion of the population is employees. Those who are not employees go to offices from time to time for various purposes.

There are some days when employers and employees spend more time at their offices than at home. Therefore, it's important to remember that work isn't a place to forget manners.

Having etiquette at a workplace is essential to foster a professional and civilized environment for anyone who interacts there.

Workplace etiquette is a set of standards on how to act with colleagues, bosses, business partners, and clients.

▪ Employee's etiquette:

·   Regardless of one's job rank, any employee should remember they are assigned to their job and receive a salary to serve the workplace, company, citizens, and customers.

·   An employee should be punctual and arrive on time. It is bad form (and possibly grounds for termination) to

---

3   Vincent Van Gogh (1853-1890), a Dutch Post-Impressionist painter who became very influential in the history of Western art. His paintings are characterized by bold colors and expressive brushwork.

frequently show up late. Sure, some extenuating circumstances may cause someone to be late occasionally, but that should not be the norm. Anyhow, it's important to call ahead to let people know when one is running late.

· At work, one should treat all clients equally regardless of their different statuses and ranks.

· One should follow the office dress code. If the dress code is "casual," employees should still come into work smartly dressed.

· Clothes should be well-maintained, clean, and without logos.

· At meetings, if the employee is unsure of what dress code would be suitable, the safest option is to opt for classic attire with colors such as black, dark blue, or dark grey.

· At work, one should know the etiquette for introductions and greetings, telephone etiquette, correspondence etiquette, conversation etiquette, clothes etiquette, banquet etiquette, and communication skills in general.

· At work, one should be friendly when entering the office each morning, and it's the norm to greet co-workers.

· At work, one should be open-minded, calm, and never arrogant or nervous with others. They should not overstep boundaries.

· Whether one works in a private office, a desk in a cubicle workplace, or sits in an open space with dozens of co-workers,

an employee should respect everyone else.

· At work, one should make eye contact, give attention, and turn towards people when they are conversing.

· At work, one should be alert. Sleepiness looks bad in the workplace.

· At work, one should interact with others gently, and genuinely smile.[4] There's no reason for anyone to act snobby. Kindness and courtesy count.

· During meetings, an employee should speak without interrupting others and be mindful of taking turns. One should allow each person to complete a thought and interject only when they have something constructive to say.

· As a rule, one should put their cell phone away or on silent mode at work. If one needs to take a personal call, they can step away from their desk to avoid distracting coworkers. Using a cell phone during meetings is a major distraction for others. Plus, it makes the person using the phone appear distracted and inconsiderate.

· At work, one should be a team player. Their coworkers and supervisors will appreciate that, which makes the employee a more valuable candidate for future promotion.

· When working in an open office space, an employee should keep their computer and phone muted, so that every email or message does not alert everyone on the floor.

---

4 Some companies, hotels, and banks conduct periodic competitions to choose the employee who smiles the best. It encourages employees to be gentle with clients and everyone they come across.

- Most companies exert major effort, in many ways, to provide a bright image of their headquarters as well as the services offered to their clients, colleagues, and everyone with whom they interact. Such an effort will be in vain if clients come to find a sullen receptionist or indifferent or brusque employees.
- With open office environments becoming the norm, personal workspaces are more public than ever.
- The employee's office should be clean, neat, and tidy, regardless of the availability of luxury furniture or not. Keeping an office orderly does not require big funds. One can imagine how annoying it would be to enter someone's office to find a careless employee with documents and papers scattered here and there, dust on shelves, and dirty curtains that have not been washed for a long time.
- If an employee has a cubicle, it's also good to be mindful of co-workers when it comes to maintaining that space. Messes should be kept to a minimum.
- While it is good to foster positive relationships between supervisors and subordinates, an employee should be aware of crossing professional boundaries.
- Trying to become the best friend of your boss is generally not a good idea. Other people may perceive a supervisor as showing favoritism. This can damage the career of the best employees.
- Similarly, even if an employee is friendly with peers, they should be aware of crossing boundaries. Oversharing details of one's personal life is unprofessional no matter how close the team is.
- An employee should not gossip about a coworker or boss. One only hurts themselves by doing so. Moreover, today, in the era of social media, an employee should remember that nothing is "private" anymore. They should not complain about fellow workers or work on social media. Even if an account is private, what is posted could get back to colleagues.
- If an employee is mistaken or makes an error, they should be humble enough to take responsibility and apologize. The boss will see them as an honest, humble person who doesn't try to cover their tracks.
- Most workplaces and businesses require a certain amount of confidentiality. Trustworthiness is one of the most valuable commodities an employee can have, and they will be more valued for keeping their lips zipped.
- By entering the boss's office, the employee should be formally dressed (if there is no special uniform).
- When entering the manager's office, it is inadmissible for a male employee to have a jacket on his shoulders and his shirtsleeves rolled up.
- Unless a boss asks an employee to sit down in their office, one is expected to remain standing.
- It is not permissible for an employee to sit in a relaxed posture or cross-legged in the presence of their bosses.
- When a boss is discussing and giving instructions, an employee should not interrupt even if they know more than the boss.
- Whether in a meeting or one-on-one, a boss should be given the chance to finish what they're saying.
- If the employee is not convinced or even does not agree with a boss, they should

wait for the proper time to speak and politely express an opinion.

· Under all conditions, an employee should not quarrel with any peers in the presence of the boss. Criticism can be made in another civilized way.

· When it comes to opening doors and getting in and out of elevators, an employee is supposed to show respect to people who have seniority in the workplace.

· If entering a floor or the elevator at the same time as one's boss, an employee should be sure to hold the door open and allow the boss to enter first.

· If the elevator's full when someone is trying to get out, an employee who is in the way should not block the elevator door. The employee should simply exit the elevator altogether and then re-enter.

- **Etiquette of the boss:**

  A boss should understand that all parts of the headquarters should be elegant, neat, and tidy.

· A boss should not think having a luxurious office is enough to give a good impression about the company if the subordinates' offices are in complete disorder.

· A boss should always be well-dressed and set the tone for business and work attire. Clothes count.

· A boss, whether they like it or not, should set an example and be a role model. Employees will observe how the boss acts, dresses, and demonstrates other important professional traits.

· A boss should be modest, calm, and offer a friendly greeting each day, being

sincerely interested in anything subordinates say concerning work. A boss shows empathy during a conversation. Nevertheless, a boss should maintain a professional demeanor.

· If a boss, directly or through a secretary, receives a call from someone, they should not leave the person waiting too long on the phone, even if they are of a lower rank. This behavior has nothing to do with etiquette and requires an apology.

· Unless there's an emergency, an effective boss doesn't cancel meetings with subordinates or others at the last minute. This is especially unacceptable when traveling to meetings is involved. Canceling for any reason is a way of showing subordinates their time doesn't matter.

· If a subordinate commits a mistake, a boss should not consider that strange.

· The best way to handle a mistake is to call the employee alone to draw their attention to the error and inform them how to do things correctly. Consequently, the employee would maintain respect for a boss and would be less likely to feel insulted or embarrassed.

· In case a mistake is committed deliberately and intentionally, there are specific administrative and legal procedures to apply.

· Under all circumstances, a boss has no right to rebuke, reprimand, or yell at any subordinates in front of others. Such a behavior would never reflect strength. This would only cause subordinates to lose respect after witnessing clear evidence of weakness, lack of leadership skills, and a lack of self-confidence.

· It is natural for a boss to stay behind their desk for meetings, reports, conversations about work, and the like. But for anything not part of the daily routine, such as meeting a client or an interview, it is far better to greet others standing up. Some business executives keep a separate table in their offices for events like this.

- Similarly, a boss should sometimes ask employees to sit on a side sofa or chair, pull his chair around from behind the desk, and have more relaxed conversations with them. It can remove a barrier that might intimidate them.

- A boss is supposed to give feedback to subordinates positively. A boss should offer more compliments than complaints or attention to mistakes.

- A boss should encourage and recognize employee talents whenever something is accomplished well, keeping in mind that happy employees drive business success.

- Without paying compliments to employees, any boss will soon end up with a disgruntled herd.

- A boss should not forget facial expressions and work on their "boss face and smile." A boss who scowls, or maintains a harsh look, drives employees away. Nevertheless, a boss with too many grins encourages an overly lax atmosphere.

- A boss should not gossip or share too much of their personal life and, likewise, avoid pointed questions to employees about personal matters, such as marriage, finances, and children. A gossipy boss can seem insincere and even untrustworthy.

- A boss is supposed to stick to discussing the business world, competition, or other broad topics. And if a rumor spreads about the inner workings of the workplace, a boss should address it directly.

- A boss should be available when needed. They should not hide and sit in their office behind a closed door all day. This gives employees the impression they either do not care about them or do not want to be bothered with day-to-day workplace matters.

- It is said that a boss who treats employees with no compassion will lose both employees and customers. They are a "toxic boss."

- At social events, a boss is supposed to be the first to leave rather than hanging around a party too long. A boss needs to conduct themselves in a way that represents their status, which means no excessive drinking or telling off-color jokes.

- **Client etiquette:**

  A client/customer/citizen is expected to understand that employees are available to serve them but that employee time is limited and valuable. This takes into consideration that an employee has many tasks to do and many other clients as well. Therefore, any client should be precise, brief, and cooperative.

- The client's cell phone should be kept on "silent mode" until finishing their business and leaving. Otherwise, the client would disturb both other clients as well as employees.

- The motto, "The customer is always right" urges employees to give a high priority to client/customer satisfaction. Nevertheless, many argue that customers are sometimes right and sometimes wrong. So, a client should not misuse such concepts to violate good manners or harbor unrealistic expectations.

- Although not justified, an employee might lose their temper at times. This might be caused by stress, fatigue, or a variety of other reasons. Nevertheless, a client is expected to stay calm and perhaps try to find some manner of alleviating the distress.

- By having a calm reaction amidst an employee's bad behavior, the client would not allow things to deteriorate and would enable the employee to restore calmness, take responsibility, apologize, and do their best to again fulfill their duty.

Elevator Etiquette

"The elevator to success is broken,
take the stairs."[5]

Like other public places such as restaurants, workplaces, buses, trains, airplanes, etc., an elevator has best practices and rules to follow. These rules ensure everyone stays safe and comfortable and moves through the environment as efficiently as possible.

Elevator rides do not last long, but the space is small and the crowd can be large.

To make these short rides in a confined space bearable we all need to be courteous and considerate.

> **Etiquette tips:**

- Unless injured or unable to climb stairs or carry heavy objects, one shouldn't take the elevator for one or two floors (either up or down).

- While waiting for the elevator, always stand to the right outside the doors (never in front of the doors) so the left and middle are clear for those exiting the elevator.

- Only when everyone exits the elevator can one enter.

- If there are people in line ahead of you or people waiting before you let them enter first. It is not proper to cut the line.

- When the elevator doors open and you see it is full, don't try to squeeze into the elevator.

- Even if you have been waiting in line and the elevator fills with the person before you, wait patiently for the next.

- Don't be the person asking for the elevator to be held. If you cannot enter before the elevator doors close, then wait for the

---

5 Jenifer Jeanette Lewis (Born, 1957) is an American actress, singer, comedian, and activist.

next elevator politely instead of rudely asking someone to hold the elevator. The time of the people in the elevator is just as important as yours.

– When you step into an elevator, file in so others can board behind you or board on another floor.

– Stay farthest from the door if you will be the last person to step out. If you are traveling to the ground or topmost floor, it's better to stand farthest from the elevator doors after you board. This way you will avoid inconveniencing others.

– If you happen to be riding in the front, make sure to step off the elevator when the doors open on each floor. When in this position, hold the elevator with your hand as the people from the back of the elevator make their way out, and then go back inside.

– If you see someone running towards the elevator and it is not crowded inside, keep the door open for him.

– Men should allow women to enter and exit first by stepping aside and holding the door if possible. However, if the elevator is very crowded it is acceptable for men to exit before women.

– Similarly, to maintain a respectful environment, it is a best practice to allow elderly people and persons with disabilities to board elevators first.

– It is not proper to stand very close to people if the elevator is overcrowded and you can wait for the next one.

– If the elevator is crowded and you are near the buttons, you should push the buttons for the floor numbers for people not near enough to do so themselves. You can also ask someone who has entered what floor button they need pressed.

– Don't ask someone else to push the button for you unless you cannot reach the button yourself.

– Any elevator passenger should be mindful of and respect others' personal and intimate spaces in an elevator.[6]

– If the elevator is not crowded, stand at a distance from other people in separate corners.

– As a rule, it is best to face the elevator doors.

– If only two people are in the elevator, it's best to stand on opposite sides.

– If there are three to four people, stand in a corner.

– If there are five or more, spread out so each person has equal space.

– Arms and hands should be kept at your sides to avoid contact as you're already in someone's personal space.

– It is advisable to reconsider heavy colognes and perfumes, especially if you take elevators regularly.

– The smell in confined spaces can draw attention and annoy others.

– Try not to belch while riding in the elevator. If you do, excuse yourself.

– In elevators, quick eye contact, a smile, and a nod are appropriate. This is usually

---

6 During pandemics, such as the COVID-19 outbreak, wear a mask and do not get onto an elevator with more than three people. While boarding, stand on opposite ends of the elevator. However, members of the same family from the same residence can board an elevator regardless of number.

well-received by fellow riders. However, minimal eye contact is a standard.

- It never hurts to offer a simple greeting, like "Good Morning" or "Hello," especially if you're boarding with coworkers or neighbors.

- After entering an elevator, turn around and face the door. Keeping your back towards the door and facing the passengers is a huge break in etiquette and can make some people feel extremely awkward.

- Once you're on board, turn your focus to something/anything else in the elevator and give others the chance to enjoy the ride without inconvenience. Entering the elevator and staring into the face of someone else can be quite uncomfortable.

- Elevators contain limited space, but in busy office buildings, many people try to fit into one car. Unnecessary movements can annoy fellow passengers or cause you to make unwanted contact. Jiggling your leg, pacing, moving your arms, or other movements can result in bumping into other passengers.

- In elevators, most people are hesitant to engage in conversation. There is no need to start a conversation with people in the elevator, you can say a quick hello and wait for your floor.

- Whether to hold the elevator door for someone or not, has been a long-debated question. On one hand, it might seem like a matter of compassion (as you feel inclined to hold the door). On the other hand, you risk holding up the elevator for fellow passengers.

- Logically, if you're alone in the elevator, do what you think is right (holding the door or not). If you're riding with others, have a quick thought and decide whether to hold it or not.

—**When deciding whether to hold the elevator door or not, it can be helpful to use the following suggestions:**

- Don't hold the door if you are in an elevator full of people. You will be delaying everyone in the elevator and cramming one more person into a tight space.

- If you are alone in the elevator, it's good elevator etiquette to hold the elevator for a person approaching.

- Don't hold the door for a friend or colleague who has taken a quick side trip, such as to get coffee or go to the restroom.

- Never hold the door for more than 15 to 20 seconds on a crowded elevator.

- If the elevator is full, there's no shame in giving an apologetic expression and letting the doors close.

- If you are with someone, don't continue conversations while riding the elevator with someone else. Put the conversation on pause until you get to your destination.

- If you want to speak to a colleague in the elevator, do not do so loudly, and keep the conversation light.

- Never gossip or discuss personal or private information. Other riders do not necessarily want to hear or be part of that conversation.

- In the elevator, the cell phone should be holstered in a pocket. Talking on your cell phone while riding is an embarrassing and tactless act. Therefore, end all conversations before entering the elevator, and put the phone on mute until you exit again.

- If you're on a call with someone as you approach an elevator, tell them you'll call right back.
- Similarly, if you receive a call in the elevator (if there is a signal/WiFi coverage) you can answer and tell them you'll call back or decline the call and text that you'll return their call as soon as possible.
- Texting or looking at your phone is a common way to avoid eye contact with strangers. However, do not text in a crowded elevator. Operating your phone takes up space, which is limited in an elevator, and the movement can cause you to bump into people.
- When the elevator is packed and full of riders, the two closest riders to the doors should step out at any requested stops to allow riders in the back to exit without requiring them to squeeze out.
- When you step out of the elevator to make room for those leaving, be considerate and hold the doors to make reentry smooth.
- If you are in the back, announce your floor is coming up as it approaches. A simple "Excuse me, my floor is next," is enough. Then, make your way to the front, or wait until the elevator stops.
- When you reach your floor, get out in a quick and orderly fashion so those waiting to board can do so. Do not shove your way out or knock people over in the process.
- It is almost forbidden to eat or drink in the elevator because it can be messy and dangerous if the elevator is crowded.
- Furthermore, don't bring extremely smelly food onto the elevator. Instead, bring your food in containers.
- If you are carrying a bag or a briefcase, it should be set on the floor in front of you, or held close to your front.
- When carrying briefcases, purses, backpacks, shopping bags, or other bulky materials, keep them low, either directly in front of you or beside you. Legs take up less space than upper bodies, so there is more space for bags. Announce your exit as the floor nears, and excuse yourself if you accidentally bump someone when exiting.
- Inside the elevator, you may encounter people who have no regard for etiquette. Either ignore them or politely ask them to stop whatever is annoying you.
- If you are riding with children, never let them push all the buttons.
- If you are accompanied by a dog or other animal, let the elevator go and wait for the next one unless they are well-behaved and calm.
- If the elevator gets stuck, press the alarm button, call the fire department, sit inside, and wait patiently for them to arrive.

Section Ten

,

Travel and Transportation
Etiquette

"If you love your son, let him travel."[1]

In addition to etiquette inside the various forms of public transportation, such as cars, buses, ferries, trains, and planes, etiquette applies to people on the streets and roads. The following rules, standards, and behaviors are common in most countries of the world.

• Street etiquette:

Streets and roads are public and allow everyone the right to use them. They are not private property where one can behave and act the way they like.

- It is inappropriate to make noise in the street and disturb others.
- It is inconvenient to speak loudly by phone and disturb other passersby.
- It is not permissible to call a friend by shouting. This behavior is vulgar and

might awaken people sleeping, scare children, or just cause inconvenience.

- It is not permissible to whistle to draw the attention of others.
- At any time, it is rude to walk in the street in sleepwear.
- No trash or litter should be thrown on roads or streets, even if the garbage containers are far away.
- Paper scraps, for example, could be kept in one's pocket until arriving home.
- It is not permissible to spit in the street. Napkins could be used to avoid such disgusting behavior.
- It is unacceptable behavior to think the stumps of trees on sidewalks or pathways are places to throw garbage or cigarette butts.
- It is not preferable to smoke and eat in the street, although American etiquette

1 Japanese proverb.

is not as strict in this matter. The streets are not restaurants or cafeterias.

· It is not good behavior to chew gum in the street.

Unfortunately, public utilities in many countries do not take into consideration the requirements of people with special needs. Therefore, with their permission, assistance should be provided (if needed).

· It is rude to stand at the roadside or near doors to stare at women. No respectable man allows himself to behave this way.

· With her permission, a man holding an umbrella can assist a woman if she is without one during a sudden rain.

· If one stops a friend to talk about something on the sidewalk, and the friend apologizes for not having time, this should be accepted.

· If two people stop on the street to talk, they should stand aside on the pavement to allow people to move and pass freely.

· If someone wants to stop, to talk to another person, who is accompanied by others, they should first apologize to the people accompanying him.

· According to classic English etiquette, a man should not bow to a woman of his acquaintance if he meets her on the street unless she bows first. On the contrary, the other European etiquette affirms that a man may bow first.

· According to American etiquette, men and women are not required to bow to each other on the street.

· According to previous Western manners, when a man was accompanied by a woman and another man greeted her, he could reply on her behalf, even if he did not know that man. This rule has now been superseded.

· When a man encounters a woman of his acquaintance across the street and wants to walk with her on the sidewalk, he should cross the street to join her.

· One should not hesitate to assist a woman or elderly person who needs help on the street. Such help is usually simple but reflects a noble human attitude.

· When a person walks with one or more children on the sidewalk, they must be aware of their movement. For their safety, they should not be on the side next to the street.

• Driving etiquette:

Naturally, when someone owns a car, it means they have certain rights and responsibilities. In this part, I will not talk about the legal driving requirements that must be met by drivers, but about some etiquette that should be observed.

· Speed limits must be met, whether there are surveillance cameras or not. This behavior reflects one's respect for the law and care for everyone's safety.

· Drivers must drive within the lanes marked off with painted lines.

· Drivers should not move from one lane to another before giving the necessary signal with sufficient time and distance.

· Drivers must stop before the white pedestrian lines when the traffic light is red.

· Even if there is no traffic light, drivers must stop before the white pedestrian lines when there are people who want to cross the street, keeping in mind that passersby have priority.

- Car horns should only be used in emergencies to warn of a mistake or danger; otherwise, they harass and confuse drivers and disturb pedestrians.
- A car must be clean on both the inside and outside. The sight of a dirty car disturbs other people on the street.
- One who drives a car greets passersby whom they know, even if the driver has a higher rank.
- Litter must not be thrown from car windows. Roads and streets are not trashcans.
- The amber light of a traffic light is a sign of being ready to slow down rather than beat the red light. Only the green one indicates a time to accelerate.
- **Children, especially infants, should not be left in the car alone, however short the time. This is unacceptable and illegal and poses the threat of "vehicular heatstroke" and possible fatality.**
- Leaving a child for 14 minutes in a hot car is enough to make them suffer from a brain or kidney injury. The temperature inside a car can rise, in a warm environment, one degree every ten minutes; when the body temperature reaches 40 degrees, the body's internal organs would suffer. At 42 degrees, the child dies.
- Pets should not be left alone in cars for fear of "vehicular heatstroke." Animals like dogs or cats do not sweat, so their bodies heat up faster than human bodies.
- Drivers and riders must pay attention before opening a car door; a suddenly opened door might strike a running child, a person walking beside the car, or another passing car or bicycle.

▷ **Seating precedence in cars:**

The highest-ranked person has precedence and sits in the right rear seat.

If a host, a friend, a colleague, or the like are driving the car themselves, the person of precedence sits in the front passenger seat.

A wife sits beside her husband if he is driving the car, while the children sit in the rear seats.

With wife and mother, precedence is given to the mother, who sits in the right rear seat.

With wife, mother, and mother-in-law, precedence is given to the mother, who sits in the right rear seat.

• **Etiquette in Taxis/cabs:**

A wide variety of people, of different statuses, genders, and ages use taxis, which provide an important service.

While people must respect taxi drivers, and deal with them gently and tactfully, drivers in return are required to provide their services professionally while considering the following etiquette tips:

- Taxi users pay for the service offered; therefore, drivers must perform their duty toward them with care and commitment.
- Taxi drivers are expected to drive quietly, observe speed limits, and stop at specified places.
- It is impermissible for drivers to shout or dispute with passengers or other drivers.
- If there is a certain uniform chosen by an operating company, a taxi driver

should adhere to it and show respect for regulations.

- A plate should be installed inside the taxi, including the driver's picture, name, and car number.
- The tariff monitor should be kept in good condition and installed in a place that allows the passenger to see it.
- Drivers must not talk by cellular phones while driving; it is against the law and risks safety.
- It is impermissible to charge an amount exceeding that recorded on the tariff monitor.
- Taxi drivers are supposed to keep coins and small amounts of cash to make change; some passengers might have only large amounts of cash.
- When the passenger pays money that exceeds the charge, they still have the right to ask for the rest back. The driver should not ignore that.
- If the passenger offers money to the driver voluntarily for gratuity, the driver can accept it.
- Taxi drivers are supposed to consider the tastes of the passengers when they listen to music; in any case, it is preferable to keep the volume down on the stereo; for safety reasons, it is a priority to pay attention to sounds outside the car.
- While driving, the taxi driver should not maintain extensive dialogue with passengers, as talking could distract the driver's attention.
- The taxi driver should not overload the car trunk and leave its lid open.

- ## Etiquette in buses, ferries, metros/subways, and trains:

Public transportation, such as buses, ferries, metros/subways, trains, and airplanes has become an essential part of daily life, subjecting us to some of its circumstances and challenges. Public transportation could be a comfortable experience if everyone observes some relevant etiquette.

› ## Etiquette tips:

- In bus, metro, and train stations, as well as airports, people are expected to line up in queues when buying travel cards, checking documents, getting boarding tickets, etc.
- Passengers disembarking the bus, ferry, metro, and train station always have priority; therefore, new passengers should wait at both sides of the doors to avoid impeding the disembarking passengers. Parking time is limited so expedited movement is essential.
- Disembarking passengers should step off using the nearest door.
- Disembarking passengers should not stop on the platform near the doors, making it easier for new passengers to embark.
- Usually, buses have stop buttons that passengers nearing their destination press to alert the driver to stop.
- Priority is for people with special needs to get in and out of all means of transport.
- Seats should be given to pregnant

- women, parents with children, people with special needs, elderly people (over 60), and people who show signs of illness.
- It is impermissible to use obscene words or argue with someone rude or drunk; this might worsen the problem.
- Food is prohibited aboard public transportation, except for some light and dry foods that do not emit odors.
- Drinks stored in containers with caps that do not allow spilling are permitted.
- On board, mobile phones should be kept on silent or vibration mode, to avoid disturbing other passengers.
- Smoking is prohibited on all public transportation and in stations.
- Paper tissues or the like should be used to sneeze and cough.
- At bus and train stations, a passenger is supposed to keep silent except to ask for directions or about a destination.
- On short journeys, it is advised to keep silent, as there is no guarantee any of the other passengers will have time or the desire to talk.
- On long-distance trains, ferries, and buses, some travelers prefer silence but most travelers do not. Long-distance travel is exhausting and tedious, and it is possible to reduce burdens with some conversation.
- A passenger could start a conversation with a nearby passenger by tactfully introducing themselves as a means of discovering whether another would like to converse.
- It is not appropriate to speak loudly with friends and acquaintances at stations or on public transport.
- It is not permissible to go beyond the specified colored safety line on the platforms at bus, ferry, train, or metro stations. For reasons of security and safety, passengers should only proceed beyond the line after the carriage doors are open.
- After boarding, one should not stand close to the door, but move as far as possible toward the inner side and rear of the carriage to facilitate the movement of others.
- Passengers should be careful their bags and other objects do not hit others.
- In order not to impede the movement of passengers, bags, and sacks should not be left in the aisles of a bus or train.
- When a passenger stops, for any reason, on the stairs, escalator, and corridor of a station, they should be on the right side (in most countries) to give space for those in a hurry to pass on the left side.
- Pets and birds are generally not allowed in public transportation, but some small pets might be permitted if they are in pet carriers.

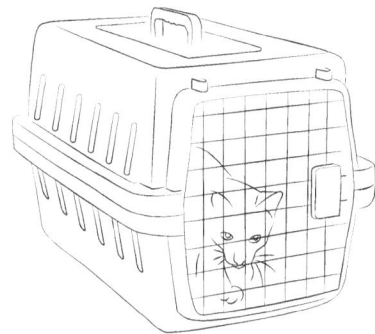

- In case of emergency, passengers should follow the printed and announced instructions.
- In case of an accident or a person falling on the track, for example, someone should immediately press one of the emergency buttons and wait for the security staff to come to help.
- It is advisable to avoid staring at others or showing surprise toward clothes, colors, hairstyles, etc.
- Men are supposed to offer help to women in lifting their bags to shelves and upper cabinets.
- Etiquette rules provide that a man ask the woman next to him to choose between his and her seat.
- If something falls from someone's pocket or bag, it is advisable to help them or at least not to obstruct them from picking it up.
- If a passenger loses something without noticing, they should be gently alerted or handed the item.
- The starting movement of trains or buses and their stops might be sudden and cause passengers to lose balance. Therefore, standing passengers are expected to hold the overhead handles or vertical and horizontal bars rather than nearby people.
- It is natural to apologize when someone bumps another inside a carriage when stepping on and off, or while moving among a crowded platform.
- Unfortunately, many men sit in public transport with their legs separated and take more space than necessary. This inappropriate behavior should be avoided.

- The ideal sitting posture for a man is to have the two feet crossed and knees slightly apart (ankle-lock position); or with his shoe soles on the floor, legs combined, and two hands on his knees.
- Trash, litter, food remnants, and other wastes should only be disposed of in trash bins to keep the seats, carriages, and stations clean.
- It is impermissible to write on carriage walls or cause damage to seats and signboards.
- **Public transport carriages are often crowded and might encourage opportunist pickpockets. Therefore, tourists should not give the impression they are foreigners by taking pictures and opening maps. If one does not live in the region or speak the language, they can become a target.**
- Some stations might not have elevators or escalators, or they might not be operating. It is nice and tactful to help others who need it, such as a woman with a heavy bag or lifting her baby's carriage up the stairs.
- In some stations, there might be musicians or painters (many who are talented), who perform for passengers while being rewarded with money. If possible, it would be kind to give these artists money.
- When giving money to musicians and painters in stations, the donor should not throw coins, but instead bend to put them in the hat, instrument case, or other container for this purpose. Respect is always required, with all people.

- ## Air travel etiquette:

It is said that one who has only seen their own country has only read the first page of the universe book.

Indeed, travel itself is considered a school, and many writers have mentioned the link between travel and knowledge, including the Egyptian writer Mustafa Amin [2], who suggested:

"One trip abroad equals one thousand books."

Travel expands people's knowledge and experience of other cultures. It is said, "He, who lives long may see so many things; but he who travels may see much more." [3]

Air travel has become common and various airlines try to convince passengers they offer the best services. Yet, air travel that provides enjoyment at times still includes many challenges and tension.

The mere standing in the queue, checking documents and bags, and being personally inspected, scanned, and even touched by security personnel, can be disturbing procedures and enough to put a passenger in a bad mood before boarding.

Furthermore, a passenger would face a greater challenge if seated next to a sullen person.

In any case, there is no fast travel between countries without aircraft; fortunately, the significant challenges of air travel can be largely reduced by observing some etiquette tips.

- ## Etiquette tips:

- A passenger is supposed to remain optimistic and try to convince themselves the trip will be fine and the person sitting next to them will be kind.
- The space next to the side exits of the cabin is the widest. Therefore, tall or large passengers are advised to book their seats there.
- Many passengers prefer to stay silent, listen to music, or read during flights. Therefore, it is recommended to avoid talking to a passenger, unless they show a desire for conversation.
- During a flight, a passenger is expected to refrain from speaking loudly or making noise with friends on board; this is a courtesy to other passengers.
- On board, the passenger with a wheeled handbag may either proceed through the aisle drawing his handbag toward his seat or carefully carry it, so as not to hit the hands, shoulders, or heads of already seated passengers.
- Each passenger should put their handbag in the compartment (bin/overhead locker) above their seat without using the compartments of others.
- Using the other passengers' compartments will cause them to look for other compartments. This behavior might delay the start of the flight and the debarking of passengers after landing.
- If there is not enough space in the passengers' compartments, the passenger should put items beneath the seat or

---

2 Mustafa Amin (1914-1997), an Egyptian columnist and journalist who enjoyed a great deal of popularity in the Arab world.

3 An Angolan proverb.

between their feet rather than in the aisle. Otherwise, the item will hinder movement.

- A passenger may put some small objects in the backseat pocket of the seat in front of them.
- The seatback should not be leaned back until permission is announced.
- The seatback should be slowly tilted, so as not to bother the passenger behind them.
- The passenger is expected not to tilt their seatback at all, or just tilt it slightly if the passenger behind them is tall or has a baby on their lap.
- The seatback must be kept upright when food and drinks are served and until the meals are over and the trash is cleaned.
- Passengers with children should pay attention so they do not hold or kick the seats in front of them and cause inconvenience for those seated ahead.
- It is recommended to bring some books, toys, and possibly electronic devices for children, to keep them busy and reduce their movement.
- The passenger accompanying one or more of their children should not book the seats next to side exits.
- During the journey, when a passenger wants to stand up, they should use their seat arms to support themselves, rather than the back of the seat in front of them. Otherwise, they would disturb another passenger who might be asleep.
- When walking through the plane aisles, a passenger can hold the compartments for balance rather than the seatbacks.
- To think that drinking alcoholic beverages before and during the journey can

make it less inconvenient is a big misconception. It may increase the trouble for both the drinker and other passengers.

- If a nearby passenger behaves oddly (perhaps when drunk), they should never be argued with. A flight attendant could be asked to find a solution or might offer them another seat.
- For health reasons, passengers are recommended to move and walk, from time to time, during long-distance flights. Yet too much movement might cause confusion or inconvenience for others.
- To reduce movement in the flight aisles as much as possible, passengers should try to refrain from going to the plane toilets often.
- A window-seated passenger, or the one seated between two or more passengers, should gently ask their neighbor if they would like to leave their seat.
- An aisle-seated passenger should not lean over a passenger in a window seat to see the view.
- The passenger should pay attention to the movement of their elbows if reading a newspaper or using a laptop. One does not want to hit nearby passengers or take more space at their expense.
- It is not appropriate to try reading something in the newspaper, book, or laptop of a nearby passenger.
- Passengers should treat crew members and flight attendants with courtesy and refinement, and not make unreasonable requests.
- The passengers should not have prolonged conversations with the flight attendants; their task is to serve all passengers.

- While the attendants are serving meals with trolleys, passengers are required to stay seated.
- Passengers should remain seated until everyone has finished eating and the trays are taken away.
- On board, passengers should only wear light perfumes; strong scents might cause inconvenience for some passengers, especially those allergic to some perfumes.
- During landing and taxiing on the runway, passengers should remain seated, until the plane stops, and the seat belt sign is turned off.
- When passengers collect their handbags and belongings from compartments, they should be careful not to let anything fall onto others.
- When passengers are permitted to leave the plane, they are expected to proceed immediately; some transit passengers might have little time to catch their next flights.
- If a passenger's bag is heavy, they can wait or stay seated until all passengers get off. Otherwise, they might impede the movement of others.

Section Eleven

Banquet Etiquette

"At a dinner party one should eat wisely but not too well, and talk well but not too wisely."[1]

❝ As already mentioned, humans, as social beings, always need to communicate, establish relationships, build friendships, and enjoy time with others. Banquets and dinners are important gatherings for these purposes. ❞

While such gatherings are a natural need for people of all classes and interests, they are a requirement and an integral part of the work of diplomats, businesspeople, and those working in public affairs.

It is worth mentioning that lunches and dinners have become important events where many discuss and talk about political, economic, social, and other issues, and even solve problems, as expressed by Ambassador Caulaincourt[2] who mentioned in one of his letters to Napoleon, that **"so many problems could be solved on dining tables."**

- **Invitations procedure:**

Before going into banquet etiquette, it is practical to mention some procedural items related to formal invitations, such as accepting or declining, means of responding, canceling, changing the reply, and the thank-you note.

---

1 William Somerset Maugham (1874-1965), an English playwright, novelist, and short-story writer.

2 Armand-Augustin-Louis, Marquis de Caulaincourt (1773-1827), a French officer, diplomat, and close personal aide to Napoleon Bonaparte

- **Extending invitations:**

Invitations should be extended well in advance so the invitee can arrange their schedule and other appointments. This way, they can accept the invitation without hesitation or at the expense of other pre-scheduled programs.

Previously, the invitation was sent one month before the event's due date; now, the period has been shortened to two weeks. With the rapid development of the media, this period has become closer to 10 days or even a week. However, the longer the invitation is extended, the better.

It is unacceptable to invite someone on the same day or one day before an event. This behavior would make them feel forgotten or neglected until the last minute.

You can re-invite a person who did not accept your invitation previously, but it is not permissible to invite them a third time if your invitation has been declined twice, unless there are justified reasons, such as illness or travel.

It is justifiable to decline invitations extended too late.

Regardless of one's relation with the host, it is impermissible to invite oneself to any event; that would embarrass the host.

It is impermissible for the invitee to propose other names to the host to invite.

It is not advisable to invite a friend in the presence of other friends; they might think that they are all invited.

- **Accepting or declining invitations:**

If the French short code "RSVP"[3] is indicated in the invitation card, the invitee should respond to the host about their acceptance or apology.

Unless there is a good reason, like illness or urgent travel (for example), when an invitation is accepted, it should be met.

If the invitee declines, they should apologize and explain why.

If indicated in the invitation card, the invitee wears the kind of clothing mentioned (formal, informal, or casual).

▷ **Responding means:**

· If an **RSVP** is indicated and no response card is inserted within the envelope, a handwritten response should be sent to the host at the return address on the envelope.

· If a response card is included, the invitee fills it in and returns it in the enclosed envelope.

· If both an **RSVP and a phone number** are listed, the invitee is supposed to call to inform the host about their acceptance or apology.

· If both **RSVP and email** are indicated, the invitation could be accepted or declined electronically.

· It is unusual to receive an invitation without a reply request; yet, it is tactful to inform the host. A **phone call** would be sufficient.

---

3   RSVP: The French short code RSVP (Repondez s'il vous plait), which means (please reply), has been internationally used to indicate that the invitee should reply within a day or two of receiving an invitation, or by the RSVP deadline at the latest (if designated).

- **Canceling or changing the reply:**

It is only acceptable to change a "yes" (acceptance) to "no" (decline) in case of illness, injury, urgent travel, death in the family, or something similar.

It is shameful if one cancels an invitation because there is a more tempting one. It is unacceptable behavior, and the host will likely drop them from future guest lists.

Accepting an invitation without attending (no-show) is unacceptable.

After declining an invitation, it is only acceptable to change to a "yes" if it is still possible for the host's arrangements.

- **Saying "Thank You":**

The invitee should thank the host twice, once before leaving the event, and another by phone or note (Thank-you note) the next day.

Banquets

Banquets are either formal, semi-formal, or informal.

- **Formal banquets:**

Formal banquets are dining events that adhere to protocol and etiquette which are part of the social functions of public and private, businesses, and diplomatic bodies, which include, inter alia:

- Dinners in honor of visiting delegations.
- Dinners in honor of a special guest who might be a politician, businessperson, artist, etc.
- Some receptions and wedding parties include protocol and etiquette rules for formal banquets.

> **Etiquette tips at formal dinners:**

Those in charge of seating arrangements should observe strict precedence.

- Customarily, formal dinners are often preceded by a cocktail hour where guests drink cocktails while mingling and conversing.
- Usually, wine is served throughout the meal, often with a different wine accompanying each course (this does not apply in many Muslim countries).
- In formal dining, many courses are carefully planned and served to complement each other gastronomically.
- The various courses are paired with different wine, beer, liqueur, or other spirits.
- At formal dinners, the dining table has symmetrical place settings for guests.
- Dining tables should have place cards, each with a guest's name.
- Speeches are usually exchanged in case of state official banquets (if the host is a head of state, prime minister, minister, ambassador, or the like).

In large formal banquets, if there is a main table facing many round tables, the number of chairs on the main table is either odd, if the host's rank is higher than that of the guest of honor, [4] or even in the case when the ranks of both the host and guest of honor are equal.

– The place of honor at the dining table is usually given the best view, whether through a window or toward a painting; this is even observed in the case of round tables, which some might think do not have a specific place of honor.

When the banquet is mixed, a husband does not sit next to his wife at the dinner table. Generally, if the guest of honor's wife accompanies him, he sits to the right of the host, and his wife sits on the left. The wife of the host (hostess) sits on the right [5] of the guest of honor:

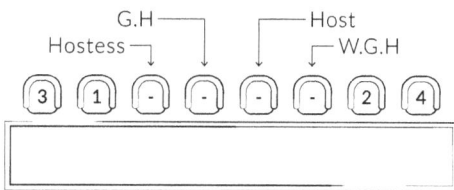

• Formal receptions:

A formal reception is a good choice when there are many guests.

Formal receptions usually take place in the evening, at 7:00 or 7:30 p.m.

According to the order of precedence, the hosts and the guests of honor stand in a receiving line near the entrance.

Each arriving guest greets the host and others in the line before joining the other guests who have already arrived.

For the line of guests to progress without delay, each guest may speak little more than their name (if necessary) and offer a conventional greeting or congratulation to each person in the receiving line.

After standing in line for about 15 to 20 minutes and receiving the guests, the hosts may mingle.

Generally, receptions may be accompanied by a buffet meal.

• Informal/Semi-formal banquets and parties:

Some informal/semi-formal banquets and parties include cocktail parties (or receptions), wedding receptions, birthdays, garden parties, commencement parties, charity events, etc.

Usually, informal banquets are held for friends and close family members.

In such cases, no protocol and etiquette rules are binding.

Telephone, email, or a visit card could be used for events such as lunch or dinner, birthdays, wedding anniversaries, tea parties, cocktail parties, etc.

Like formal receptions, informal receptions usually take place in the evening, yet it has become common for informal receptions and cocktails to take place at other times such as a lunch break for instance. [6]

---

4 The guest of honor is a person who is especially eminent at an event, ceremony, party, dinner, festivity, gathering, etc. They are usually given precedence.

5 There are many other arrangements that will be shown afterwards.

6 In many Latin American and Western countries, it is normal to be invited to receptions and cocktails at lunchtime (at noon or 1 p.m.).

- **Some table service systems:**

▷ **Already filled plates system:**

At most common formal dinners, already filled plates are brought in large individual food portions to each guest in sequence, without an opportunity to request something different or ask for more than a single serving. In this case, food presentation is focused on individual portions.

▷ **"Service à la Russe" system:**

At formal "Service à la Russe," only empty plates are set in front of each guest, and courses are sequentially brought to the table on platters, so diners make selections and fill their plates from a variety of dishes. In this case, the food presentation is focused on the platters.

▷ **"Service à la Française" system:**

At formal "Service à la Française," food courses are served on the table at the same time and guests serve themselves. It is almost a "family" style meal.

▷ **Rodizio system:**

In many countries, a rodizio restaurant refers to a Brazilian-style steakhouse restaurant (traditionally called "churrascaria").

It is an "all-you-can-eat" (AYCE) restaurant service system.

In this service system, a diner pays a fixed price, and from the serving counter selects rice, beans, fried potatoes, collard greens, fried bananas, etc. (similar to buffet style).

At the table, from time to time, a waiter comes carrying a knife and a skewer, on which there are quality cuts and samples of grilled meat.

The samples are cut from a certain part of the body of the cow, according to a figure [7] already present in front of the diners showing the part where the meat was cut from.

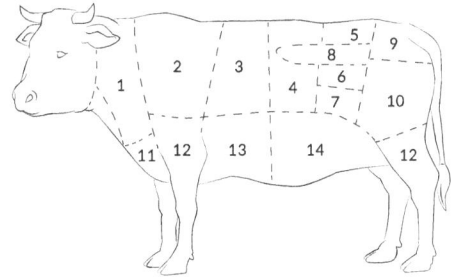

1. Neck and Clod
2. Chuck
3. Rib
4. Shortloin
5. Sirloin
6. Top Sirloin
7. Bottom Sirloin
8. Tenderloin
9. Rump
10. Round
11. Brisket
12. Shank
13. Plate
14. Flank

The waiter slices as much as the diner requests.

Other times, the waiter may bring various types of meat, such as pork (and perhaps more exotic choices) according to the diner's appetites.

Usually, each diner is provided with "yes" and "no" colored cards. Green on one side shows they want more meat, and red indicates they have finished.

This system has recently been developed to include pizzerias. Instead of grilled meat, waiters serve different types of pizza from which one can choose what they desire.

---

7 The figure embodies a cow including parts that represent specific regions of its body and the cuts of beef provided from that area.

▷ "Comida por quilo" system:

"Comida por quilo" or "Comida a quilo" system, meaning "Food by Kilo": It is a combination of a buffet style and a food by kilo procedure.

"Comida por quilo" restaurants are popular in Brazil, where diners are billed by the weight of the food selected.

▷ Buffet system:

The buffet system is an effective and practical system for serving large numbers of people at once. In this system, the customers select what kind of food they like to eat and directly serve themselves from serving trays placed on a "serving counter."

It is an internationally common system followed at various restaurants, where diners pay a set price (unless formally invited by someone) for "all-you-can-eat" (AYCE) food.

Due to the nature of the buffet dining system, usually, it is acceptable to start eating as soon as a diner sits down with their plate.

› Buffet etiquette tips:

- The buffet system requires lining up in a queue. It is inappropriate to reach around or cut in front of another person in line.
- Diners in the queue should be given enough personal space and elbow room.
- It is acceptable to walk around the serving counter and look at the items on the serving counter before selecting them.
- Diners should keep the line moving.
- One should not hover while trying to figure out whether they want something or not.
- One should not crowd others when they are serving themselves.

- On the plate column, for sanitary reasons, one should not touch any plate other than the one they use.
- Diners can move several times from their tables to the serving counter:
  1. To get soup.
  2. To get appetizers.
  3. To get the main course.
  4. To get fruits and sweets.
- One should not stack everything on one plate. It is tantamount to gluttony.
- It is better to under-serve oneself and return than to over-serve and not finish what is taken.
- It is unacceptable to eat from one's plate in front of the serving counter.
- One should not use fingers to touch or pluck something off the serving counter.
- The provided utensils on the serving counter should only be used to put food on one's plate.
- For whatever reason, once a food item is put on one's plate, it should not be returned to the counter.
- One should not lick their fingers, touch their hair, sneeze, or cough in front of the serving counter.
- To let others know one is returning to the buffet, one should place their napkin on the seat of their chair.
- Used plates should be left on the table for servers to take them away.
- Every time a diner leaves their table for the serving counter, they use a new clean plate.
- As young children are not yet prepared to care for themselves entirely and their hygiene is sometimes lacking, they are not allowed to serve themselves.
- Buffet-style restaurants do not allow doggie bags with leftovers.

• Eating styles

In most regions of the world, people use one or more of the following eating styles:

— The Continental style.
— The American style.
— The Chopstick style.
— The Eating-by-Hand style.

▪ Continental style:

Today, the Continental eating style is the most common, applied in Europe, Latin America, Russia, Australia, parts of Africa and Asia, and other places.

Continental style
I'm resting position

Continental style
I'm finished position

With the Continental style (sometimes called the European style), the fork stays in the left hand, with the tines pointed down, and the knife is held by the right hand. Once a bite-sized piece of food is cut, it is carried straight to the mouth by the fork in the left hand.

In between bites, the "resting position" is shown by setting the knife and fork crossed, with handles in at 5 and 7 o'clock positions, and the fork tines turned downwards on the plate.

While placing them together with the fork tines turned down, the blade of the knife facing inwards, and the handles at the 4 or 5 (even 6) o'clock position, is the position to indicate one is "finished."

▪ American style

The American eating style is applied in the United States of America and Canada. British colonists who used this system in Europe until the middle of the Eighteenth century brought it there.

American style
I'm resting position

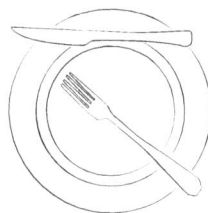

American style
I'm finished position

The American style is sometimes known as "the zigzag method."

After the knife is used to cut the food held by the fork, the knife is then set down on the plate and the fork is taken by the right hand to bring the food to the mouth for consumption (tines up). The fork is then transferred back to the left hand and the knife is picked up with the right, and so on until the diner is satisfied. In this style, the fork is held much like a spoon or pen once it is transferred to the right hand (with tines up) to carry food to the mouth.

To indicate the "resting position," the knife is placed on the right side of the plate in the 2 o'clock position, blade in, and the fork placed in the 5 o'clock position, tines up.

While, placing them together (with the fork tines up, the blade of the knife facing inwards) and the handles at the 4 or 5 (even 6) o'clock position, is the position to indicate one is "finished."

- ## Chopsticks style:

The chopsticks style is used in many Asian countries like China, Japan, Korea, and Vietnam.

The food utensils used are chopsticks, which have become well-known worldwide, but one needs some practice to use them properly.

- ## Eating-by-hand style:

The eating-by-hand style is a common tradition in many parts of Asian and African countries.

Usually, one bite-sized piece of flatbread is used to carry food from a communal platter (or from one's plate) to one's mouth.

Only the right hand is used.

• Dinner serving

Today, the most formal dinner is served from the kitchen.

Dinner serving takes place according to a right and left practice.

Left and right Food serving: [8]

A. From the Left:

The server approaches the diner from the left in order:

1. To present a platter of food from which he/she will serve them, or the diner will help themselves. By standing to the left of the diner, the waiter holds the platter at a safe distance as the diner leans forward to reach it.
2. To place side dishes (such as vegetables, dinner rolls, and the like) while leaving the right side free for the main dish.
3. To clear the side dishes placed from the left.

B. From the Right:

The server approaches the diner from the right:

1. To serve ready-filled plates (except for side dishes).
2. To place empty plates and clean utensils.
3. To clear plates.
4. To present and pour wine and other beverages. (To do this service from the left would force the server to reach in front of the guest).

---

8 The old rule of "all food should be served from the left and removed from the right" is no longer practiced. Nowadays, formal dinner serving is characterized by having pre-plated food offered to guests directly from the kitchen. They are served from the right and not from the left as the case was a long time ago, when all food was served in large trays and each guest was served individually.

• Table Etiquette/Table manners:

Different cultures observe different rules for table etiquette (or table manners), and each culture, to some extent, sets its standards for applying these rules.

Anyhow, there are some common behaviors, which have evolved over centuries to make the practice of eating with others pleasant and sociable.

› The most common etiquette tips:

– Naturally, the host should arrive at the restaurant before the guests.
– The host (and spouse) may wait for the guests in the foyer of the restaurant (if there is one) or at the dining table. In the second case, the host informs the maître d' of the restaurant and asks for the guests to be directed to their dining table.
– Punctual guests can order drinks and examine the menu once they are seated.
– Dinner might normally be held after 15 to 20 minutes of the appointed dinner time (no longer), allowing for late guests to arrive.
– A lighted cigarette is never taken to the table.
– Cocktail glasses (from cocktail hour) should be left in the place where they are taken.
– Cellphones should be turned off. If that is forgotten, and a cellphone rings, it should immediately be turned off.
– One should wait to check calls and messages until they are finished with the meal, and away from the table.
– At an informal dinner, the guests enter the dining room in whatever order is convenient.
– With a large group, place cards always designate individual seats.
– Usually, the host or hostess enters the dining room first to tell everyone where to sit if the seating arrangements are not designated by place cards.
– If the guest of honor is a high-ranking female dignitary, she enters the dining room first with the host. Her husband follows with the hostess.
– If the guest of honor is a high-ranking male dignitary, he enters the dining room first with the hostess. The host enters the dining room second with the dignitary's wife.
– Generally, the place of honor is the right side of the host, although there are many other different seating arrangements.
– At the dining table, women sit first, and men should help them by sliding out and pushing in their chairs.
– When seated, one should not hunch their shoulders over the plate, or slouch back in the chair.
– The "no elbows on the table" rule should be applied.
– In some upscale restaurants, steamed hand towels are brought to diners at the beginning and end of meals to wipe their hands.
– To speed up the pace of a meal if the guest of honor has another engagement, the host may order something that can be prepared quickly.
– To lengthen a meal, the host informs the server they want guests to finish drinks before ordering the first course.
– To have a more sociable time the host can inform the server there is no need to rush between courses.

- Napkins should be placed on the lap and not tucked into clothing.
- Napkins should not be used for anything other than wiping the mouth.
- Napkins should be placed unfolded on the table when the meal is finished.
- If wearing gloves or carrying a fan, a woman should remove her gloves and put them together on her lap under the napkin.
- When eating indoors, it is not proper table manners to wear a hat.
- Some may advise taking off a hat even when eating outdoors.
- To avoid misunderstanding or creating suspicion, men should avoid placing their hands under the table in banquets with women in attendance.
- Before coming to the dining table, a female should refrain from replenishing lipstick to prevent an imprint from appearing on the rim of a glass or napkin.
- By closing the menu and placing it on the table, the diner shows the server they are ready to order.
- The guest selects a wine in the category they are interested in at a fairly decent price. (More details in the "Wine Etiquette" chapter.)
- At a meal served buffet style, guests begin eating when they are ready. They do not need to wait for others to sit.
- At banquets with less than eight people, one may begin eating only after all other guests are served and the host or guest of honor has started to eat.
- At informal banquets, eating commences as soon as those on either side of a diner are served.
- To enjoy the company and cuisine, the diner should take part in the conversation at the dining table.

- It is impolite to scrape a plate or chew, smack, or slurp food loudly. It is best to be patient.
- At the beginning of the meal, the host usually offers the first toast as a welcome to guests.
- Toasts offered by guests generally start during the dessert course.
- When eating with other people, it is acceptable to pour one's drink first, but it is more polite to offer to pour drinks to those sitting on either side.
- Before drinking, the lips should be blotted with a napkin, so as not to leave some food remains on the rim of the glass.
- When drinking, one should look toward the bottom of their glass, not at the people around them. Otherwise, they might look impolite.

- When drinking, the glass should be picked up with all fingers; crooking the pinky could be considered a signal of some kind.
- At the dinner table, utensils are used by applying the "outside-in" rule.
- The fork is held generally with the tines down.
- The knife is used to cut food and help guide the food onto the fork.
- When no knife is being used, the fork can be held with the tines up (to eat rice, for example).

Service Plate
Salad Plate

- The fork should not be held like a shovel, with all fingers wrapped around the base.
- The knife should be held with the base in the palm, of the hand, not like a pen with the base resting between the thumb and forefinger.
- To avoid soiling the tablecloth, utensils should never touch the table during the meal.
- It is improper to allow the handle of a utensil to touch the table while the other end rests on the plate.
- When a course is complete, both the used and unused utensils for that course should be placed on the plate. Otherwise, the waiter will do that.
- When a fork and spoon are presented together with a bowl, the fork is used to steady the portion, and the spoon to cut and carry the bite to the mouth.
- If a utensil is dropped, one can pick it up and let the waiter know they need a new one.
- If the diner cannot reach a dropped utensil, they can ask the waiter for a replacement.
- If a napkin is dropped, the diner can pick it up themselves. If not, they can ask the waiter for a replacement.
- If part of one's food is dropped, they may either lift it with a utensil and place it on the side of their plate or use a napkin to retrieve it from the table and ask the waiter for a replacement napkin.
- If a glass of wine or water is spilled, one can use a napkin to dry the mess.
- At an informal buffet meal, if one spills food on another person, they apologize and offer to pay for cleaning. They should let the person wipe the spill, though.
- In a restaurant, if one is offered a soiled utensil, they can ask the waiter for a clean one.
- In a private residence, it is embarrassing to show that a utensil is not clean. Therefore, without being noticed, the guest may drop it and ask to be served another one.
- It is improper to play with utensils or gesture with a knife or fork in your hands.
- Adding salt and condiments or seasoning before the food is tasted might be considered an insult to the chef's ability to prepare a meal.
- It is advised to savor the meal and eat slowly; this encourages conversation and conviviality.
- Before talking, one is supposed to swallow their food.
- While eating, food is cut into only one or two bite-sized pieces at a time.
- It is acceptable for diners to ask for items to be passed along the table to them.
- It is improper to lean past the person sitting nearby to reach for a certain item.
- When asked to pass the salt, one passes both the salt and pepper.
- When pouring, glasses should not be filled to their rims, but to about three-quarters.
- If the waiter is pouring water or a drink, the diner leaves the cup on the table.

- If a diner sitting nearby offers to pour water or a drink, the recipient is expected to raise the cup a little off the table.
- At informal meals, a piece of bread could be used to push wayward food onto a fork.
- If an unfamiliar menu item is served, the diner can ask about it.
- In a formal dinner, if an unfamiliar item is offered, the guest watches those around and proceeds accordingly or avoids the food.
- When in doubt about whether to use fingers or a utensil to eat a particular food, the guest can wait until someone else starts to eat. If still in doubt, the guest uses a fork.
- Unwanted food should be removed from the mouth with a utensil.
- If something is caught between the teeth, one can wait to remove it privately.
- If there is a speck of food on a diner's face, one can subtly call their attention to it. They might use their index finger to tap their chin lightly or the affected part of the face.
- If a diner is unable to avoid sneezing or coughing, they should cover their nose or mouth with a napkin and proceed as quietly as possible.
- It is inappropriate for a diner to use a napkin to blow their nose. They should excuse themselves from the table and use a handkerchief instead.
- When an unavoidable burp is coming on, the diner covers their mouth with the napkin, quietly burps, and says, "Excuse me."
- If there are repeated hiccups, the diner excuses themselves from the table until the hiccups have passed.
- If a diner cannot suppress a yawn, one covers their mouth.
- While serving, if a waiter makes a certain mistake, they should be treated with respect calmly.
- It is acceptable to send a dish back if it is not what was ordered.
- It is acceptable to send a dish back if it is not cooked to order or if its taste is spoiled.
- Discreetly, the waiter could be asked for a replacement if a hair or an insect is discovered in the dish.
- When leaving for the restroom, it is best to excuse oneself.
- It is not acceptable to lick one's fingers after placing a "finger food" on a plate; instead, a napkin can be used.
- If there is a finger bowl available, the diner dips his fingers into the water after eating lobster, "finger food," or some kind of dessert. The diner then dries them with the napkin.
- To test the temperature of a hot beverage, it is safe to take a single sip from the side of the spoon.
- To decrease the effect of the burn if a very hot beverage is sipped, one takes a sip of water.
- At an informal meal, it is possible to sop up extra gravy or sauce with a piece of bread on the end of a fork and then eat the soaked bread.
- The diner can stir the soup to reduce the heat. It is improper to blow on it.
- To eat soup, one uses the soup spoon to scoop the soup in outward movements before carrying it to their mouth.
- To eat soup, it should be sipped from the side of the spoon, not its end.

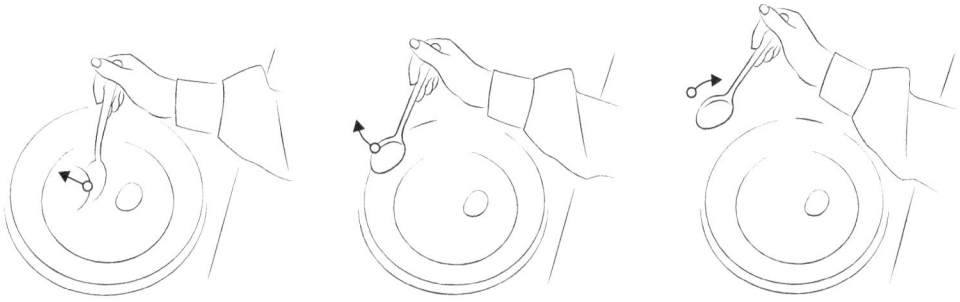

- Between bites or after finishing eating from a cup, stemmed glass, or soup bowl, the diner rests the spoon on the saucer or soup plate. They do not leave it in the cup or bowl.
- Cheese should be cut and placed on the side plate before eating.
- When the waiter offers a platter, the diner helps themselves with the serving fork in the left hand and the serving spoon in the right.
- From a platter, the diner takes a portion nearest to them.
- When a platter contains a combination of foods, the diner takes a moderate serving of each.
- To squeeze a piece of lemon without squirting the nearby dinner companion, one pierces the pulp of the piece on the fork tines, cups his free hand over the lemon, and gently squeezes the fruit.
- Netting the pieces of lemon should capture all the seeds, depending on how fine the netting is.
- At an informal meal, a diner can pass the dishes and breadbasket to the nearest dinner companion.
- To avoid congestion, passing the dishes and breadbasket always goes to the right.
- To cut a piece of bread from a loaf in

a breadbasket, the diner uses the cloth in the basket to cover one end of the loaf before grasping it to cut a few slices.
- At a formal dinner, it is not proper table manners to ask for a second helping (a refill).
- At an informal meal, it is permissible to ask for a second helping.
- At a buffet, it is not appropriate to go back to the service counter with a dirty plate for a refill. It should be left for the wait staff to pick up.
- At an informal dinner, the waiter may place coffee or tea on the table without filling the cups. In this case, the person nearest the pot should offer to pour, filling their cup last.
- Generally, the host signals the end of the meal by placing the napkin on the table.
- If there is a problem with the bill, it could be discussed quietly with the waiter. If the waiter is uncooperative, it is best to consult the manager.
- Children younger than 10 years old should not participate in official or semi-official banquets. At family meals, children are often expected to ask permission to leave the table at the end of the meal.
- It is acceptable table manners to take

leftover food (doggy bag) home from a restaurant, except if one is invited or on a date or business meal.

– If smoking is allowed, cigarettes may be passed after the main course or just before the dessert course. Smoking, however, is now illegal in many restaurants across the world.

– A compliment on the cuisine is always appreciated.

– According to some diplomatic practice at formal banquets, when a diplomat feels that a mistake, especially regarding their precedence, has been made, they turn over their charger plate (the large decorative plate that acts as a base for other tableware) and do not take the first course. It is a silent signal of protest.

– **At formal house dinners, if a guest wishes to express their impression about the food and the meal arrangements, they may employ the following:**

· To express high appreciation, they place the fork on its side and insert the knife's blade between the two upper tines.

· To say things were acceptable, they insert the blade of the knife between the two middle tines of the fork.

· To express dissatisfaction, they insert the knife's blade between the two lower tines of the fork.

· Nevertheless, it is untactful and impolite to resort to this sign of dissatisfaction unless there is a flagrant problem.

• Tableware

Tableware is mainly the items used for setting a table, serving food, and dining.

To achieve performance and elegance, such items are used for practical as well as decorative purposes.

Tableware consists of plates and bowls, glassware, cutlery/utensils, table covers, candles, and flowers.

▪ Table setting:

The table setting is concerned with the manner of setting a dining table with tableware for serving and eating.

▪ Place setting:

The formal place setting is the arrangement for a single diner.

For this purpose, utensils are placed to the right and left of the dinner plate in the "outside in" order, following the sequence of the courses as well as the way the diner will use them.

With fewer utensils and dishes, an informal setting generally uses the same formal layout.

- **Right & left tableware:**

To the left of the charger plate	To the right of the charger plate
The forks	The knives
The butter plate and knife	The spoons
(The napkin (or on the charger's center)	Stemware and tumblers
	Cups and saucers

Tableware is lined up and at the same distance from the edge of the table (about two to three centimeters for the plates).

Utensils in the outermost position are to be used first.

Utensils are placed either upon the same invisible baseline or the same invisible median line.

Glasses are placed about two-and-a-half centimeters above the knives.

Glasses are placed in the order of use: white wine, red wine, dessert wine, and water tumbler.

The lower edges of the utensils should be aligned with the bottom rim of the plate.

Formally, dessert spoons and forks are brought on the dessert plate just before dessert is served.

In a less formal dinner (not served from the kitchen), the dessert fork and spoon can be set above the plate (fork pointing right, spoon pointing left).

Although colored or patterned tablecloths (table covers), placemats, and napkins can be elegant, white linens are still considered the most formal.

The average drop of the table cover, on each end and the sides of the table, is 30 to 45 cm.

The table cover should not hang too low or end up in the diners' laps.

Placemats (if used) are placed in front of each chair, about three to five centimeters from the edge of the table.

Place settings should be evenly spaced around the table.

Formally, the table should be strictly symmetrical and have an even number of candlesticks and flower arrangements.

The table should not be overcrowded.

Decorations should be arranged in a way that diners seated opposite can see each other.

The following chart shows the distribution of a place setting with its dishes, glassware, and utensils:

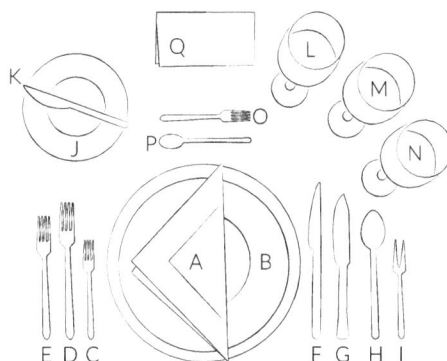

(**A**) *Napkin,* (**B**) *The Charger,* (**C**) *Salad Fork,* (**D**) *Dinner Fork,* (**E**) *Fish Fork,* (**F**) *Dinner Knife,* (**G**) *Fish Knife,* (**H**) *Soup Spoon,* (I) *Oyster Fork (if shellfish are served),* (**J**) *Butter Plate,* (**K**) *Butter Knife,* (**L**) *Water Goblet,* (**M**) *Red Wine Glass,* (**N**) *White Wine Glass,* (**O**) *dessert fork,* (**P**) *dessert spoon,* (**Q**) *place card.*

– The napkin is usually placed on top of the charger (if one is used) or in the space of the plate.

– The napkin can also be to the left of the forks, or under the forks if the space on the table is tight.

– The water goblet is placed directly above the knives.

– A butter plate is to be used for both the butter knife as well as bread.

– The fish knife has a special shape.

– The oyster fork is the only fork ever placed on the right of the plate.

– If the meal includes seafood or prawn salad (all of which are served in a bowl or cup), a special fork (two or three tines) is placed to the right of the spoon and knives. Here, the diner holds the stem of the cup with the left hand and eats with this special fork using the right hand.

• Seating arrangement:

In this section we will discuss:

Framework of the guests' names.

Table diagram.

Seating cards.

Place cards.

Table number cards.

▪ Seating Framework for Guest Names:

At a formal dinner, a seating framework makes it easy for guests to know where they are seated.

The seating framework is usually in the form of a rectangular leather tablet.

It is a frame with side slots through which pieces of paper or slim cards, with the guests' names, are inserted and show the seating locations at the dining table.

It is placed on a table at the entrance of the dining room so guests can see it before entering.

This framework is usually available in a variety of models and sizes that can accommodate up to 30 names.

The framework enables each guest to find their seat at the table themselves and know who sits next to them on both sides.

With the framework, the host will not need to tell or show each guest where they are seated.

Additionally, place cards with the names of guests are already on the table.

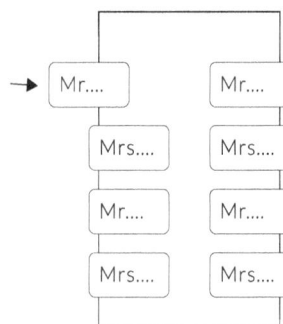

- **Table diagram:**

When using rectangular or U-shaped tables for a large number of guests (70 or more), a table diagram makes it easier for guests to know where they are seated. Each guest is given a card with their name upon arrival, which includes a U-shape diagram on one side. The card reads, "The red dot indicates your place at the table."

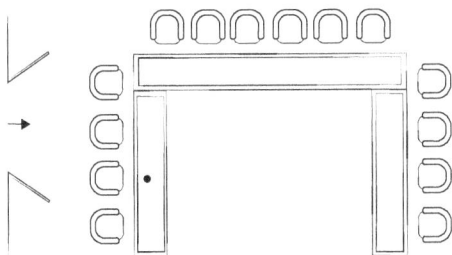

When the guest goes to the table, they have no difficulty finding their chair, keeping in mind the place cards are already there.

- **Seating cards:**

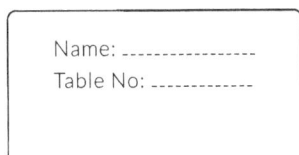

With a large number of guests (as many as hundreds), the best seating option is that the people in charge of dinner arrangements make the seating plan for their use and distribute the seating cards for all guests upon arrival.

Each card includes the guest's name and the number of their dining table.

When the guests are called to the dining hall, each one proceeds to the table indicated on their seating card and sits according to the place cards there.

- **Place cards:**

For formal events, the place cards used are usually white or beige (possibly, with gold beveled edges) rectangles that are folded. The size of the place card usually does not exceed the size of an ID card (Identity Card).

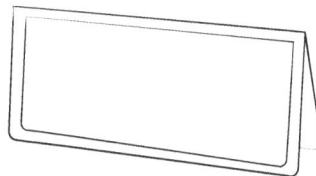

Full name and title are used are used.

The place card is intended to identify an individual at a table and inform dinner companions of their identity.

It is either white or beige and without trimmings.

In certain cases, an official emblem, logo, or flag might be embossed on the upper corners or top center of the card.

The state flag or emblem should not be added on place cards unless the host is of a very high rank (a head of state, prime minister, speaker of parliament, minister, ambassador, etc.).

- **Table number cards:**

At a large dinner gathering with many guests and dining tables, each table should have a clear table number (that guests can see) fixed on a cardholder or supporter in the middle of each table.

• Dining tables & seating arrangements

▪ Dining tables:

In restaurants, houses, gardens, etc., the tables have various shapes and capacities:

- Square tables are for a limited number of people, usually 4 to 12.
- Round tables are for a limited number of people, not exceeding 12.
- Rectangular tables are for a larger number of people, up to 36.
- U-shaped or horseshoe tables, suitable when the number of people exceeds 30.

▪ Seating arrangements:

The seating arrangements are important to ensure a proper application of protocol and etiquette to make any kind of event enjoyable and successful.

At formal dinners, seating arrangements observe the guests' precedence.

All kinds of tables have a forefront seat or seats usually afforded the best view.

The guest of honor or the highest-ranking person is usually given the forefront seat (with an ideal view).

Care should be taken that the place of a guest of honor and other senior guests or dignitaries should not be toward the service or kitchen doors.

Most often, the guest of honor is also the highest-ranking person.

At informal dinners, seating might be arranged according to the guests' interests and backgrounds.

It is worth reminding that the clergy and the elderly should be given a kind of precedence.

Usually, the guest of honor sits to the right of the hostess, and the wife of the guest of honor sits to the right of the host.

It is common to have the host and guest of honor sitting facing each other.

Men and women guests are seated alternately [9], according to precedence.

As much as possible, people of the same sex are not seated next to each other.

At formal banquets, to exchange opinions and experiences and get acquainted with others, it is not permissible for a man to sit next to his wife.

Regarding seating arrangements at large banquets, it is not tactful to have a woman seated at the end of a dining table. In this case, the rule of "alternating seating" can be ignored.

▪ Seating diagrams:

The following diagrams can help us visualize how guests are seated according to precedence order:

▷ **When the number of people is 2 to 4,** they can sit at the dining table the way they like.

▷ **At a round or rectangular table, if the number of people is five,** including one man, he takes seat No.1 and women sit according to their precedence.

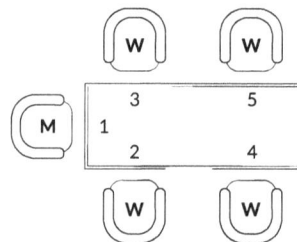

---

9 The alternate seating rule stipulates that (except in very special cases) at formal banquets people of the same sex should not be seated next to each other at a table.

▷ **The same order is followed if there is one woman and five men.** She takes seat number one and the men sit according to their precedence.

▷ **At a round or rectangular table, if there are two men and three women,** the highest-ranking woman takes seat No.1, two men take seats No. 2 and 3, and the other two women take seats No. 4 and 5.

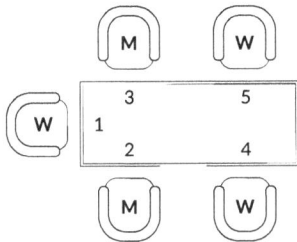

▷ **At a round or rectangular table, if there are three men and two women,** the highest-ranking man takes seat No. 1, two women take seats No. 2 and 3, and the other two men take seats No. 4 and 5.

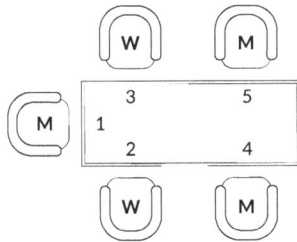

▷ **At round or rectangular tables, if the number of guests is 6:**

The host and hostess sit facing each other.

- The guest of honor sits to the right of the hostess.
- The wife of the guest of honor sits to the right of the host.
- Then, the other guests fill the remaining seats.

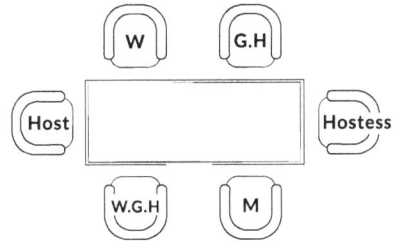

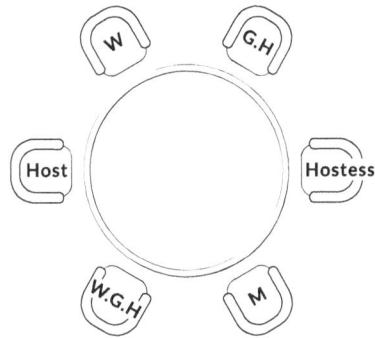

▷ **At a round table, if the number of guests is 7:**

The guest of honor and wife sit on the two forefront seats.

- The host sits to the right of the guest of honor's wife.
- The hostess sits to the left of the guest of honor.
- Then, the other guests fill the remaining seats.
- Contrary to the rule of "alternating seating," if there are 4 men and 3 women, two men will be next to each other.

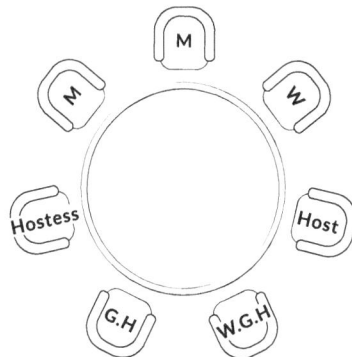

– Similarly, contrary to the rule of "alternating seating," if there are 4 women and 3 men, two women will be next to each other.

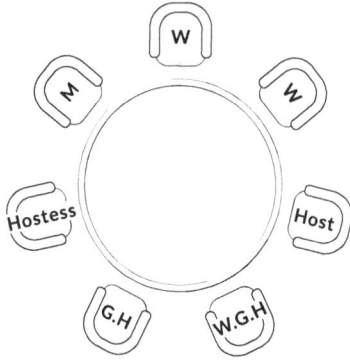

▷ **At a rectangular table if the number of guests is 7:**

The hostess and wife of the guest of honor sit at the two ends of the table facing each other.

– The guest of honor sits to the right of the hostess.
– The host sits to the right of the wife of the guest of honor.
– One seat at the table center will be vacant.
– If the guests are 4 women and 3 men, a woman will sit to the left of the wife of the guest.

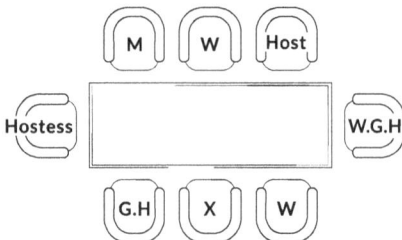

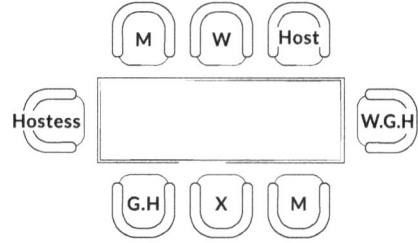

— **Another option:**

The hostess takes the seat at the head of the table.

– The guest of honor sits to the right of the hostess.
– The host and wife of the guest of honor face each other at the other end of the table.
– Contrary to the rule of "alternating seating," two men will be next to each other.

–

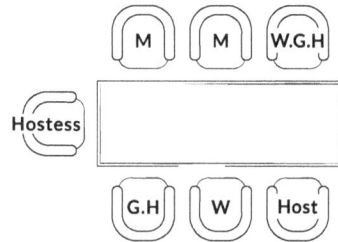

3 women + 4 men

— **One more option:**

The host takes the seat at the head of the table.

– The wife of the guest of honor sits to the right of the host.
– The guest of honor and the hostess face each other at the other end of the table.
– Also, contrary to the rule of "alternating seating," two men will be next to each other.

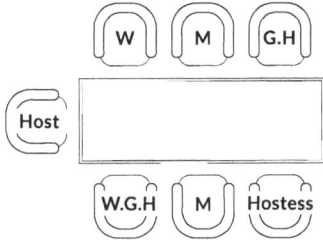

At a round or a rectangular table, if the number of guests is 8:

The host and the guest of honor sit facing each other (at the two ends of a rectangular table).

- The wife of the guest of honor sits to the right of the host.
- The hostess sits to the right of the guest of honor.
- The other guests sit according to their precedence.

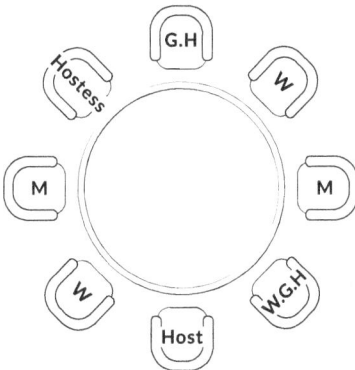

At a round table if the number of guests is 9:

At one curve of the table sits the host and to his right sits the wife of the guest of honor.

- At the opposite curve sits the guest of honor and to his right sits the hostess.
- The other guests sit according to their precedence.
- If there are 5 men and 4 women, two men will sit next to each other.
- If there are 5 women and 4 men, two women will sit next to each other.

* Note:
With this number of guests, there is no way, in any seating arrangement, but to have two women or two men sitting next to each other.

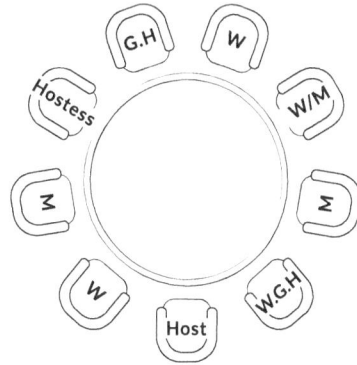

At a rectangular table if the number of guests is 9:

First option (5 women + 4 men):

- The hostess sits at the head of the table.
- The guest of honor sits to her right.
- The wife of the guest of honor and the host sit next to each other at the center (on the left side) between a man and a woman.

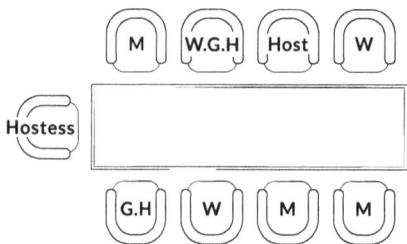

5 women and 4 men

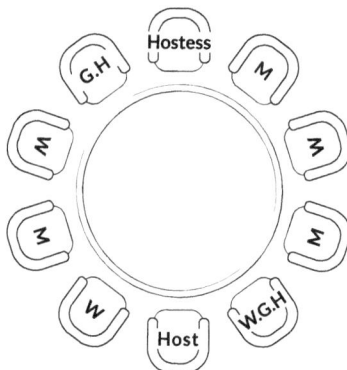

— **Second option (5 men and 4 women):**

The host sits at the head of the table.

- The wife of the guest of honor sits to the right of the host.
- The hostess and the guest of honor sit next to each other at the center (on the left side) between a woman and a man.

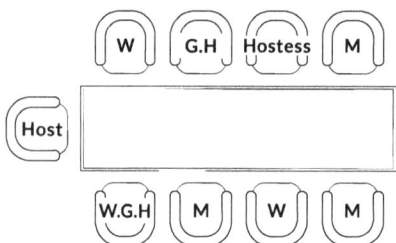

5 men and 4 women

▷ **At a round table if the number of guests is 10:**

The host sits at one curve of the table.

- The hostess sits at the opposite curve facing the host.
- The wife of the guest of honor sits to the right of the host.
- The guest of honor sits to the right of the hostess.
- The other guests sit according to their precedence.

▷ At a rectangular table if **the number of guests is 10:**

The host and the guest of honor sit at the center of the table facing each other.

- The wife of the guest of honor sits to the right of the host.
- The guest of honor sits to the right of the hostess.
- The other guests sit according to their precedence by applying the "Rule of Spacing."[10]

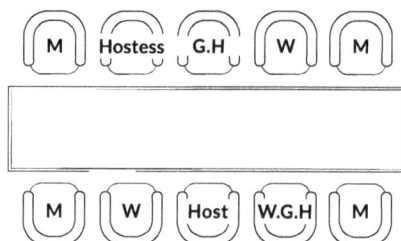

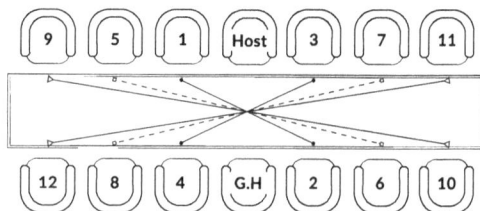

The "Rule of Spacing"

10 The "Rule of Spacing" is a form of the multiplication sign X X X X repeated from the center to both ends of the table (regardless of the number of guests).

▷ **At a round table if the number of guests is 11:**

— **First option (6 men and 5 women):**

The hostess and the guest of honor sit next to each other at one curve of the table.

– Facing them, the host and wife of the guest of honor sit next to each other at the opposite curve.
– The other guests sit according to their precedence.
– In this case, two men sit next to each other.

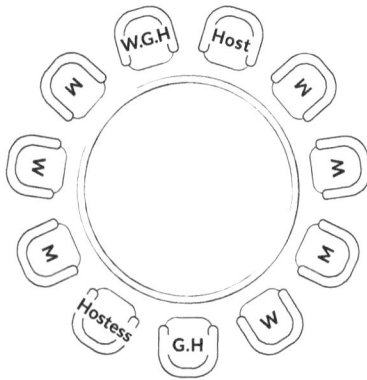

5 men and 5 women

— **Second option (6 women and 5 men):**

The Host and wife of the guest of honor sit next to each other at one curve of the table.

– Facing them, the hostess and the guest of honor sit next to each other at the opposite curve.
– The other guests sit according to their precedence.

*Note:
At round tables, when the guests are 11, there is no way, in any seating arrangement, but to have two women or two men sitting next to each other.*

▷ At a rectangular table if **the number of guests is 11:**

The host and wife of the guest of honor sit next to each other at the center of the table.

– Facing them, the hostess and the guest of honor sit next to each other on the opposite side.
– The other guests sit according to their precedence by applying the "Rule of Spacing."

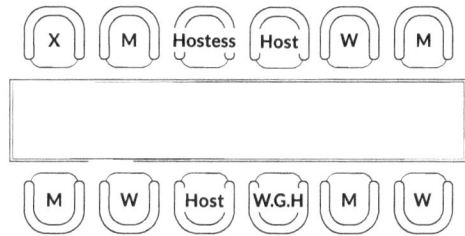

(One seat is vacant).

▷ At a round table if **the number of guests is 12:**

The host and the guest of honor sit facing each other.

– The wife of the guest of honor sits to the right of the host.
– The hostess sits to the right of the guest of honor.
– The other guests sit according to their precedence.

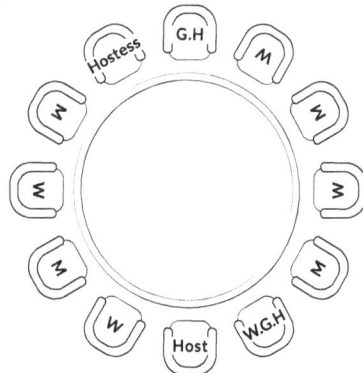

▷ At a rectangular table if **the number of guests is 12:**

— **First option:**

– The Host and wife of the guest of honor sit next to each other at the center of the table.

– Facing them, the hostess and the guest of honor sit next to each other on the opposite side of the table.

– The other guests sit according to their precedence, by applying the "Rule of Spacing."

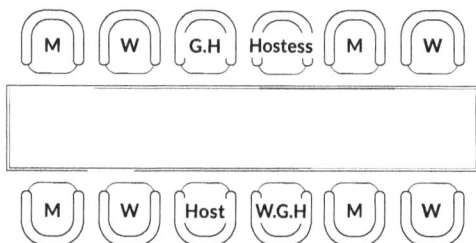

— **Second option:**

– The host and the guest of honor sit facing each other at the two ends of the table.

– The wife of the guest of honor sits to the right of the host.

– The hostess sits to the right of the guest of honor.

– The other guests are seated according to their precedence by applying the "Rule of Spacing."

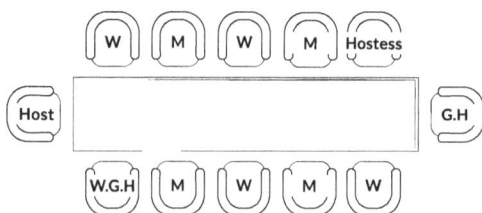

▷ **Guests of the same gender:**

If the guests are only men or only women, the seating arrangement can be as follows:
At round tables (up to 12 seats):

— **First option:**

– The guest of honor (man or woman) sits at one curve of the table.

– The host/hostess sits facing the guest of honor at the opposite curve.

– The other guests sit according to their precedence.

— **Second option:**

– The host/hostess and the guest of honor sit next to each other at one curve of the table.

– The other guests sit to the right and left of the host/hostess and the guest of honor according to their precedence.

– At rectangular tables:

– At the center, on both sides of the table, the host/hostess sits facing the guest of honor (man or woman).

– The highest-ranking guest sits on the right of the host/hostess.

– The second high-ranking guest sits to the right of the guest of honor.

– The other guests sit according to their precedence by applying the "Rule of Spacing."

* Note:

1 Usually, at rectangular tables with a number of guests between 14 to 36, the host and wife of the guest of honor face the hostess, and the guest of honor is seated at the center at both sides of the table while applying the "Rule of Spacing" concerning the other guests.

2 It is worth mentioning that, in addition to the aforementioned traditional and commonly used seating arrangements (and depending on the number of guests) there are still many arrangements, for example, the option of two separate tables. This is especially useful at houses.

▷ **The options of two separate tables:**

— **The first option:** At one table, the host sits facing the guest of honor, while at the other table, the hostess sits facing the wife of the guest of honor.

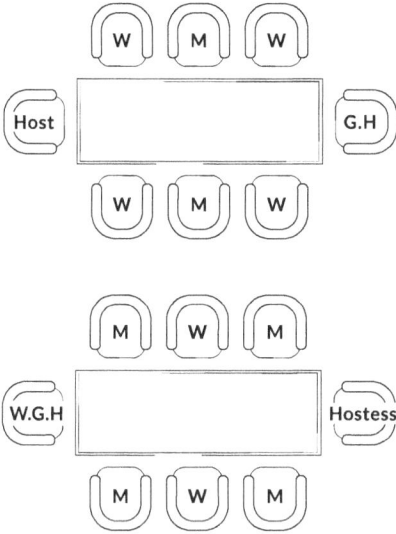

— **The second option:** At one table, the guest of honor sits to the right of the hostess, while at another table his wife sits to the right of the host.

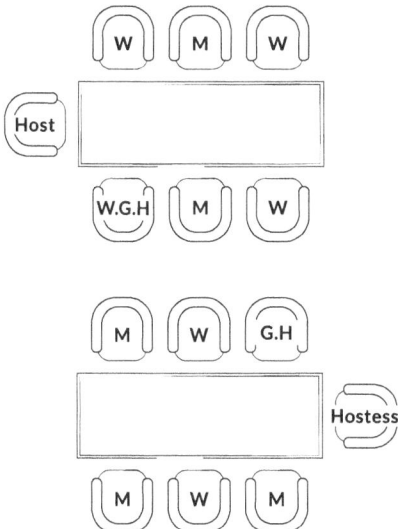

▷ **Horseshoe and U-shaped tables seating arrangements:**

At large formal banquets, horseshoe tables, and U-shaped tables (open boxes) are good options.

The simple horseshoe or U-shaped table arrangements require that:

— **First option:**
- The guest of honor and his wife sit at the outside of the curving center (of the horseshoe table) or the center (of the U-shaped table).
- The host sits to the right of the wife of the guest of honor.
- The hostess sits to the left of the guest of honor.
- The other guests sit in an alternating pattern.

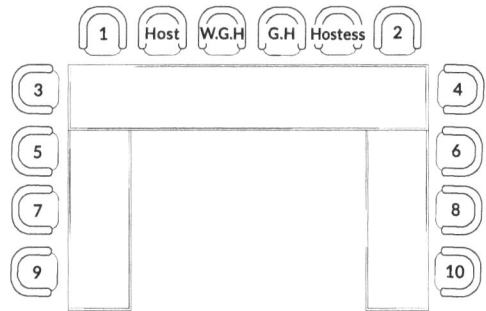

— **Second option:**
- The guest of honor sits to the right of the host at the outside of the curving center (of the horseshoe table) or the center (of the main side U-shaped table).
- The wife of the guest of honor sits to the left of the host.
- The hostess sits to the right of the guest of honor.
- The other guests sit, in an alternating pattern, along the sides of the table.

— **Third option:**

- The host sits at the center of the outside curve (of the horseshoe table) or the center (of the main side of the U-shaped table).
- The guest of honor sits to the right of the host.
- The hostess sits to the right of the guest of honor.
- The guest of honor's wife sits to the left of the host.
- Then the other guests sit right and left, according to their precedence.

This seating arrangement can be resorted to especially when the host is the highest-ranking person among all the guests (including the guest of honor).

According to this kind of seating arrangement, the number of chairs on the outside of the main table (of the U-shaped table) is odd, and the number of guests is consequently equal to the right and left of the host.

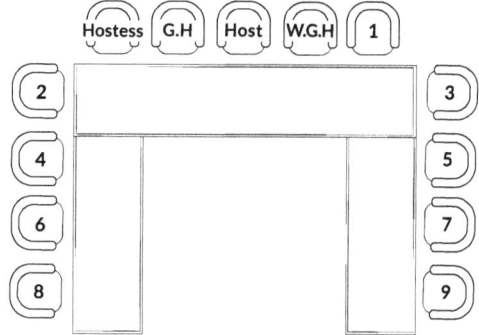

▷ **Using the interiors of the two sides of the U-shaped table:**

When the space is limited and does not allow the extension of two sides of the U-shaped table, the interiors of the sides themselves can be used to increase the number of chairs to accommodate a larger number of guests.

In this case, two or four chairs at the interiors of the inner sides of the U-shaped table should be removed (one or two from each side), due to the proximity of these chairs to the main side of the table.

Keeping the chairs there means that those who sit in them will have their backs toward the high dignitaries/senior guests (including the host, hostess, and their guests of honor) at the main side of the table.

Sometimes, at formal banquets, it is tactful to slightly ignore the alternating seating rule to avoid having a woman sitting at the end of a table.

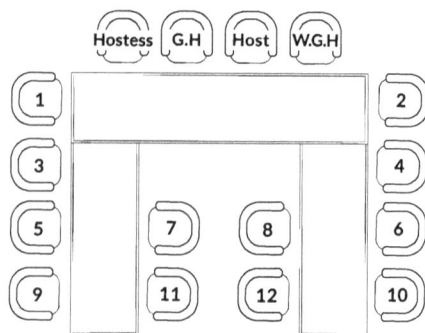

▷ Head tables:

For banquets held with a very large number of guests, the most common arrangement is having a rectangular head/main table facing many round tables.

The number of chairs at the head table is not supposed to exceed 14 or 15.

The chairs of the head table are only on one side of the table (facing many round tables).

The head table chairs are usually allocated for a few high-ranking dignitaries/senior guests (and their wives) in addition to the host and hostess, the guest of honor and wife.

The round table chairs are for the rest of the guests.

For a functional reason, the nearest two round tables to the head table have at least two chairs less than the other tables, so as not to have some guests' backs toward the senior guests on the main table.

A substantial space should be left directly in front of the head table. Therefore, at least two round tables are removed from in front of it. Otherwise, the vision of the persons at the head table will be limited and they will not be able to see the other guests in front of them well.

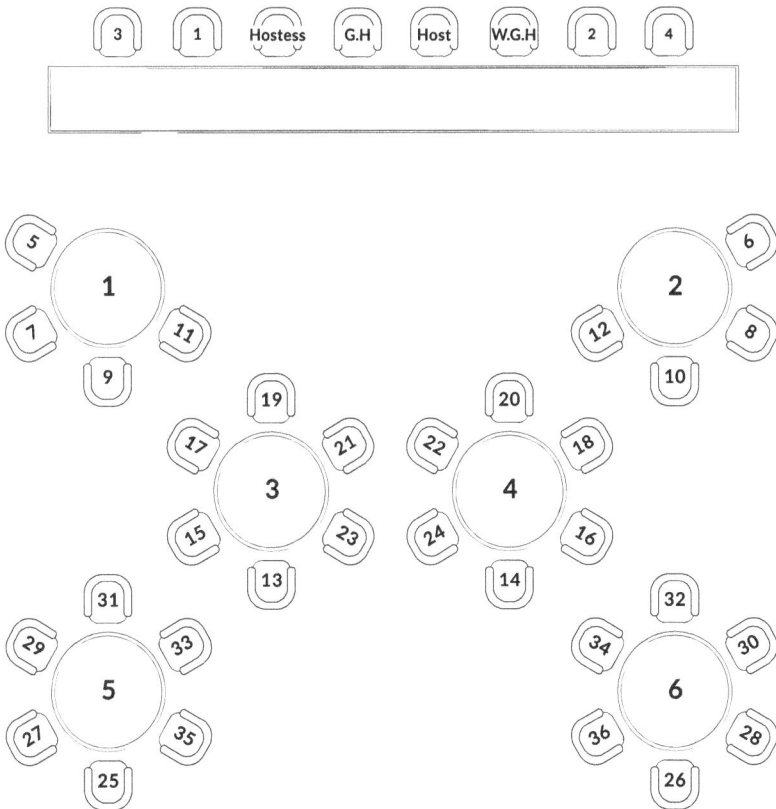

If the host and the guest of honor are of the same rank and therefore both have the same precedence, the number of head table chairs should be even.

The host and the guest of honor are seated at the center, and an equal number of guests are seated to their right and left sides.

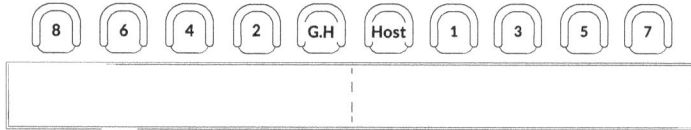

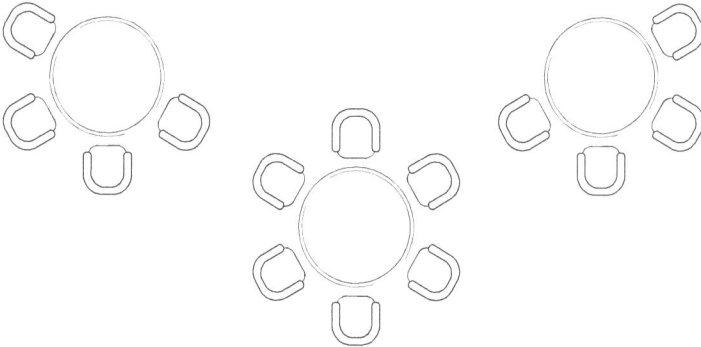

If the host is the highest-ranking person, the number of the head table chairs should be odd.

The host sits at the center and the guest of honor sits to his right. Consequently, the number of guests to his right and left will be equal.

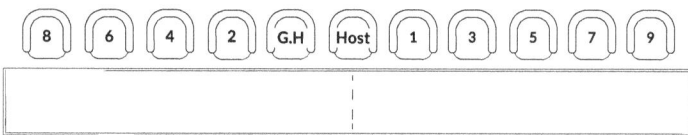

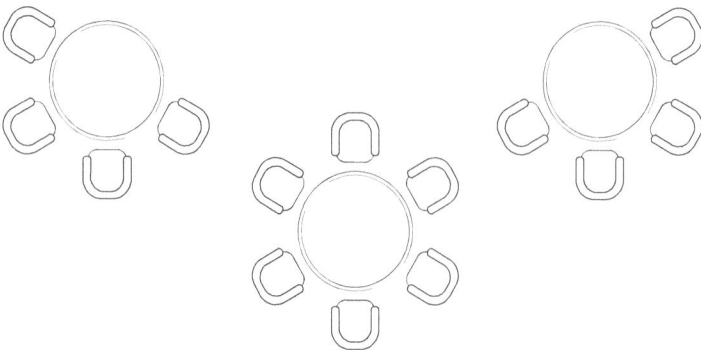

Children's Eating Etiquette

"Children are great imitators.
So, give them something great to imitate."[11]

❝ *Parents and school teachers should not wait until kids are older to stress the importance of etiquette and proper table manners. Table manners are best taught to children early and often, and should be explained clearly and patiently.* ❞

In addition to showing respect, children should know that good table manners make sharing a meal a pleasant and neat experience for everyone.

The following are some etiquette tips for children who already know how to use tableware properly.

— A child should:

· Come to the table with clean hands and face.
· Watch the host to see when to unfold the napkin.
· Put the napkin on their lap.
· Wait until everyone is served before eating.
· Stay seated during the meal and sit up straight.
· Not rest their elbows on the table.
· Take small bites and never stuff their mouth.
· Chew with mouth closed.
· Not talk until finished chewing and swallowing food.

——————— 11 Anonymous.

- Not pick their teeth, smack their lips, or pick their nose.
- Not make rude noises like burping or slurping.
- Not lick their fingers.
- Not complain about the food.
- Ask politely for things to be passed if they cannot reach them and say, "Please pass the..."
- Chat, at least, with those who are next to them at the table.
- Should not interrupt when someone else is talking.

It is said: "Teach your child to hold his tongue; he'll learn fast enough to speak."[12]
- Put the napkin on the chair if excusing themselves to go to the restroom. It should not be put on the plate or table.
- Should not push in their chair when finishing and getting up from the table.
- Ask to be excused when they want to leave the table (at family meals).
- Thank the host.
- Make eye contact with the waiter and say, "Thank you" (at a restaurant).

---

12 Benjamin Franklin (1706-1790) was an American statesman and scientist. He has also been called "The First American." He was a very important person in the American Revolution and helped make the Thirteen Colonies one nation.

Coffee Etiquette

"Coffee should be black as hell, strong as death, and sweet as love." [13]

** Coffee is certainly one of the most popular drinks in the world, and can be prepared and served in a variety of ways including; Espresso, French Press, Café Latte, Cappuccino, Arabic Coffee, Turkish Coffee, etc. **

Once brewed, coffee may be served hot, although iced coffee is a popular alternative.

Drip-brewed, percolated, or French-pressed/cafetière coffee may be served as white coffee with a dairy product such as milk or cream, or as black coffee with no addition.

In some Arab countries such as Syria, Lebanon, Jordan, Palestine, Iraq, and Egypt, cardamom can be added. In others, such as Kuwait, Saudi Arabia, the United Arab Emirates, Qatar, and Bahrain, coffee is prepared from cardamom as the main ingredient, to which mixtures of other types of spices, especially saffron, are added.

Coffee may be served bitter or sweetened (with sugar or sweetener).

---

13 Brazilian proverb.

- **Cup Sizes and Formalities:** [14]

Coffee is typically served in three-cup sizes.

1. **Small** or demitasse cups, used to serve espresso and strong black coffee, often used after a formal dinner.

2. **Medium**-sized cups, known as teacups, are most often used at meals.

3. **Large** coffee cups, only used at informal family meals and during breakfast.

   Any coffee cup sits upon a saucer, regardless of its size. A spoon should be included on each saucer.

   In addition to the cups, saucers, and coffee spoons, a coffee set usually includes a coffee pot, a pitcher of cream, and a bowl of sugar.

- **Serving coffee:**

– Traditionally, coffee comes at the very end of the meal.

– Some people assume that coffee and dessert go together.

– The more formal option is to serve dessert first and serve coffee once the dessert plates have been cleared.

– The second, more casual possibility is to serve coffee with the dessert. Those who like it this way think coffee helps to cut some of the sweetness and richness of dessert.

- **Informal Coffee Etiquette:**

· At home meals, guests leave the dining table and move to the living room to have coffee.

· Guests proceed to a table where the coffee tray is set and take their prepared coffee.

· If the house or apartment is small, it is acceptable to serve coffee at the dining table itself.

· The host or hostess may set the coffee tray down by their place setting and serve each guest after adding cream and sugar, upon request.

· The host or hostess may also choose to pass the cream and sugar after the coffee cups have been distributed, allowing guests to help themselves.

14 Mustache cup: In the 1860s, the British potter Harvey Adams invented what was called the moustache cup. It is a coffee and teacup with a semicircular shelf across it that has a half moon-shaped opening to allow the passage of coffee or tea and serves as a guard to keep moustaches dry. From 1860 to 1916, it was obligatory for the British soldiers to sport a moustache. To keep the moustache stiff, moustache wax was applied. When drinking hot liquids, steam from the drink would melt the wax, which would drip into the cup. Sipping hot tea or coffee would also often stain moustaches. The shelf or ledge of the moustache cup was important to allow the moustache to rest safe and dry on the guard while sipping a hot beverage through the opening.

- **Formal coffee etiquette:**

  At a formal dinner table, coffee could be served in one of several ways:

1. The waitstaff presents a tray of filled cups to each guest who selects one and then adds sugar and cream to taste, from sugar and cream dispensers placed around the table.

2. A tray of empty cups, presented by the waitstaff. Each guest puts the amount of sugar into one of the cups and then carefully picksup the selected coffee setting.

   A table assistant fills it. The guests at the table may add cream, from a conveniently situated cream dispenser.

3. At a sideboard,[15] coffee is poured by the waitstaff and presented to each guest by a table assistant.

   Guests may add sugar and cream, if desired, from the sugar bowls and cream dispensers, which are already placed conveniently around the table.

---

15 A sideboard is a movable small table-like furniture used in a dining room or a restaurant for serving drinks and coffee.

Wine Etiquette

*"If you have wine and money,
your friends will be many."*[16]

Wine, with its many brands and flavors, is generally the most popular alcoholic beverage to serve with dinner.

Contrary to some misconceptions, wine is not that mysterious, despite all its apparent complexities. One is not required to be a specialized wine connoisseur before uncorking a bottle of wine; they are simply supposed to know a few basics.

• Wine's defining elements:

Four basic elements define every wine:
- The grape: An Italian proverb says, "Bad grapes can't give you good wine."
- The region.
- The vintage: The year in which the wine, especially one of high quality, was produced.
- The producer.

• Choosing wine:

As a host, if the guests' preferences are not known, both a red and a white should be stocked.

Easy-to-drink wines that pair well with the food being served should be provided.

• Evaluating wine:

The process of evaluating wine starts from the first moment it is poured into the glass.

This process involves four basic steps: looking, swirling, smelling, and tasting.

1. Looking:

To evaluate its color and clarity, one holds the wine glass up against a white background.

Red wines usually range in color from deep purple to red-brown; white wines usually range in color from pale yellow to pale brown.

Notes:

Red wines generally fade in color with age.
White wines usually darken with age.
If the wine is discolored or cloudy, it might be bad.

2. Swirling:

To aerate and release its aroma, one swirls the wine in the glass.

3. Smelling:

One can properly smell a wine by putting his nose in the glass and taking a deep breath. Generally, older wines have subtler aromas than younger ones.

4. Tasting:

To taste a wine, one should fill the mouth about ½ full and subtly move the wine around. By doing so, the wine releases its aroma and coats the mouth.

- **Basic Taste Components in Wine:**

It is worth mentioning that wines contain three tastes of acidity, sweetness, and bitterness in varying degrees, but lack the other three tastes of fatness, spiciness, and saltiness. Accordingly, wines could be grouped into three different general categories:

Red wines that have more bitterness. White, rosé, and sparkling wines that have more acidity. Sweet wines that have more sweetness.

- **Wine and food pairing:**

"Wine and food pairing" is the process of creating a balance between both the food and beverage to best taste and enjoy meals. Yet, the question of enjoyment and taste is very subjective and varies from one person to another.

For food and wine pairing, one should take into consideration all the interacting elements of both food and wine, such as texture and flavor, in addition to sugar, acid, alcohol, and tannins.

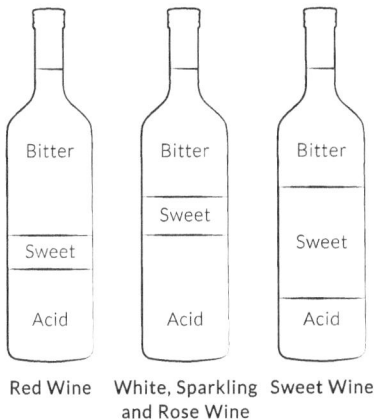

Red Wine   White, Sparkling and Rose Wine   Sweet Wine

Wine can be accentuated or minimized when paired with certain types of food. Therefore, food is the real determining factor, according to which one should choose the wines and their sequence of service.

Hence, the food menu is to be set first, and then the wine is chosen based on how it will complement the food.

Today, the old rule "White wine with fish and chicken, and red with meat" is no longer applicable, because every dish usually consists of more than just one component.

Chicken, for example, is not just chicken, but rather a chicken with herbs or spices. Therefore, one should keep in mind that there are many things to think about when pairing a dish.

Anyhow, the safest way for a food and wine pairing is to choose which part/element of the dish one wants to emphasize and then match the wine to that element.

> **Some tips for pairing wine and food:**

– The wine should be more acidic than the food.
– The wine should be sweeter than the food.
– It is better to match the wine with the sauce than with the meat.
– The wine should have the same flavor intensity as the food.
– Red wines pair best with bold-flavored meats, such as red meat.
– Bitter red wines are best balanced with fat.
– Red wines create congruent pairings.
– White wines pair best with light-intensity meats, such as fish or chicken.
– White, sparkling, and rosé wines create complementary pairings.
– Most cheeses pair well with white wine. However, some cheeses (like Gouda or Roquefort cheese) are best paired with red wine.

- **More details:**
- Wines, which are light-bodied but full of savory[17] depth, taste great with dishes of earthy flavors and ingredients like mushrooms and truffles.
- Delicate wines[18] seem to have a good flavor when paired with light fish and seafood dishes.
- Wines, which are classified as silky,[19] are delicious with fatty fish or fish in a rich sauce.
- Champagne and most dry sparkling wines have a slight touch of sweetness and are more refreshing when matched with salty foods.
- Red wines, which have firm tannins, are terrific with red meat steaks or lamp chops with frizzled herbs.
- Cheering and energetic wines are great with tangy foods that have piquant flavor and smell as well as with tart dressings and sauces.
- Bold wines[20] are good enough to drink with foods brushed with heavily spiced meat, as in barbecue sauces.
- Demi-Sec champagne, which is a moderately sweet sparkling wine, matches nicely with fruit desserts. It helps emphasize the fruit, rather than the dessert's sugar.
- Syrah wines[21] match well with highly spiced dishes, especially with heavily seasoned meat.
- Wines that have a citrus and clover scent are fine when there are many fresh herbs in a dish.
- Rustic[22] and rich wines (usually red) can pair with pâtés,[23] mousses,[24] and terrines.[25]
- Wines that have slight sweetness can pair with sweet and spicy dishes.
- Although some cheeses go better with white wine and some with red, almost all pair well with dry rosé, which has both the acidity of white wine and the fruit characteristic of red wine.

---

17 Savory wines lean towards the vegetable-fruit end of the spectrum. They are the ones that don't leave the impression of sweetness. In fact, they may not taste like fruits at all, except for citrus and possibly apple flavors, which are more acidic than sweet.

18 Delicate wine is a wine that contains several flavors, but none are strong or bold. It does not contain the rough and harsh elements of wine. Delicate wine is typically found in white wine.

19 Silky wine is soft, smooth, and fruity with low tannins but plenty of flavor.

20 Bold wines are forceful and fill the mouth with their taste; they are richer and creamier than an elegant wine. Higher alcohol wines tend to taste bolder.

21 Syrah also known as Shiraz, is a dark-skinned grape variety grown throughout the world and used primarily to produce red wine.

22 A "rustic" wine is one that can be described as hearty, earthy, or rough-edged. The opposite of a rustic wine would be one that's refined, elegant or smooth. "Rustic" is also a good way to describe tannins that have a chewy or coarse texture.

23 Pâtés: A rich, savory paste made from finely minced or mashed ingredients, typically seasoned meat or fish.

24 Mousses: A sweet or savory dish made as a smooth light mass with whipped cream and beaten egg with chocolate, fish, etc., and typically served chilled.

25 Terrines: A meat, fish, or vegetable mixture that has been cooked or otherwise prepared in advance and allowed to cool, typically served in slices.

– Rosé sparkling wines match with hors d'oeuvres as well as with some dinner dishes. They have the depth of flavor and richness to go with a wide range of main courses.

• Wine serving sequence:

Traditionally, when serving more than one kind of wine with the meal, the following general sequence works best:

· Sparkling wines are served before still wines.[26]
· White wines are served before red wines.
· Light wines[27] are served before heavy wines.[28]
· Dry wines are served before sweet wines.
· Ordinary or lesser wines are served before better or fine wines.
· Young red wines are served before mature red wines.
· With salad, no wine is served.

• Opening a bottle of wine:

· The first step is to remove the foil from the wine bottle's neck or cut it below the lip.
· It is easier to cut the foil by using a foil cutter (some corkscrews contain small blades for cutting the foil away).
· Second, insert the screw in the center of the cork.
· Then, rotate the corkscrew for six half turns.
Finally, pull or lever the cork out slowly.

Note:
When opening a bottle of wine, the host uncorks it quietly without bringing attention to themselves.
When serving champagne at dinner, the host should avoid sending the cork flying across the room.

• Pouring wine:

Unlike many other beverages, pouring and drinking wine comes with ritual and etiquette. This, by itself, gives more attention to wine.

When pouring, the bottle is held toward the base.

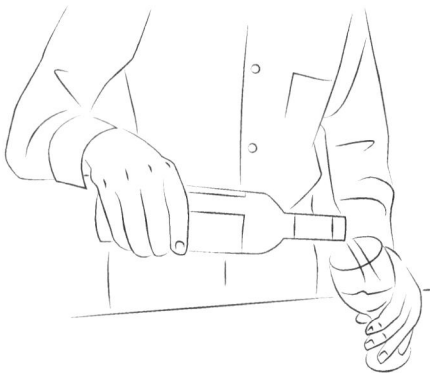

To avoid dripping while pouring wine in glasses, the following simple technique is followed:

For insulation, a napkin or towel is wrapped around the bottle's neck or draped over the left hand.

---

26 Still wine is a type of table wine absent of any carbon dioxide, which is what makes them still, rather than bubbly, sparkling, or fizzy.

27 Light-bodied wines (usually with an alcohol content of less than 12.5 percent and low tannins) are easy to drink and pair well with a variety of foods.

28 Heavy (or full-bodied) wines are a little heavier with bold tasting notes, complex flavors, and a powerful aroma. They are typically meant to be sipped over a prolonged period since they are so bold.

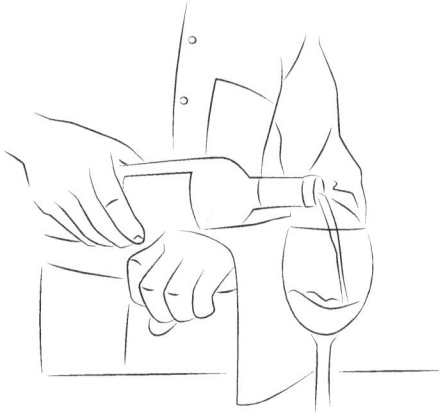

The bottle is held by the right hand, the label facing outward, so the diner can see what is being served.

After pouring the wine, the bottle is twisted a half-turn over the glass to halt the drops on the bottle lip and avoid spills. Furthermore, the napkin will absorb any drip.

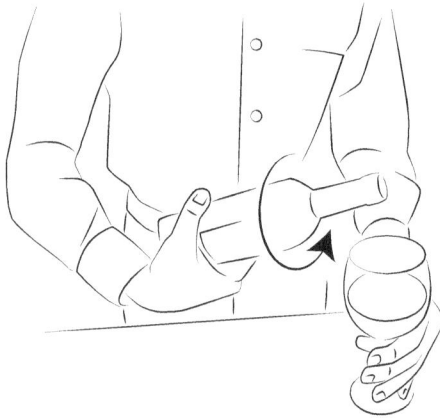

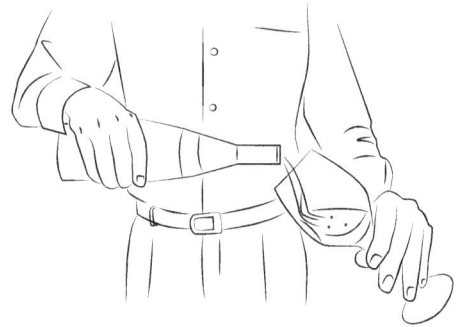

- · Still wine is poured into the center of the glass to let the bouquet (aroma) float upward in the vessel.
- · If it is planned to sample many wines throughout a meal, less than half per glass should be served.
- · For white wine and rosé, it is okay to pour less than two-thirds of the glass. For sparkling it should be about three-quarters-full.

- · For red wine, it is adequate to pour less than half-full. Some recommend pouring wine to the broadest point of the glass.

- **The amount of wine to pour:**

Generally, wines could be classified into bubbled and still (devoid of bubbles).

- · Sparkling wine is poured down the side of the glass to protect the precious bubbles.

- ## Wine glassware:

A wine glass should have four important characteristics:

1. It should have a clear bowl to best see the wine's color.
2. It should also have a long stem so the warmth from one's hand does not heat the wine.
3. The glass should also have a thin rim, to make sipping easy.
4. It should have enough capacity, providing room to swirl the wine.

- ## Differences between glasses / Main types of wine glasses

It is important to mention subtle differences between the glasses for red wine and white wines.

A red wine glass has a bowl wide enough to allow swirling of the wine and sampling the bouquet, which is concentrated around the rim of the glass.

Full-bodied red wines,[29] which have strong, satisfying taste and quality, with heavier tannins, are often served in tall, large bowl glasses that help let the wine "breathe."

A white wine glass has a longer stem and a more slender globe than a red wine glass. The slender globe helps maintain the wine's liveliness.

Champagne glasses and other sparkling wines have narrow shapes (flutes), which help preserve bubbles and direct them up the glass.

Port wines,[30] typically sweet reds, are often served as a dessert wine in slim tapered glasses that are still large enough to swirl.

Sherry wine[31] is served in a small, narrowly tapered glass.

---

29 Full-bodied red wines: Any red wine with more than 13.5 percent alcohol is considered a full-bodied wine. Full-bodied wines have more complex flavors and a richer mouthfeel.

30 Port wine is originally a Portuguese fortified wine. It is typically a sweet red wine, often served with dessert, although it also comes in dry, semi-dry, and white varieties. Port wine is typically rich, sweet, heavy, and high in alcohol content (usually 19 to 20 percent alcohol). Port is commonly served after meals as a dessert wine in English-speaking countries, often with cheese, nuts, and/or chocolate; white and tawny ports are often served as an aperitif. In Europe, all types of port are frequently consumed as aperitifs.

31 Sherry wines are fortified wines, often drunk as an aperitif. There are three groups or families of Sherry: the "Dry Sherry Wines," the " "Naturally Sweet Wines," and the "Sweet Sherry Wines." The wines are fresh and crisp on the nose with a very dry flavor and low acidity. Their alcohol content is usually about 15 percent.

• Storing wine:

I. Storing corked bottles:

– It's a common misconception that all wines improve with age.[32]

– More than 95 percent of all wines made in the world are meant to be consumed within one to five years.

– In fact, less than 5 percent of the world's wines are meant to be aged for more than 5 years.

– Wine bottles should be stored in a horizontal position to keep the corks moist, and prevent air and bacteria from entering the bottles.

– If wine bottles are stored upright for a long amount of time, the corks will dry out, and air will eventually get to the wine and spoil it.

– All wines should be stored away from light, especially direct sunlight and fluorescent fixtures.

– Darker bottles are better protected, and some bottles have UV filters built into the glass. Still, enough UV rays can penetrate a bottle to ruin the wine.

– If it is not possible to keep a bottle entirely out of the light, it could be wrapped up in a cloth, or simply put inside a box.

– An ideal temperature for storing a varied wine collection is 12.2°C. It should not go over 24°C; otherwise, it begins to oxidize.

– Letting the temperature drop below 12.2°C won't hurt the wine; it'll only slow down the aging process.

– White wine, rosé, and sparkling wine are stored at cooler temperatures than red wines.

– The following table shows proper wine-storing temperatures:

Type of Wine	Celsius (°C)
Sparkling	6 - 10
Rosé	9 - 12
White	9 - 14
Sherry (light)	9 - 14
Red	13 - 20
Fortified (Port)	13 - 20
Sherry (Dark)	13 - 20

32 Wine aging distinguishes it from most other consumable goods. Yet wine is perishable and capable of deteriorating due to complex chemical reactions involving sugars, acids, and phenolic compounds that can alter its aroma, color, and taste. The ability of a wine to age is influenced by many factors including grape variety, vintage, viticultural practices, wine region, winemaking style and storing conditions.

II. Storing already opened bottles:

If there is no wine cellar, wine can be put in the fridge after opening, for three to five days.

There are some ways to ensure wine stays good for longer:

- Minimize its exposure to air.
- If there is only a little wine left, it could be transferred to a smaller bottle.
- Keep it away from excess amounts of light and heat.

• Wine flaws:

· Due to various bottling, transporting, or storing, wine might have flaws that make it undrinkable.

· Wine might be "corked"[33] and smell nasty (two to seven percent of wines are "corked").

· If oxidized, wine might taste dull or cooked and smell like vinegar.

· Wine might smell like decay if yeast from the grapes used in the winemaking process infiltrates the wine.

· If a wine has been exposed to too much heat, it might look brown and smell like it has been cooked.

• Etiquette of ordering wine:

· When ordering wine for guests, a half bottle per person is the average.

· If there are at least three guests, the host may order two bottles, one red and one white.

· When ordering, guests are supposed to choose decently priced wines.

· To show the wine selection to the sommelier, the diner is advised to place their finger on the price, rather than the name.

· If a diner is doubtful about what kind of wine to order, they can ask the sommelier for an opinion.

· Diners are advised to select food-friendly wines that pair well with almost all courses.

· When ordering wine by the glass, one should expect that they might be getting wine from a previously opened bottle.

· Before ordering wine by the glass, it is acceptable to ask the sommelier when the bottle was opened.

· In the case of ordering wine by glass, it is possible to choose another selection if the bottle has been opened for more than one day.

› Etiquette tips:

- At house banquets, a host pours equal portions of wine into the guests' glasses and their own.
- The host leaves plenty of room in the glass for the wine to breathe. Instead of pouring a full glass, the host pours just half or a bit less, depending on the kind of wine and how many samples are offered throughout the meal.
- Before pouring for themselves, the host offers seconds to guests.

---

33 A corked wine does not mean a wine that has tiny particles of cork floating around in the glass. Corked wine is the term for wine that has become contaminated with cork taint. Cork taint is not simply the taste of a cork. Rather, it is caused by the presence of a chemical compound called TCA (2,4,6 – trichloro anisole). TCA is formed when natural fungi (of which many reside in cork) contacts certain chlorides found in bleaches and other winery sanitation/sterilization products.

- The host is expected to make sure of pacing their serving so that everyone gets to try all the varieties.
- A wine glass should be held only by the stem of the glass.
- When toasting, one holds their glass by the stem, making sure to clink bell to bell. This reduces the chance of breakage and spillage.

- A diner is advised to drink from the same location on the wine glass to avoid mouth marks, especially when a woman is wearing lipstick.
- It is recommended to take the time to sniff the wine to test it and enjoy its bouquet.
- The first taste of wine tells a lot about it.
- Therefore, one should let their taste buds pick up the subtle flavors of the wine.

- Hence, instead of drinking the first sip in full gulps, one lets their palette experience the full taste of the wine.
- When bringing a bottle of wine to a host, the guest is supposed to take it in stride if their bottle is not shared during the meal.
- If the dinner was planned with a particular wine and food pairing, a guest's bottle may not be shared if it does not fit into that scheme.
- When empty, wine bottles should not be turned into the ice bucket.
- Sorbet[34] is a palate cleaner; it should not be considered a dessert.
- At formal dinners, Sorbet is usually served after the first course or entrée and is eaten before the next course.

- **Toasting etiquette:**[35]

- In addition to its main purpose of demonstrating thanks, appreciation, honor, and goodwill, toasting provides a festive touch and adds an air of class.
- Internationally, toasting is usually made as a straightforward gesture to wealth, happiness, love, and friendship but most commonly to health.
- Toasts are generally offered in many formal, semi-formal, or informal events, and at times of celebrations or commemorations.
- One should clink with the nearby diners, not necessarily with everyone at the table. Otherwise, it can be wearisome.
- The host should always be the first one to initiate toasting, after making sure that all the guests' glasses are filled.

---

34 Sorbet, is a frozen dessert made from sugar-sweetened water with flavoring – typically fruit juice, fruit purée, wine, liqueur, or honey. Generally, sorbets do not contain dairy ingredients.

35 Since the beginning of recorded history, toasting has been part of almost every culture. The clinking of glasses was traditionally a custom believed to drive away evil spirits.

- Traditionally, the first toast offered by the host is considered as a welcome to guests.
- The host is expected to attract the guests' attention before making a toast, by standing and raising their glass rather than by tapping on the glass with a utensil.
- The host should ask, "May I have your attention." They might need to repeat this several times, politely, patiently, and with a smile.
- When the host stands for toasting, everyone else remains seated, unless they ask everyone to "rise and drink to ..."
- When a guest offers a toast, they stand to give some short and simple comments.
- Informally, the toaster may remain seated if the group at the dinner table is small.
- At a formal event, the host and the guest of honor-making toasts should keep comments no longer than three minutes.
- It is acceptable for a toaster to prepare notes, but only glance at them occasionally, and not to read them.
- If the toast is honoring someone, the person being honored remains seated, smiles, and says "thank you" without drinking; otherwise, it would be like applauding themselves.
- The person honored should then stand and respond with thanks or by offering another toast.
- A toast offered by someone other than the host or guest of honor usually happens during the dessert course.

- Traditionally, champagne is the choice for the first toast, but it is possible to use other beverages.
- Non-drinkers may toast with water, juice, or a soft drink.
- It is acceptable to participate with a non-alcoholic beverage or water rather than not at all. However, for some, according to the world of superstition,[36] you'd be better to toast with an empty glass than with water.
- When toasting, one must make eye contact, but avoid clinking glasses.
- It is advised not to initiate the 'clinking' of glasses.
- If someone is set on 'clinking' glasses, the other person should not retract his glass away.
- When toasting, one takes a sip from the glass rather than draining it.
- When toasting, one leaves at least a little wine remaining in case a subsequent toast is proposed.
- It is inappropriate to refuse to participate in a toast.
- If the diner has only an empty glass, it is better to raise it than raise no glass at all.
- At a wedding reception, the best man usually leads the toasting.
- Except for the bride and groom, everyone should rise for the toasts being made. The bride and groom should only smile and thank people.
- The bride and groom make their toast by standing, each giving a toast and commenting with a few words.

---

36 According to Greek mythology, the dead would always drink from the River Lethe in the depths of the Underworld, in order to forget their past, corporeal lives. As a result of this story, the Greeks would always toast to the dead with glasses filled with water to symbolize their voyage, via the river, to the Underworld.

Smoking Etiquette

"The true face of smoking is not glamour and stylishness; it is disease and death."[37]

A few years ago, smoking was allowed nearly everywhere at any time. On the contrary, due to the great health problems it causes, the fight against smoking is now one of the main concerns of governments, health associations, and institutions, as well as national and international organizations.

Although countries all over the world have adopted many anti-smoking laws, including forbidding it inside closed quarters, the number of smokers is still high in most parts.

Regardless of the different opinions about smoking, it is important to recognize relevant etiquette rules.

• General etiquette tips:

▪ Cigarettes:

– A smoker should choose the appropriate time and place to smoke.

– Smoking apart from others is always a matter of both politeness and safety.

– A smoker should ask permission before smoking, as many people cannot tolerate the smell of smoke and find it bothersome.

– Smoking around people may increase their health problems and the chance of developing lung cancer, respiratory infections, and asthma.

– A smoker should freshen their breath with a toothbrush, mint, mouthwash, or breath spray after smoking. There is nothing worse than engaging in conversation with someone with bad breath.

– A smoker should not take a drag right before they speak. It looks odd when his words come out mingled with snakes of smoke.

– If asked to stop smoking, a smoker should either excuse themselves and find a different spot or stub the cigarette. Reacting badly or objecting will be rude and awkward.

– While smokers are eating a meal or engaging in social activities but desire a smoke break, they politely excuse themselves before leaving. This will allow them to politely disengage from the host, guests, and activity.

– They say, "What goes around comes around," and cigarettes are no exception. Hence, in the presence of other people and regardless of the quality of cigarettes, the smoker should offer their cigarettes to the others next to them; otherwise, they would be considered selfish and stingy.

– It is always tactful to light cigarettes for others, especially for women. Realistically, it's a simple gesture that takes minimal effort, yet it makes a big impression.

– Tapping a cigarette or a cigarette pack against one's hand is a vulgar behavior.

– One should not take out a cigarette and place it in their mouth without intending to smoke it.

– While talking to someone else, it is unacceptable to keep a cigarette between one's lips. The words uttered would be unclear and incomprehensible, and it is inappropriate behavior.

– It is not preferable to smoke on the street; when meeting someone in public, the smoker should refrain from smoking and keep the cigarette in their left hand to greet another.

– At a friend's house, guests should not smoke at the dining table before asking the host's permission, and they should smoke only at the end of the main course.

– In official banquets held where smoking is permitted and ashtrays are on the table, smoking should only happen after the main course.

– Due to its great harm to children, smoking is impermissible in their presence.

– Smoking around children should be avoided at all costs. [38]

– It is impermissible to smoke in elevators. Regardless of how good an elevator's ventilation system is, its air takes some time to change, and the other elevator riders could be annoyed by the smoking smell.

– It is impermissible to extinguish a cigarette in a cup of coffee or tea and the like; this inappropriate behavior shows disregard for the person who will wash it.

– A cigarette butt should be extinguished and disposed of in an ashtray. Throwing it away elsewhere allows the cigarette remnants to continue burning and emitting foul odors.

– When smoking outdoors and the wind movement is somewhat strong, a smoker should be extra careful when disposing a

---

38 Smoking may increase a baby's risk of dying from sudden infant death syndrome (SIDS), or trigger asthma attacks. Furthermore, smoking around children may cause several illnesses, such as bronchitis, pneumonia, and ear infections.

cigarette butt, making sure it is fully extinguished.

– Outdoors, to avoid the scattering and spread of ashes, it is advised to put some water in an ashtray.

– In a restaurant, the waiter usually puts an inverted clean ashtray over the used one, so that ashes and other residue do not scatter. They take both to the trash after; they place the clean ashtray on the table.

- **Cigar:**

– It is well known that smoking one cigar produces more smoke and odors than several burning cigarettes.

– Even in places where smoking is permitted, one should make sure that ventilation in the room or space is very good before smoking a cigar.

– Before smoking a cigar, its tip should be cut with a cigar cutter rather than with one's teeth.

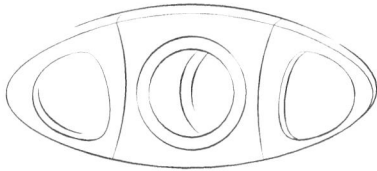

– According to cigar etiquette, and the recommendations of Cigar Clubs, this is the only correct method.

– The cigar's label should be removed before smoking for two reasons:

– First, the entire cigar only consists of tobacco. When smoked, if the flame were to reach its label, made of paper or cellophane, a foul odor would be released.

– Secondly, the label refers to the type of cigar, and it is known that the price of cigars is linked with its type. It could be very expensive, average-priced, or cheap. Removing the label reduces boasting for some and embarrassment for others.

– Cigar smokers should avoid (as much as possible) smoking at official banquets, even if smoking is permitted. The strong odor might even upset cigarette smokers.

– Smoking on the street is generally undesirable, and smoking a cigar is inappropriate if a woman accompanies the smoker.

- **Pipe:**

– The tobacco pipe implies a certain kind of privacy.

– Usually, it is more appropriate to smoke a pipe in the designated smoking area or lounge within a house rather than in public places.

– Smoking a pipe is impermissible at official banquets. The odor of a pipe is stronger than cigarettes and cigars, especially when the tobacco remnants are removed.

– It is not permissible to use the pipe at receptions and cocktail parties, otherwise, both hands of the smoker will be busy if they have a glass in the other hand. Furthermore, the pipe smoker with two busy hands would be unable to greet and shake hands with others.

– If the pipe smoker smokes in an office, they must make sure the space is well-ventilated, and they must not remove the tobacco remnants in the presence of others. Again, the odor of the pipe and burned tobacco can be bothersome.

- **Narghile:**

In many countries around the world, smoking narghile has increased in recent years, particularly among young people. Previously, it was used only by adults, the elderly, and retired men.

Although narghile is not considered a favorable practice in some parts of the world, it is now an unrivaled trend in Syria, Lebanon, Turkey, Iran, Iraq, the Gulf States, Saudi Arabia, Egypt, and Arab North African countries, as well as in countries where there are expatriates and immigrants from the aforementioned countries (in Latin America, for example).

Reliable research shows that smoking one narghile is equivalent to smoking a pack of cigarettes.

It is not permissible to smoke narghile in official banquets, even if smoking is permitted.

When the "narghile person" presents a narghile to someone in a restaurant or cafeteria, they do that while the hose tip (mouthpiece) is folded toward their direction; otherwise, it would be impolite behavior. ·

In houses, narghiles should only be used on balconies and well-ventilated lounges.

Etiquette Toward
Obesity and Dieters

*"Obesity affects every aspect of people's lives,
from health to relationships."*[39]

Although obesity has existed long before today's globalized world, it has become a major concern.

In many countries of the world (for example, about 30 percent of Americans are obese), it has been exacerbated by eating habits, fast food, job types, "screen obsession," environmental pollution, etc.

The foundation of good manners and etiquette is kindness, respect, and consideration for every human being. Exhibiting these traits often depends on our belief in the dignity of all individuals and our ability to put ourselves in another person's shoes.

Unfortunately, we all know how rude some people can be when it comes to physical appearance; the more overweight a person is, the more people seem to feel entitled to preach or scorn.

Due to the obesity epidemic, the issue of dieting has become a common feature everywhere. Many people are applying certain dieting systems and restricting themselves to special kinds of food to lose weight.

Hence, good etiquette can help address this issue with a mind toward helping obese people, those on a diet, and others interact properly.

---

39 Jane Velez-Mitchell (Born, 1956), American television and social media journalist and author.

> **Etiquette tips:**

– It is improper to look surprised when meeting an obese person.
– During conversation, it is impermissible to focus on a person's diet, especially at dining tables.
– It is not proper to ask an obese person about the cause of their obesity.
– With a person following a diet, it is inappropriate to tell them what to eat or avoid.
– As a host, one should avoid places where there are only folding chairs.
– As a host, one is expected to check that the restaurant has chairs without arms.
– Chairs without arms make it easier for an obese person to sit and stand.
– Being on a diet is a purely personal thing.
– When invited to dinner or lunch, a person on a diet can eat a little bit, apologize (if necessary), and explain to the host that they are on a diet.
– A person on a diet should not inform the host that they prefer one kind of food over another.
– A person on a diet should not ask for a special type of food if the event is in the host's house.
– At a restaurant, a person on a diet can tell the waiter: "I am on a diet, what can you offer me?"
– A person on a diet should neither criticize nor negatively comment on the types of food provided.

Section Twelve

Pet Etiquette

"The better I get to know men,
the more I find myself loving dogs."[1]

The concepts and behaviors related to this subject vary from one region and culture to another. The strictness and reservations that prevail in this or that part of the world regarding animal acquisition have diminished. Consequently, contempt is no longer a common reaction toward someone accompanying a dog on the street or garden or having it in his flat.

Despite the gradual change in this regard, it must be recognized that the views of societies are not all the same.

Many people, everywhere, still do not feel comfortable with the acquisition of dogs inside houses, considering that such animals are expected to be in backyards, gardens, and farms, for security and guarding purposes.

Regarding cats, the prevailing concepts often accept their presence in and outside houses, although they need the same care requirements as dogs.

Some people are interested in the acquisition and breeding of undomesticated animals, such as monkeys, squirrels, turtles, lizards, mice, rats, etc.

Some reactions to these pets are mixed, including consent, astonishment, disdain, revulsion, and even disgust.

---

1   Charles De Gaulle (1912-1970), a French army officer and statesman who led Free France against Nazi Germany in World War II and chaired the Provisional Government of the French Republic from 1944 to 1946. In 1958, he was appointed President of the Council of Ministers (Prime Minister) and in 1965 he became president of France until his resignation in 1969.

> ## Some general considerations:

The inclination to like or dislike pets, as well as the decision to acquire pets, is not indicative of closed- or open-mindedness, or any other criteria used to assess people and societies. Therefore, it is important to accept and respect different opinions and attitudes.

- Acquisition of pets should be considered part of one's freedom that allows certain rights but includes certain obligations.
- The acquisition of pets, especially dogs and cats, requires special attention concerning hygienic conditions, regular consultation with a veterinarian, and the ability to provide specific types of food on a routine basis.
- Dogs should always be kept under control.
- Off a leash, dogs might act beyond verbal control.
- Whether the dog is well-behaved or not, the owner should use a leash near people, especially around children, elderly people, or other dogs and animals.
- A dog leash is required everywhere and there are strong laws against dog attacks with serious consequences for the offending animal and its owner.
- In parks and gardens, if there is a fenced "off-leash area," the dog leash can be removed in this area.
- Owners are required not to let their dogs urinate on other people's lawns, shrubs, trees, mailboxes, or any other piece of property.
- Owners should clean up waste as it occurs, and always bring extra plastic bags.
- To make them a pleasure to be with, dogs should be taught the basic manners to sit, stay, down, bed, and quiet.
- Before the arrival of guests, a host should keep their pet in a separate place. Otherwise, if it is well trained, it can stay on its mat in sight of its owner.
- Due to the possibility of being irritated by noise or the presence of unfamiliar people, dogs might bark, cats might scratch clothes and socks, and so on. Such animals do not forget their instincts, no matter how well-behaved they are.
- Dogs should be taught to sit when the doorbell rings or company walks through the door and should only be allowed to rise when it is clearly in control of their excitement.
- Dogs should be trained to greet others in a calm manner rather than jumping and licking.
- During mealtime, pets should always be separated from the group and away from the dining table so they are not underfoot. Anyhow, dogs might be intimidating to some guests and annoying to others.
- Dogs begging at the dinner table is bad pet etiquette and may embarrass or annoy the guests even if they smile indulgently or offer the animal tidbits from their plates.
- If the owner has created a food beggar, the dog will consistently be a beggar.

- If dogs are uninvited or unannounced, one should not visit others with their dog, and it is not fair to ask for permission.
- Pets have their own needs, and owners should be sure the places they are going to with their pets provide the possibility to fulfill such needs. Anyhow, the owners should always carry plastic bags with them and clean any mess.
- When one goes to a certain place accompanied by a pet, it is usually permissible to bring some of its food.
- Pets and birds are generally not allowed in public transportation, but some small pets might be permitted if they are in pet carriers.
- It is not preferable to talk a lot about one's pet and its characteristics. Such a topic is not necessarily important to others.
- Some people have an innate fear of dogs, cats, and other pets that may amount to a certain degree of phobia. Therefore, people's fears should be considered.
- A pet's owner should not show astonishment or disagreement with other people's reactions and fear toward their pet. They should instead try to diminish their fear by holding the pet.

References

- Alkon, A., 2014. *Good Manners for Nice People Who Sometimes Say F*ck. Macmillan.*
- Baldrige, L., 1990. *Letitia Baldrige's Complete Guide to the New Manners for the 90's. Simon and Schuster.*
- Barnes, J., 2001. *Etiquette for Wine Lovers. Copper Beech.*
- Black, R., 2014. *Dining Etiquette: Essential Guide for Table Manners, Business Meals, Sushi, Wine and Tea Etiquette. CreateSpace Independent Publishing Platform.*
- Bolton, M., 1968. *Complete Book of Etiquette. W. Foulsham & Co.*
- Bowman, J., 2009. *Don't Take the Last Donut: New Rules of Business Etiquette. Red Wheel/ Weiser.*
- Bridges, J., 2012. *How to be a Gentleman: A Contemporary Guide to Common Courtesy. Thomas Nelson.*
- Bridges, J. and Curtis, B., 2012. *50 Things Every Young Gentleman Should Know: What to Do, When to Do It, & Why. Thomas Nelson Inc.*
- Clayton, N., 2016. *A Butler's Guide to Table Manners. Batsford.*
- Cook, G., 2010. *Guide to Business Etiquette. Pearson.*
- Cook Ross Inc. (Author), 2012. *Disability Etiquette Guide. Cook Ross.*
- Dariaux, G.A., 2004. *A Guide to Elegance: For Every Woman Who Wants to Be Well and Properly Dressed on All Occasions. Harper Collins.*
- Davison, I., 2008. *Etiquette for Women: A Book of Modern Manners and Customs. Chancellor.*
- Dresser, N., 2011. *Multicultural Manners: Essential Rules of Etiquette for the 21st Century. John Wiley & Sons.*
- Eberly, S., 2011. *365 Manners Kids Should Know: Games, Activities, and Other Fun Ways to Help Children and Teens Learn Etiquette. Harmony.*
- Forgays, D. K., Hyman, I., & Schreiber, J. (2014). *"Texting Everywhere for Everything: Gender and Age Differences in Cell Phone Etiquette and Use." Computers in Human Behavior, 31, 314-321.*
- Forni, P.M., 2008. *The Civility Solution: What to Do When People Are Rude. Macmillan.*
- French, A.M.M., 2010. *United States Protocol: The Guide to Official Diplomatic Etiquette. Rowman & Littlefield.*
- Harrington, R.J., 2007. *Food and Wine Pairing: A Sensory Experience. John Wiley & Sons.*
- Harshbergern, K.H., 2019. *Etiquette Still Matters. Berryfield.*

– Hartley, F., 2017. *Ladies' Book of Etiquette, and Manual of Politeness.* CreateSpace Independent Publishing Platform.

– Hayes, C.C. and Miller, C.A., 2010. *Human-Computer Etiquette: Cultural Expectations and the Design Implications They Place on Computers and Technology.* CRC.

– Herrington, E., 2008. *Passport Brazil: Your Pocket Guide to Brazilian Business, Customs & Etiquette.* World Trade.

– Hurt, A.E., 2016. *Cross-Cultural Etiquette.* The Rosen Publishing Group.

– Ingram, L., 2005. *The Everything Etiquette Book: A Modern-Day Guide to Good Manners.* Simon and Schuster.

– Innis, P.B., McCaffree, M.J., Sand, R.M. and Höfer, M.D., 2002. *Protocol: The Complete Handbook of Diplomatic, Official & Social Usage.* Durban.

– James, M., 2017. *Elegant Etiquette in the Nineteenth Century.* Grub Street.

– Johnson, D. and Tyler, L., 2013. *Modern Manners: Tools to Take You to the Top.* Clarkson Potter.

– Kallos, J., 2004. *Because Etiquette Matters!: Your Comprehensive Reference Guide to Email Etiquette and Proper Technology Use.* Xlibris.

– Lotter, V., 1966. "Epidemiology of Autistic Conditions in Young Children." *Social Psychiatry, 1(3), pp.124-135.*

– Martine, A., 2013. *Martin's Handbook of Etiquette, Guide to True Politeness.* Dick & Fitzgerald.

– Matlins, S.M., Magida, A.J. and Feiler, B., 2010. *How to Be a Perfect Stranger.* Skylight Paths.

– Meier, M. 2020. *Modern Etiquette Made Easy: A Five-Step Method to Mastering Etiquette.* Tantor and Blackstone.

– Miller, S., 2001. *E-Mail Etiquette: Do's, Don'ts and Disaster Tales from "People" Magazine's Internet Manners Expert.* Grand Central.

– Munzenmaier, Cecilia M., 2012. *Write Better Emails.* CreateSpace Independent Publishing Platform.

– O'Doherty, D., 2016. "Manners, Taste, and Etiquette: New Practices of 'Politesse' in Business and Management." *The Routledge Companion to Reinventing Management Education.* Routledge.

– Pachter, B., 2013. *The Essentials of Business Etiquette: How to Greet, Eat, and Tweet Your Way to Success.* McGraw-Hill Education.

– Pachter, B. and Coleman, E.S., 2006. *New Rules @ Work: 79 Etiquette Tips, Tools, and Techniques to Get Ahead and Stay Ahead.* Penguin.

– Patterson, K., 2002. *Crucial Conversations: Tools for Talking When Stakes Are High.* Tata McGraw-Hill Education.

– Post, E., 2017. *Emily Post's Etiquette in Society, in Business, in Politics, and at Home.* Open Road Media.

– Powell, M., 2005. *Behave Yourself!: The Essential Guide to International Etiquette.* Globe Pequot.

– Pramezwary, A., Lee, E. and Oktalieyadi, V., 2021. *Etiquette and Protocol in Hospitality.* Penerbit NEM.

– Ramesh, G., 2010. *The Ace of Soft Skills: Attitude, Communication, and Etiquette for Success.* Pearson Education India.

– Rucker, D., 2019. *Workplace Etiquette.* Newman Springs Publishing.

– Scapp, R. and Seitz, B. eds., 2012. *Etiquette: Reflections on Contemporary Comportment.* SUNY.

- *Shackelford, E.L., 2011. Disability Etiquette Matters. Xlibris.*
- *Sheardy, P., 2015. Airplane Etiquette: A Guide to Traveling with Manners. CreateSpace Independent Publishing Platform.*
- *Shepherd, M., 2007. The Art of Civilized Conversation: A Guide to Expressing Yourself with Style and Grace. Crown.*
- *Sioli, M., 2016. Rules of Civility and Decent Behaviour in Company and Conversation. Colonial Williamsburg Foundation.*
- *Spade, K., 2004. Manners. Simon and Schuster.*
- *Traxler, S.L., 2016. Office Etiquette: The Unspoken Rules in the Workplace. Traxler Marketing.*
- *Vanderbilt, A., 1954. Complete Book of Etiquette: A Guide to Gracious Living. Doubleday & Company.*
- *Visser, M., 2015. The Rituals of Dinner: The Origins, Evolution, Eccentricities, and Meaning of Table Manners. Open Road Media.*
- *Warkentin, T., 2010. Interspecies Etiquette: An Ethics of Paying Attention to Animals. Indiana University.*
- *Winters, C. and Winters, E.A., 2010. The Official Book of Electronic Etiquette. Skyhorse.*

- *Aboushi, Salah, 1990. Protocol Book. Publications Company for Distribution and Publishing.*
- *Ahmed, Jamal El-Din, 2000. The Art of Successful Business Administration Etiquette. Ibn Sina Library.*
- *Al Midan, Aida Abdulkarim. 2018. Etiquette, the Art of Courtesy and Decorum. Intellectual Creativity Company.*
- *Fareed, Mona. 2012. Social and Diplomatic Etiquette. Osama Foundation for Publishing and Distribution.*
- *Hassan, Kamel Sarmak, 2003. Protocol Administration. Yazodi Foundation.*
- *Hilal, Mohamed Abdul Ghani Hassan. 2012. Reference in Protocol Management, Etiquette, and Ceremonies. Performance Development Center for Publishing and Distribution.*
- *Samouhi, Fauq Al-Adeh. Diplomacy and Protocol. Dar Al-Yaqza for Authorship, Translation, and Publishing.*
- *Shammo, Daoud Soliman, 2013. Etiquette and the Art of Communication. Al-Warraq Foundation for Publishing and Distribution.*
- *Nofal, Riad, 2008. Public Relations and Protocol. Al Wahda Establishment for Printing, Publishing and Distribution.*
- *Al-Alam, Safwat Mohamed, 2017. Etiquette Arts and Protocol. Dar Al-Maarif.*

Riad Nofal

An academic, professional and diplomatic career for about 35 years, as a high-ranking official, diplomat, lecturer, trainer and visiting lecturer in many countries, in several universities, higher institutes, diplomatic institutes and training centers. A long experience that was deepened through academic and professional visits to about 60 countries, and participation in about 40 regional and international conferences (parliamentary and governmental). Hence, it was possible to integrate scientific knowledge with practical experiences, and to teach others on the one hand and to learn from them on the other.

- Doctorate of Arts in International Relations, LaHaye University ,The Hague, Holland.
- Bachelor's degree, English Language and Literature, Damascus University, Faculty of Literature, Syria.
- George Mason University, Arlington Virginia, USA Diploma on Diplomacy, Negotiations and Conflict Resolution
- The Chartered Institute of Public Relations (CIPR), London
- Diploma on Public Relations
- The Inter-Parliamentary Union IPU, Geneva Diploma on Organizing Conferences
- The Indian Institute of Parliamentary Studies, New Delhi
- Diploma on Parliamentary Studies

KHAYAT®
Publishing House

WASHINGTON, DC
UNITED STATES

www.khayatpublishing.com
www.khayatbooks.com

www.ingramcontent.com/pod-product-compliance
Lightning Source LLC
Chambersburg PA
CBHW080606270326
41928CB00016B/2949